Mesoamerican Mythology

A Captivating Guide to Maya Mythology, Aztec Mythology, Inca Mythology, and Central American Myths

Free Bonus from Captivating History (Available for a Limited time)

Hi History Lovers!

Now you have a chance to join our exclusive history list so you can get your first history ebook for free as well as discounts and a potential to get more history books for free! Simply visit the link below to join.

Captivatinghistory.com/ebook

Also, make sure to follow us on Facebook, Twitter and Youtube by searching for Captivating History.

Contents

Section: 1 Maya Mythology

Captivating Maya Myths of Gods, Goddesses and Legendary Creatures

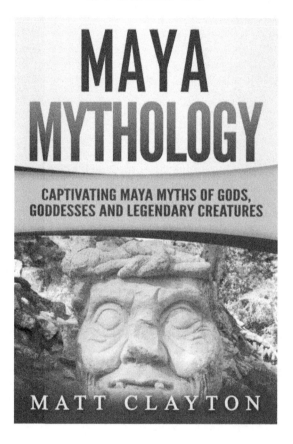

Introduction

The story of Maya culture extends in an arc that reaches back nearly four thousand years, with the first small settlements being established around 2000 BCE, through to the zenith of Maya civilization between about 250 and 900 CE, and ending with the gradual collapse of Maya cities beginning in the tenth century, which became complete with the Spanish incursions into southern Central America in the sixteenth and seventeenth centuries. Unlike their Aztec cousins to the north, the Maya were able to hold out against the Spanish until the late seventeenth century, and since that time have been more successful than their cousins at maintaining their languages, many of their traditional religious practices, and other important aspects of their culture, despite colonial rapacity and influences.

Unfortunately, the amount of information about ancient Maya myth and culture that still survives today is shockingly small. Under Spanish rule, all but four Maya codices were destroyed, and early Spanish historians and chroniclers such as Diego de Landa (1524-1579)—who as Bishop of Yucatan oversaw the burning of Maya books—declined to record Maya myths and other literary forms, although their writings do relate quite a bit about Maya culture, society, and religious practices.

What little Maya myth we have today is recorded in two sources: the *Popol Vuh*, the main book of K'iche' Maya myth; and the *Books of Chilam Balam*, which were compiled by Yucatec Maya redactors in the seventeenth and eighteenth centuries. The latter are named after the places where they were compiled (e.g. *Chilam Balam of Chumayel*; *Chilam Balam of Mani*).

The K'iche' are one of several branches of Maya culture. They took up residence in the highlands of what are now Guatemala and El Salvador after the fall of Chichen Itza, probably sometime in the early thirteenth century. Today, they live in Guatemala. The *Popol Vuh* continues to be a touchstone for the K'iche' of Guatemala today, as well as for other Maya peoples, and was declared the national book of Guatemala in 1971.

Compiled around 1550, the *Popol Vuh* is an important sacred text preserving ancient epic tales of the creation of the world, a mythical early history of the Maya people and their culture, and the adventures of Hunahpu and Xbalanque, the Hero Twins who overcome monsters and giants, play the sacred ballgame against the Lords of Death themselves, and eventually are transformed into the sun and moon.

The Books of Chilam Balam (Books of the Jaguar Priest) are written in a Yucatec Maya dialect, and reflect the culture and traditions of the Maya from the Yucatan Peninsula. There are nine extant *Books of Chilam Balam*, all of which were compiled in the seventeenth and eighteenth centuries by Maya redactors. The three most important of these are the books in Chumayel, Tzizimin, and Mani. While the *Popol Vuh* is a coherent set of epic myths, the *Chilam Balam* books are more miscellanies or commonplace books, containing varied collections of ancient myth, history, ritual, almanacs, and other information, including prophecies about the advent of the Spanish. Looking at the myths that the *Books of Chilam Balam* contain gives us a hint of the variety of ancient Maya traditions and beliefs, as these Yucatec myths are substantially different from those preserved in the K'iche' *Popol Vuh*.

Although the Yucatec and K'iche' Maya traditions are different from one another, neither were isolated from other Mesoamerican cultures. For example, the K'iche' and Yucatec pantheons both include an analog of the Aztec Quetzalcoatl, the Plumed Serpent, who is called *Gucumatz* by the K'iche' and *Kukulcan* by the Yucatec Maya. However, while the Plumed Serpent functions as a creator god for the K'iche', he does not appear in the Yucatec creation myth at all.

Another point of contact with Aztec myth that differs between the K'iche' and Yucatec Maya is that the Yucatec creation myth conceptualizes the material of the earth as having been made out of the body of a crocodilian creature called *Itzam Cab Ain* (lit. "Iguana Earth Crocodile"), which recalls Aztec myths about Cipactli and Tlaltecuhtli, both of which were water-dwelling monsters who were turned into the earth by the gods. A monster such as this is entirely absent from the K'iche' tales of creation.

Myths from the Yucatec and K'iche' traditions make up the bulk of the tales presented in this book, which also contains other Maya folktales. The first section of this volume is devoted to creation myths, one from the *Popol Vuh* and the other from the *Books of Chilam Balam*. The second section relates the tales of Hunahpu and Xbalanque, the Hero Twins from the *Popol Vuh*, and the third section contains three traditional Maya folktales unrelated to either the *Popol Vuh* or the *Chilam Balam* sources.

Since many translators and editors of these stories tend to present the names of gods and other characters in English translation rather than the Maya original, I have maintained that convention here, with two exceptions: the first is in cases where accurate translations are not available, and the second is in the Yucatec creation myth, for reasons of prosody.

From the fantastic exploits of the Hero Twins, to the stories of how the world came to be, to folktales about people, animals, and supernatural beings, Maya myth presents us with a fascinating variety of characters, plots, and imagery. All of these tales, whether from an ancient or more modern source, show us the great richness and beauty of Maya literature.

The Maya Calendar

For the Maya, as for other Mesoamerican peoples, accurate timekeeping was of paramount importance, primarily for agricultural and religious reasons. And similarly to other Mesoamerican cultures such as the Aztecs, the Maya kept both a 360-day solar calendar with five intercalary days tacked on to the end of the year and a 260-day ritual calendar.

The structure of the Maya calendar is nearly identical to the Aztec one. The 260-day ritual calendar is known as the Sacred Round and is often referred to by the Yucatec Maya term *Tzolk'in*, or *Chol Q'ij* in K'iche'. This calendar is comprised of an interlocking round of twenty sacred day names and thirteen day numbers. The day names are used in a recurring specified order, preceded by the day number. Each day is called by number and name, for example, 5 Ix or 11 Ahau. When the thirteenth day is reached, the count begins again with 1 on the next day name in the series. This produces a set of 260 unique day designations. Below is a table that gives an idea of how the number and day systems interact with one another.

Table 1: The Sacred Round

Day Name	Translation	Day Counts		
Imix	Water Lily	1	8	2
Ik	Wind	2	9	3
Akbal	Darkness	3	10	4
Kan	Yellow	4	11	5
Chicchan	Snake	5	12	6
Cimi	Death	6	13	7
Manik	Deer	7	1	8
Lamat	Venus	8	2	9
Muluc	Water	9	3	10
Oc	Foot	10	4	11
Chuen	Monkey	11	5	12
Eb	Tooth	12	6	13
Ben	Cane	13	7	1
Ix	Jaguar	1	8	2
Men	Eagle	2	9	3
Cib	Buzzard	3	10	4
Caban	Earth	4	11	5
Etznab	Flint	5	12	6
Cauac	Rain	6	13	7
Ahau	Lord	7	1	8 *etc.*

Translations of day names from Prudence M. Rice, Maya Calendar Origins: Monuments, Myth History, and the Materialization of Time *(Austin: University of Texas Press, 2007), p. 34.*

The solar calendar is called *Haab'*, and consists of eighteen months of twenty days each, plus an additional five intercalary days at the end of the year. These five additional days are considered to be very unlucky.

Table 2: Haab' MonthNames

Yucatecan Name	Translation
Pop	Mat
Wo	Frog
Sip	Stag
Sotz'	Bat
Sek	Skull
Xul	End
Yaxk'in	Green Day
Mol	Gather
Ch'en	Well
Yax	Green
Sak	White
Kej	Deer
Mak	Cover
K'ank'in	Yellow Day
Muwan	Owl
Pax	Drum

K'ayab'	Turtle
Kumk'u	Dark
Wayeb'	Specter

Wayeb' is the set of five unlucky days at the end of the year. All other months have twenty days.

After Prudence M. Rice, Maya Calendar Origins: Monuments, Myth History, and the Materialization of Time *(Austin: University of Texas Press, 2007), p. 41.*

In addition to the 365 days of the solar calendar and the 260 days of the Sacred Count, the Maya recognized other important blocks of time. The chart below shows how the system builds up from a single day, or *k'in*, into larger and larger units up through the *b'ak'tun*. This reckoning of large units of time is known as the Maya Long Count.

Table 3: The Long Count

Unit	Value	Number of Days	Approximate Gregorian Value
k'in		1 day	
winal	20 k'in	20 days	
tun	18 winal	360 days	1 year
k'atun	20 tuns	7,200 days	20 years
b'ak'tun	20 k'atuns	144,000 days	396 years

Table compiled from information in Prudence M. Rice, Maya Calendar Origins: Monuments, Myth History, and the Materialization of Time *(Austin: University of Texas Press, 2007), p. 44.*

PART I: TWO CREATION MYTHS

The Creation Tale from the *Popol Vuh*

For the K'iche' Maya, creation did not happen in one fell swoop, but rather in stages. The gods make several failed attempts at creating people who might speak to and honor them before they finally arrive at beings that are complete, and they succeed only when they create the people out of maize, the most important Maya staple food. We also see in this story the central importance of speech and timekeeping to the Maya, since it is through speech that the gods wish to be honored and addressed, and since they wish the people to keep a sacred calendar so that they might know when to honor the gods. The Maya gods therefore are not infallible, nor are they entirely self-sufficient: they can make mistakes, and they require the attention and adoration of sentient beings for their own sustenance.

In the beginning, there was nothing but sky and the waters beneath the sky. And the waters were still, the waters of the great sea of the beginning, but the sea was empty and void, and no creatures lived within it, there under the sky. There was no earth. There were no fish, no birds, no animals, no people. All was water and sky, there alone in the dark.

But far down within the waters, down deep at the bottom of the bottomless sea, were Tepeu the Ruler and Gucumatz the Plumed Serpent. The Ruler and the Plumed Serpent were with the other Creators, The One Who Bears and The One Who Begets, and The One Who Makes and The One Who Molds. Together all these Creators were hidden at the bottom of the bottomless sea under a great many quetzal feathers and cotinga feathers, bright feathers of blue and of green, of black and ruby, and there only was light. And up high within the sky, high above the bottomless waters, was Heart of Sky. Heart of Sky was both one and three, and the three are Thunderbolt Hurricane, Youngest Hurricane, and Sudden Thunderbolt.

Heart of Sky sent their word to the Plumed Serpent, and together they spoke of the world. "The world is empty," they said. "How shall we fill it?"

Together Heart of Sky and the Plumed Serpent spoke of all the things they would make with Tepeu and the other Creators who lived at the bottom of the bottomless sea. They planned and they thought, they talked of the things they would make, of the plants and animals, and of the people. This happened because Heart of Sky sent their word to the Plumed Serpent; it was their word that began the beginning of things.

When all had been planned, when the shapes of all things had been decided and agreed upon, the Creators first moved aside the waters. They parted the sea, they emptied it out, they bent their thought to their creation and lo! the earth came into being. From the earth sprang mountains and hills, and on the mountains and hills were forests of green trees, and between the mountains and hills the creators let flow the rivers and the streams, and the waters of the sea surrounded the earth.

The Plumed Serpent looked upon the earth that was made and said, "Heart of Sky! This was a fine thought you had, to create new things. I am pleased with this earth."

Heart of Sky replied, "Yes, it is good. But still we must make the people, for without the people, there will be no one to thank us or praise us for what we have done and what we have yet to do."

And so, it was by the thoughts and words of the Creators that the earth came into being out of the waters of the sea, and the sky was set above the earth and the waters.

Next the Creators took counsel among themselves as to what manner of beasts and birds should live upon the earth. The One Who Bears and The One Who Begets said, "The world is silent. There only is earth, and water, and trees, and bushes. We should make guardians for these things."

And when they had said this, the deer and the birds came into being. The One Who Bears and The One Who Begets gave homes to the deer. They said to the deer, "Live in the forests and along the rivers. Go into the meadows. These places are to be your home, and there shall you bear your young. You will walk on all fours."

Next The One Who Bears and The One Who Begets gave homes to the birds. They said to the birds, "Live in the trees and the bushes; make your nests in them. There shall be your homes, and there shall you bear your young. You shall fly in the sky."

In this wise, the One Who Bears and The One Who Begets gave homes to the deer and the birds, to the jaguar and the serpents, to all the birds and all the beasts.

When that was done and all the creatures were in their proper places, The One Who Bears, The One Who Begets, The One Who Makes, and The One Who Molds said to them, "Speak! Talk to one another! Say our names to us, for we have created you. Pray to us, and keep sacred our holy days."

The jaguar heard the command of the Creators, but it did not say their names. It only roared. The birds heard the command of the Creators, but they did not say their names. They only sang their songs and called their calls. None of the birds or beasts was able to say the names at all, for they did not have languages to speak with.

"Oh!" cried the Creators. "Oh, this has gone badly. The birds and the beasts cannot say our names, even though it is we who have created them."

The Creators then said to the birds and the beasts, "From now on, the canyons and mountains shall be your homes. From now on, you shall provide a service, and that is that your flesh shall become food. This we ordain, for you failed to give us the proper honor that is our due; you did not say our names, and you cannot keep sacred our holy days."

And thus it was that the Creators made the birds and the beasts, and gave them homes, and thus it was that the flesh of the birds and the beasts became food, because they could not speak, but only make the sounds that belong to each kind of creature.

Again, the Creators took counsel among themselves about what to do. The One Who Makes and The One Who Molds spoke together with The One Who Bears and The One Who Begets. They said, "We must try again. The birds and the beasts cannot do for us what is needful. We must make a new creature, one that can speak, one that can keep sacred our holy days, one that can praise us and nurture us as we deserve."

So, the Creators took up some earth, they took up some mud. They patted it, they shaped it, they made it into a form of a body. No matter how they tried to shape it, it crumbled. The body crumbled, it became soft, it fell apart. They could not get the head set upon it in the correct way. It could not see properly. It spoke, but it had no understanding. And when it went into the water, it dissolved away, it flowed away with the current of the water.

The One Who Makes and The One Who Molds said, "This was not successful. The body we made was not strong enough. It could speak, but it dissolved too quickly in the water. It could not bear young. It could not keep holy our sacred days. We must try again."

And so, the Creators went to the other gods for aid. They went with Ruler and Heart of Sky and Plumed Serpent, to those who were seers and keepers of time and of days. They went to Xpiyacoc, who is Grandmother of Day. They went to Xmucane, who is Grandmother of Light. They went to Hunahpu Possum and Hunahpu Coyote. They called upon Great Peccary and Great Tapir. They called upon those who are Masters of their Art.

"Tell us," said the Creators. "Tell us how we might make beings to care for us and worship us. Cast maize and the seeds of the coral tree for divination. Tell us how it shall go if we make beings out of wood, for you are the ones who have the wisdom to see."

Xpiyacoc and Xmucane cast maize in divination. They cast the seeds of the coral tree. They worked their art of divination, and they said to Heart of Sky and the Plumed Serpent and to all the Creators, "Yes, your thought is good. Make new beings from wood. Make them so that they might speak and live."

The Creators said, "Let it be thus," and from those words creatures come into being, people made from wood. The One Who Makes made the man from the wood of the coral tree. The One Who Molds made the woman out of reeds. These creatures could walk, and talk, and bear young, and walk upon the earth, but because they were made of wood and reeds they had no souls, and their bodies were poorly fashioned and very dry. They did not know their Creators. They did not know Heart of Sky. They went about their daily business without thinking at all of those who had created them, without saying their names.

Heart of Sky therefore made a flood and a disaster to destroy the people made from wood. Heart of Sky sent a flood to wash them away, and the destroyers to destroy the people made from wood, to gouge out their eyes and cut off their heads, to eat them and to rend their bodies. This was done because the people made from wood did not give proper honor to those who had created them.

Hurakan came, the one who is a great storm. The rain fell and fell and fell, all day and all night. Beasts from the forests came into the houses of the wooden people. Their household belongings turned upon them, their dogs and turkeys turned upon them. Their household belongings rose up and beat them; they hit the man and the woman in their faces.

The dogs and turkeys said, "You ate us once, but now we shall eat you!"

The stone for grinding corn said, "You used us to pound and grind, but now we shall pound and grind you!"

The dogs said, "You beat us with sticks, you wouldn't give us our food. We couldn't eat because of you. But now we shall eat you!"

The cookpots and griddles said, "You put us in the fire. We are all covered in soot. You burned us, but now we shall burn you!"

Even the hearthstones turned against the wooden people. The hearthstones jumped out of the hearth and threw themselves at the people, and at that the people turned and ran.

The people tried to hide on top of their houses, but the houses fell down. They tried to climb the trees, but the branches broke beneath them. They tried to go into the caves, but the mouths of the caves were shut.

So it was that the people made from wood were destroyed. They turned into monkeys, and went to live in the forests. And thus it is that monkeys look like people, because they come from those creatures made from wood who were but incomplete human beings.

Twice the Creators had tried to make people, and twice they had failed. Once again, they came together and took counsel among themselves, to see what might be done, for soon the sun and moon and stars were going to rise upon the earth. The Creators planned and thought, and finally they said, "Ah! We see what must be done! Now we know what we must use to make people the correct way."

The place that held what was needed to make people was called Broken Place, and also it was called Brackish Water. Inside Broken Place and Brackish Water was maize, both yellow and white. The Creators learned of the maize from four animals. The fox, coyote, parrot, and crow came to the Creators and told them where the yellow and white maize might be found. They showed the Creators how to get into Broken Place. The Creators saw the maize, and thus they know that this was the best thing they could use to make new people. The Creators used the maize to make the bodies, and water to make the blood.

Maize was not the only thing inside Broken Place. Also it held many other good foods. Cacao there was, and the fruits called *zapote* and *anona*, and sour plums. All manner of other fruits there were, and also good sweet honey.

Xmucane, the Grandmother of Light, took the ripe maize. She took both yellow and white kernels and ground them well. She took water and washed her hands with it, and the water that dripped off her hands turned into fat. Xmucane ground the maize nine times, and The One Who Begets and The One Who Bears and the Ruler and the Plumed Serpent together took the maize flour and water, and fashioned it into human beings. And thus it was that the first true people were all made of maize, were all made of food.

The Creators made four people from the maize and water. And these were their names: the first was called Jaguar Quitze; the second was called Jaguar Night; the third was Mahucutah by name; and the fourth was Wind Jaguar. These were the first people, the first ancestors of all who came after, and they had no begetting and no birth. They were made by the Creators, from their thoughts and their labor alone.

Once the four first people were made, they were able to talk. They could see what was around them, and hear. They could move about and do their work. They were well made in their bodies, bodies that were those of human males. Their understanding of the world was perfect, and it came to them unbidden and instantly. They could see everything without turning their heads, without going from one place to another. They could even see through the stones and the trees.

The One Who Makes asked the new men, "What do you see, and what do you know? Does your speech please you, and your movement? Tell me what you perceive."

And so, the four first men did look about them, and they saw everything, and they were very pleased. They said to The One Who Makes and The One Who Molds, "We can see and we can hear. We can speak and we can move about. These are the gifts of our Creators, who made us to understand what is far and what is near, what is great and what is small. For this we give thanks to our Grandfather and our Grandmother. We give thanks twice and thrice to the Ones who created us."

When the four first men had thus thanked the Creators, they then understood everything there was to know in the four corners of the world. But The One Who Makes and The One Who Molds said, "It is not good, that our new creatures understand everything so well."

The One Who Bears and The One Who Begets heard the words of the other Creators, and they also looked upon the new people and saw they had too much knowledge. And so, they dimmed the sight of the new people, so that they could only see well those things that were close by. When the four men's sight was dimmed, they also lost their understanding of all things that they had had before.

And thus it was that the first four men were made by the Creators, and were given speech and movement, but who were made to be lesser than the gods.

But the making of the people was not yet perfectly accomplished, for there were no women. So, one night when the four men slept, the Creators made four women and placed them at the sides of their men. When the men awoke and found their beautiful wives next to them, they rejoiced.

These were the names of the women: Sky Sea House was the wife of Jaguar Quitze; Prawn House was the wife of Jaguar Night; Hummingbird House was the wife of Mahucutah; and Macaw House was the wife of Wind Jaguar. And thus it was that the first four women were made by the Creators, and they became the mothers of all the K'iche' people.

There in the East the people multiplied. There in the East the K'iche' people had their beginnings, with these forefathers and foremothers.

Now the earth and sky had been made, and the earth set apart from the waters. Beasts and birds had been made. The many kinds of good food had been found, and new people were created that could speak and move and work and keep sacred the holy days of the gods. But still the sun and moon and stars had not risen, and all creation was in darkness. All of creation waited for the dawning of the sun.

When the time was ripe, the Morning Star appeared in its brilliance. The people and the birds and the beasts saw it in the sky. It was then that all the creatures knew that the sun would surely rise. And so, the people waited, and they watched, and when they saw the light of the sun begin to shine in the East, they rejoiced greatly. They prepared offerings of copal incense, and they wept as they burnt the incense in thanksgiving for the rising of the sun. At this time, the number of people had become very great, and all the tribes together praised the rising of the sun.

The birds and the beasts also saw the sun. They came out of the canyons and went up to the tops of the mountains to see this new thing, and like the people, the birds and beasts also rejoiced. Seeing the sun rise, the beasts and birds cried out, each one after its own kind. Jaguar roared. Parrot squawked. Birds took to the sky, flying about with great happiness.

The sun was very great and very hot, and he dried up the earth as he rose. At that first rising, all the creatures of the world saw the sun as he truly is; they saw him in all his grandeur and splendor, and in all his unbearable heat. But since that time the sun has diminished himself, so as not to harm the creatures or over-parch the earth.

Upon that mountain, the people made their home, that holy place from which they watched the first sunrise, and from which they first saw the moon and the stars.

And that is the tale of how the world came to be, with the beasts and birds and people that live in it.

The Creation Tale from *The Books of Chilam Balam*

Several of the nine Books of Chilam Balam *that exist today contain related versions of a creation tale. It is in the* Chilam Balam *creation myths that we see some of the diversity of Maya religious belief: the Yucatec story of how the world was made is quite different from that in the K'iche'* Popol Vuh. *For example, although both the Yucatec and K'iche' concepts of divinity include multipartite gods that seem to exist simultaneously as a single, unitary entity, the primary creator gods in these two traditions are different. In the Yucatec myth, creation is carried out by entities known collectively as* Oxlahun-ti-ku *(The Thirteen Gods) and* Bolon-ti-ku *(The Nine Gods), who seem to have been gods of the heavens and the Underworld, respectively, and by deities known as the* Four Bacabs. *The K'iche', by contrast, saw the process of creation as being overseen by a variety of both single and multipartite gods, including Heart of Sky (a trinity) and the Plumed Serpent (a unity).*

Two technical terms in this story require explanation. First is the phrase "Katun 11 Ahau," which is a calendrical reference. A katun *is a span of approximately 20 years in the Maya Long Count calendar;* 11 Ahau *designates which katun is meant. The other term is "Peten," a Maya word referring to the land inhabited by the Maya on the Yucatan Peninsula. These two elements locate the story both in place and in time.*

In reading the Yucatec creation myth presented below, it is important to note that Maya conventions of mythography and storytelling differ from those that most Western readers will be familiar with. These myths were not told and recorded for Western readers: they were made for the Maya, who doubtless considered them very meaningful and sufficient in and of themselves, and whose traditions and culture would have informed their understanding of the story.

Some translators and editors of the Chilam Balam *books present the texts as prose, while others present it in poetic form. I am choosing to present this myth as poetry, since poetry has a flavor and rhythm that seems better suited to the story than prose. Although here I combine several related versions of the Yucatec creation myth into a single story, I did not generally try to smooth over the apparent disjunctures, either of events or of time, that exist in the original.*

In the beginning

There was Oxlahun-ti-ku, The Thirteen Gods.

There was Bolon-ti-ku, The Nine Gods.

There was Itzam Cab Ain, the Great Earth Crocodile.

There was Itzam Cab Ain,

Whose body became the earth,

Whose body became the Peten,

Whose body became the earth upon which the people live

After the great flood,

After the great deluge that destroyed everything,

Before everything was made anew.

It was in Katun 11 Ahau

That Ah Musen Cab went forth.

Ah Musen Cab,

the Lord of the Bees,

Went forth.

He came to Oxlahun-ti-ku,

Ah Musen Cab seized Oxlahun-ti-ku,

He seized The Thirteen Gods

And blindfolded him.

And The Thirteen Gods did not know his name.

This happened after the world had already been made,

But before it was laid waste and created anew.

Oxlahun-ti-ku was blindfold,

And so he was seized by Bolon-ti-ku.

The Lord of the Heavens was blindfold,

Helpless.

And fire came down.

And ropes came down.

And stones and trees came down.

And the Lord of the Netherworld

Came to the one who was blindfolded.

Bolon-ti-ku struck him.

He struck Oxlahun-ti-ku in the head,

He wounded him in the head,

He buffeted him in the face,

He spat on him,

He bound Oxlahun-ti-ku

And laid him on his back,

Helpless.

Bolon-ti-ku took his regalia.

The Lord of the Netherworld

Took the scepter of the Lord of the Heavens,

He took away his ash,

The ash that marks the face of one

Who is fasting,

Who is being purified,

Who is being consecrated.

When Oxlahun-ti-ku was free,

When he was free from his bonds,

He took green shoots,

Shoots of the *yaxum* tree.

He took seeds,

Seeds of squash,

Seeds and beans,

And wrapped them up in the body of Bolon Dz'acab,

In the body of the Lord of Nine Generations.

Oxlahun-ti-ku wrapped up the seeds,

And then ascended to the thirteenth heaven.

When Oxlahun-ti-ku ascended,

On the earth remained only the husks,

On the earth remained only the corn cobs.

The heart of the earth,

The heart of the people was gone

Because of the ascent of Oxlahun-ti-ku,

But the people were in ignorance.

The people were alive on the earth,

But they had no hearts.

The people were alive on the earth,

But they had no fathers,

They had no husbands,

They had no hearts,

And so they were all destroyed,

Together they were all destroyed.

They were buried by sand,

They were drowned in the waves,

The waves of the sea.

When the insignia of The Thirteen Gods was taken,

When he was robbed of his scepter

When he was robbed of his ash,

The ash for penitence

And for consecration,

It was then that the floods came.

It was then that the sky fell.

It was then that the Four Bacabs came forth,

It was then that the Four Bacabs destroyed the world

And remade it anew.

The Four Bacabs planted four mighty trees,

Four mighty trees in the corners of the world,

Four mighty trees in the corners of the Peten.

A red tree for the East,

A white tree for the North,

A black tree for the West,

A yellow tree for the South,

Trees of abundance,

Trees for the nesting of birds,

Trees to hold up the heavens.

And when the Trees of the Four Corners were planted,

The Bacabs went to the center of the world.

They went to the center of the Peten,

And there they planted a great green tree,

The green World-Tree of abundance,

The World-Tree

That records the destruction of the world.

And so it was

After the Trees had been established

That the Morning Star

And the Evening Star

Were set in their places.

The rosy light of dawn in the East

And the fading light of dusk in the West

Were set in their places.

And Lahun Chan who is Ten Sky

Is the Evening Star,

And he is in the West.

And Lahun Chan who is Ten Sky

Is the Morning Star,

And he is in the East.

Then it was that Ah Uuc Cheknal came forth,

That The One Who Fertilizes Maize Seven Times came forth,

He came forth into the seven parts of the world,

He went to Itzam Cab Ain,

And it was then that the heavens touched the earth,

It was then that Itzam Cab Ain was made fertile,

That the earth was made fecund.

At that time there was neither day nor night.

At that time all was in darkness.

At that time there was neither sun nor moon nor stars,

But then the world began to be created.

They saw that the world was being created,

And behold! There was dawn,

And the world was made anew.

PART II: THE ADVENTURES OF THE HERO TWINS

The Downfall of Seven Macaw

The story of the downfall of Seven Macaw is the first of the stories of the Hero Twins, Hunahpu and Xbalanque, in the Popol Vuh. *In this story, the twins outsmart and defeat a boastful being who dares to think himself greater than the sun. The Hero Twins, as servants of the triune god Heart of Sky, are tasked with putting Seven Macaw in his place. This is important not only because Heart of Sky requires it, but because Hunahpu and Xbalanque are destined to themselves become the sun and the moon, as we see in the story of their battles with the Lords of Death in a later story, and it is not right that Seven Macaw should usurp their position.*

The names of the twins, Hunahpu and Xbalanque, are difficult to translate into English. In his translation of the Popol Vuh, *Allen Christenson states that "Hunahpu" can be translated as "One Blowgun Hunter." Christenson notes that "Xbalanque" is rather more difficult to translate. He says that the prefix x- can be either a diminutive affix or an indication of feminine gender, while balan is probably the same word as balam, which means "jaguar," and q'e means "sun" in one Kekchi Maya dialect. He also notes that the*

Maya "identified the jaguar with the sun, particularly in its journey through the underworld at night" (p. 81, n. 164). Christenson therefore suggests the translation "Young Hidden/Jaguar Sun" for this name, and notes that it is especially apt given the entry of the Hero Twins into Xibalba, the Maya Underworld, in a later story in the Popol Vuh.

In the time of the people made of wood, in the time when they were destroyed in the great flood, and in the time before the rising of the sun and moon and stars, there was a being called Seven Macaw. And although there was no light from the sun or moon or stars, there was a light from Seven Macaw, for he was a great being.

But Seven Macaw was over-proud of his greatness. He boasted long and loud about how great he was. He said, "What need have the people of sun and moon? I can make all the light they need, for I am truly great. I have eyes all made of bright jewels. I have teeth all made of bright jewels. My nest is made of shining metal. My feathers are made of shining metal. My greatness shines all over the whole earth." And so, he puffed himself up and boasted of his greatness, even though he could not see the whole world but only to the horizon.

At that time also there were two boys, twins named Hunahpu and Xbalanque, and they were both gods. They saw how Seven Macaw puffed himself up. They heard how he boasted of his greatness. The twins said to one another, "It is not good that Seven Macaw goes about boasting like this. It is not good that he praises himself so loudly before Heart of Sky. People will not be able to be created, or be able to live on the earth, with Seven Macaw doing as he does. People cannot live properly where jewels and precious metals are the most important things. Let us take our blowguns and put an end to Seven Macaw and all his boasting and all his riches."

And so, the twins took up their blowguns and set out to find Seven Macaw to put an end to him.

Now, Seven Macaw had two sons of his own, and these were Zipacna and Cabracan. And Seven Macaw had also a wife, whose name was Chimalmat, and she was the mother of his sons. Zipacna made great mountains, and Cabracan, whose name means "earthquake," shook them. Zipacna and Cabracan had the same fault of pride as their father did.

Seven Macaw said, "I am great! I am the sun!"

Zipacna said, "I am great! I make the mountains!"

Cabracan said, "I am great! I make the sky tremble and shake the mountains down!"

Hunahpu and Xbalanque saw how Zipacna and Cabracan boasted, just like their father did. The twins saw that this was evil, and they swore that they also would put an end to Seven Macaw's sons.

The favorite food of Seven Macaw was the nance fruit. Every day, he would go to the nance tree and sit in the boughs to eat the fruit. Hunahpu and Xbalanque found out where Seven Macaw liked to eat his meal. They arrived before him, and lay in wait for him. When Seven Macaw ascended the tree and began to eat, Hunahpu took up his blowgun and aimed a shot at Seven Macaw. The dart went right into Seven Macaw's jaw, and the force of it knocked him out of the tree. Hunahpu came running up to Seven Macaw, thinking to grab him. But instead Seven Macaw grabbed Hunahpu by the arm and bent it back, back, back. Seven Macaw pulled and pulled. He pulled Hunahpu's arm right out of its socket, and then ran away home, carrying Hunahpu's arm with him.

When Seven Macaw arrived home, his wife Chimalmat said, "Whatever happened to you? What is wrong with your jaw? And what is that you carry?"

Seven Macaw replied, "I was in the nance tree having my meal when two demons shot me. They shot me in the jaw, and now it is all broken, my teeth are all broken, and it hurts. But I showed them. I tore the arm of one of them out of its socket. I shall hang it over the fireplace until they decide to come and get it back." Then he took Hunahpu's arm and hung it over the fireplace, as he said he would do.

After Seven Macaw left with Hunahpu's arm, the twins took thought as to what they should do next. They decided they needed to get Hunahpu's arm back. They also knew they would need help to do this. Hunahpu and Xbalanque went looking for a very old grandfather who had white hair and a very humble grandmother. The grandfather's name was Great White Peccary. The grandmother's name was Great White Tapir. They were both very, very old.

Hunahpu and Xbalanque asked the grandmother and grandfather for help. The twins said, "We are going to get Hunahpu's arm back from Seven Macaw. You will tell Seven Macaw that we are your grandchildren, and that your work is curing people of toothache. That way we will trick Seven Macaw into thinking that we are mere children."

The grandparents agreed to help the twins and to do as they said.

And so Hunahpu and Xbalanque set out for Seven Macaw's house with the grandmother and grandfather. The old ones went in front. The twins went behind, playing and running about as though they were mere children. They came to Seven Macaw's house, where Seven Macaw was crying aloud with pain from his teeth and jaw. Seven Macaw saw the grandparents and the twins and said, "Where are you going? Are those your children?"

The grandfather said, "We travel about and ply our trade, my lord. And these are our grandchildren. Sadly, their parents are dead, and we must care for them."

Fighting through the pain in his mouth, Seven Macaw said, "Have pity on me, help me! Perhaps you know some way to cure the pain in my jaw, to cure what is wrong with my eyes. Can you help me?"

"We pull rotten teeth, my lord," said the grandparents, "and we cure eye diseases and set bones. Yes, we can help you."

"Oh, please, please cure my mouth," said Seven Macaw. "Heal my jaw. Fix my loose teeth. They hurt so badly I cannot eat. I cannot sleep. Also cure my eyes. I was shot by two demons, and how I have suffered ever since!"

"Ah," said the grandparents, "we shall have to remove the loose teeth in order to cure them. That is the way to cure the ills in your mouth."

Seven Macaw said, "I do not want you to pull my teeth. They are all made of precious jewels. And I will not look so fine without teeth in my mouth."

"Have no fear, my lord," said the grandparents. "We shall give you replacement teeth, even though they will be made of ground bone."

"Do what you must," said Seven Macaw, "but be sure you give me new replacement teeth."

The grandparents pulled out all of Seven Macaw's teeth, each one of them a precious jewel. And then they placed the replacement teeth in his mouth. But here they tricked him, for the teeth were not made of bone, as they had said, but of grains of white maize. Then the grandparents cured Seven Macaw's eyes. They took from his eyes all the jewels and precious metals that had been there. They took away all the things that had made him beautiful and proud. And then Seven Macaw's pain was gone, but he no longer looked fine and lordly, and he died from the shame of it, and his wife Chimalmat died with him.

Then the grandparents took Hunahpu's arm from the place Seven Macaw had hung it, and they reattached it. Soon enough, Hunahpu was good as new.

And so it was that Hunahpu and Xbalanque did the will of Heart of Sky. They brought about the downfall of Seven Macaw, whose pride had made him evil.

The Downfall of Zipacna

In his translation of the Popol Vuh, *Allen Christensen notes the ritual and cultural significance of the house lintel in Maya culture. According to Christensen, Maya people consider house lintels to have great power, and that Zipacna's transgression was taking up a powerful ritual object by himself without permission and without having first been ritually prepared to do so. It is this that leads the four hundred boys to sentence him to death, and gives the Hero Twins a legitimate reason to kill him.*

Christensen also notes that Zipacna's name might have derived from cipactli, *the Nahuatl word for "crocodile." If so, Christenson states, then Zipacna is himself a crocodile. Since crocodiles are not particularly mobile when they are on their backs, part of the Hero Twins' trick against Zipacna involves getting him onto his back, a position where he is vulnerable despite his great strength.*

Zipacna was the son of Seven Macaw. Zipacna was a maker of mountains, and a very strong giant. One day, Zipacna was bathing in the river when a group of four hundred boys passed by, dragging with them the trunk of a great tree. This was hard work for the boys, for the trunk was very big and very heavy.

Zipacna called out to them. He said, "What are you doing? Why do you carry that tree?"

The boys replied, "We have cut down this tree to make a lintel to put atop the doorway for our house. But it is so heavy, we cannot lift it. We cannot carry it."

Zipacna said, "Let me help you," and he took the great trunk of the tree up onto his shoulders and carried it to the place where the boys were building their house. Zipacna then helped them put the lintel onto their house.

When that was done, the boys said, "Do you have a mother or father?"

"I have neither," said Zipacna, for both Seven Macaw, his father, and Chimalmat, his mother, were dead.

"Then stay with us," said the boys, "and you can help us get another tree to use for building our house."

And so Zipacna agreed to stay with the boys and to help them get another tree. But behind Zipacna's back, the boys plotted against him. "Who does he think he is, lifting our log like that all by himself? We should kill him."

The boys decided to dig a great hole and ask Zipacna to get inside it. Then they would drop the tree on his head and kill him with it. When the hole was dug, they went to Zipacna and said, "We need this hole to go deeper, but we can't do that work ourselves. Will you do it for us?"

Zipacna agreed to dig. "Call us when you have dug down far enough," said the boys, and they left him to his work, thinking that they would throw the log in when Zipacna called. But Zipacna had heard the plans of the boys. He knew they intended to kill him. So instead of digging down, he dug into the side of the hole. He dug a small chamber in which to hide, in which to save himself when the boys tried to kill him.

The boys came to the hole and called down, "Are you finished digging yet?"

Zipacna replied, "Not quite yet. I shall call you when the hole is deep enough."

Zipacna kept digging until he had made a chamber big enough to hide in. Then he went into the chamber and called out to the boys. "The hole is deep enough! Please help me take away all the earth I dug. You should see how far down I have dug!"

The boys heard Zipacna's call. They took up the great tree and dragged it to the lip of the hole. They tipped the tree into the hole. Down it went, hitting the bottom with a mighty *thump*. And when the tree hit the bottom of the hole, Zipacna cried out as though in agony.

"Ha! He is dead!" said the boys, and they danced about with happiness at their victory. "It is good that we killed him," they said to one another, "because he was too strong, and he might have tried to rule us without our consent."

Then the boys decided that they would make some good liquor to drink, that they would do that for three days, and that during the three days, they would check to make sure that the giant was indeed dead. They would know he was dead when the ants began to gather in the hole. When the drink was made, and the ants had gathered, and they were sure Zipacna was dead, they would then hold a great celebration.

Zipacna sat in the chamber he had dug, and from that hole in the earth, he heard all the plans of the boys. He knew he had to convince them that he was dead. He cut his nails. He trimmed his hair. The ants came down the hole and found the hair and nail clippings. They took these up, and began taking them back to their nest.

After three days, the boys went to the hole and saw the ants carrying pieces of Zipacna's nails and hair. They said, "Surely the giant is dead! See? The ants are carrying his nails and hair. Now we may have our celebration."

The boys went into their house and drank their sweet liquor until they were drunk. When Zipacna was sure they were so drunk they would not hear him coming, he climbed out of the hole and pulled the house down upon their heads, killing them all. Not one of the four hundred boys survived. They were taken up into the heavens and became the constellation called Motz (Pleiades).

Now, it soon came to the ears of Hunahpu and Xbalanque that Zipacna had killed the four hundred boys. This made the twins very angry, for the boys had been their friends. They vowed to take revenge on Zipacna for his deed. The twins knew that during the day, Zipacna would be at the river catching fish and crabs, while at night he went about carrying mountains from place to place. The twins vowed they would trick him by using his love for crab meat. They took up some leaves and flowers of the bromeliad plant and used these to make the legs and claws, while a great stone became the body. The twins hid the false crab in a cave that was under a mountain called Meauan. Then they went looking for Zipacna.

The twins went along the river, guessing that this was the most likely place the giant would be during the day, and soon enough they found him there, fishing for crab as was his wont. "What are you doing there?" they asked him.

Zipacna replied, "I am fishing for crabs to eat."

"Have you caught any?" said the twins.

"No," said Zipacna. "I haven't had any luck for days, and I am ravenously hungry."

"Oh!" said the twins. "Oh, we know where there is a great crab that you could eat. We saw it just a little while ago, in a cave not far from here. We tried to catch it, but its claws were too strong and we had to let it go. But you seem like a very strong fellow; perhaps you could catch the crab."

"Yes!" said Zipacna. "I could catch a great crab like that with ease! Please, show me how to get to the cave."

"We have other business to tend to and cannot show you," said the twins, "but if you follow the river westward to the base of that mountain over there, you'll find the cave very easily. The crab is quite large, so you should have no difficulty finding it."

"Oh, please, please, show me the way!" cried Zipacna. "What if I get lost and cannot find the cave? I have not eaten in so long, I am very weak. Besides, if you come with me, maybe you will find birds to shoot with your blowguns along the way, and then we shall all have something good to eat today."

When the boys saw how desperate Zipacna was, they agreed to take him to the cave. Together the three walked westward along the river until they came to the place where the twins had hidden the false crab. Zipacna saw the claws showing near the mouth of the cave. He lay down on his stomach to climb in, for the mouth of the cave was very narrow. He crawled forward head first, but the false crab moved away, and he could not catch it. Zipacna came out of the cave empty-handed.

"Did you not catch the crab?" the twins asked.

"No, it moved away when I got close," said Zipacna.

"Perhaps if you go in on your back you will have better luck," said the twins.

"Yes, that is a good idea," said Zipacna. "I will try doing that."

Zipacna lay on his back and squirmed his way into the mouth of the cave. He wriggled in up to his shoulders, then up to his waist. But when he had gone in up to his knees, the mountain settled down on top of him, and he could not get out. And in this way, Hunahpu and Xbalanque put an end to Zipacna, son of Seven Macaw, there in the west of the world.

The Downfall of Cabracan

Guatemala is part of the Pacific Ring of Fire, and its western mountain range and southwestern plain are dotted with volcanoes. Guatemala therefore experiences frequent earthquakes, so it is no surprise that the Maya would have created a myth surrounding those frightening and potentially destructive natural events.

The story of the downfall of Cabracan, whose name is the Maya word for "earthquake," is a combination of a cautionary tale against excessive pride and a trickster tale. It also may be a kind of just-so story, since according to Allen Christensen, the Maya even today conceptualize earthquakes as the thrashings of a giant who is buried underground.

Cabracan was the second son of the prideful Seven Macaw. "I am the strongest!" proclaimed Cabracan. "I shake the very mountains! I bring them tumbling down!"

Heart of Sky looked down from the heavens and saw Cabracan knocking down mountains and boasting about it. "This is not right," said Heart of Sky. "This boasting is very bad indeed. He is making out that he is even greater than the sun. I shall have to do something about this."

And so, Heart of Sky went to the Hero Twins, Hunahpu and Xbalanque. He told the twins that Cabracan had become so prideful that he must be killed. "Cabracan thinks he is more important even than the sun," Heart of Sky said to the twins, "and so you must put an end to him. Bring him to the east, where the sun rises, and deal with him there."

"We will do this thing, O Heart of Sky," said the twins, "for we also disapprove of his boastful behavior, and it is our duty to do your will."

Hunahpu and Xbalanque went looking for Cabracan. They soon found him, shaking mountains down as was his wont. Cabracan was so powerful that all he needed to do was tap his foot and down would come the mountain; nothing would be left but rubble and dust.

The twins said to Cabracan, "Where are you going?"

Cabracan said, "I'm not going anywhere. I'm knocking mountains down, turning them into rubble and dust. That is what I like to do."

Then Cabracan looked closely at the twins. "I don't think I've seen you before. Where are you from? What are your names?"

"We have no names," said the twins. "We are simply poor hunters. We wander through the mountains with our blowguns looking for game. But if you're looking for mountains to flatten, maybe you should go over there. We saw a great mountain there, so large that it towers over all the others. We tried and tried to catch birds on that mountain, but we had no luck. Do you really knock mountains down?"

"Yes, I certainly do," said Cabracan. "But tell me more of this mountain. I don't see how I could have missed one that big."

"It is in the east," said the twins.

"Take me there," said Cabracan.

And so, they set out on their road together, with Cabracan in the middle and one twin on either side of him. As they walked, the twins hunted birds with their blowguns. The guns had no pellets in them. All the twins had to do was point the gun at a bird and blow, and down the bird would fall, dead. Cabracan watched the twins, and marveled at how they could kill the birds with just the force of their breath.

When the boys had killed enough birds, they stopped to cook and eat them. The boys made a fire, and began to roast some of the birds on a spit. One bird they set aside. This they covered in earth, to use to trick Cabracan. They said, "When he becomes hungry, we will give him this one to eat. When he eats the bird covered in earth, it will make him weak, and we will be able to defeat him. Cabracan will be buried in the earth, just as the bird he eats will become buried inside him."

After a time, the rich aroma of roasting bird filled the air. The skins of the birds became golden brown. Rich fat dripped into the fire and sizzled, casting up fragrant smoke. Cabracan smelled the goodness of the roasting birds. He became very hungry, and his mouth watered greatly. "What is this you are cooking?" he said. "It smells so good; let me have some."

"Certainly," said the twins, and they handed to him the bird they had smeared with earth.

The giant was so hungry that he swallowed the bird in one bite. He did not even notice that it had been covered with earth. He ate the bird, earth, skin, meat, bones, and all.

When the three had finished their meal, they continued their journey eastward. Cabracan felt strange. His limbs felt tired and weak. He could not understand what was happening. The enchanted bird covered in earth was doing its work. Soon they came to the mountain.

"There it is!" said the twins. "Bring down the mountain!"

Cabracan tried to shake the mountain, but he could not do anything to it. He was so weak that he sank down to the ground. The twins grabbed Cabracan and bound his hands behind his back. They also bound his ankles together. Then the twins dug a great pit. They cast Cabracan into it, and filled the pit with earth, and there the giant died. And so Cabracan, the son of Seven Macaw, was brought down by the Hero Twins, Hunahpu and Xbalanque, there in the east of the world.

The History of the Hero Twins

In addition to the three stories of the Hero Twins' victories over Seven Macaw and his sons, the Popol Vuh *contains an extended tale of the twins' parentage and their exploits in Xibalba, the Maya Underworld. That the twins are divine beings is attested by not only their superhuman powers but also by their blood relationship to several Maya deities, and by the unusual nature of their conception.*

Hunahpu's and Xbalanque's father is One Hunahpu, the son of Xmucane, the Grandmother of Light and one of the deities involved in the creation of the world, as we saw above. Their mother is Lady Blood, who is the daughter of Gathered Blood, one of the Lords of the Underworld. The twins are conceived when the head of One Hunahpu, who has been killed, drools saliva into Lady Blood's hand. The Maya story therefore shares with many other traditions, including those of the Aztecs and the ancient Irish, the idea that divine beings can be conceived without coitus.

The sacred ballgame, which the Maya called pitz *and the Aztecs knew as* tlatchtli, *plays a central role in the greater part of the Hunahpu and Xbalanque stories, and was an important feature of Mesoamerican social and ritual life. This game, which involved play on an I-shaped court with raised walls, used a solid rubber ball which the players had to hit with their hips, knees, or elbows through a stone hoop that was affixed to the walls of the long sides of the court.*

The twins embody some of the most common traits of divine heroes. They are prodigiously strong, skilled, clever, and can work a certain amount of magic. They can speak to animals and understand what the animals say to them. They also are superb tricksters: they not only manage to get out of tight spots that were the downfall of their own elders, but also to defeat the Lords of Death by means of a trick.

One Hunahpu and Seven Hunahpu in Xibalba

You have heard of the great deeds of Hunahpu and Xbalanque, and how they defeated the boastful Seven Macaw and his sons, Zipacna and Cabracan. And now you shall hear of the deeds of their father, and of how Hunahpu and Xbalanque were born, and of the deeds of the twins and their father in Xibalba, which is the Underworld, the Land of Death.

Two brothers there were, One Hunahpu and Seven Hunahpu, and they were the sons of Xmucane, the Grandmother of Light, who assisted with the creation of humankind. One Hunahpu was the father of Hunahpu and Xbalanque, but he also had two other sons, named One Batz and One Chouen, which mean One Monkey and One Artisan, and these were born long before the Hero Twins. One Hunahpu's wife was named Xbaquiyalo, which means Egret Woman, but she died very soon.

Seven Hunahpu had no wife, but lived with his brother as a companion and servant. Both One Hunahpu and Seven Hunahpu were wise and knowledgeable. They were men of good hearts, seers who could tell the future. They taught all they knew to One Monkey and One Artisan, and thus the boys played well upon the flute and sang with sweet voices. They knew how to make beautiful things from jade and silver and gold. They wrote well, and could sculpt in stone.

One Hunahpu and Seven Hunahpu liked to spend their days playing at dice and the sacred ball game. Every day they would go down to the ballcourt to practice. Sometimes One Monkey and One Artisan would join their father and uncle, and together the four of them would play game after game against one another. They were all very skilled ballplayers. At the times when they all played the game together, Voc, the Falcon, who is the messenger of Heart of Sky, would come to watch them.

Now, the ballcourt of One Hunahpu and Seven Hunahpu was directly over the road to Xibalba. Whenever the men and the twins played ball, the thudding of their feet and the thumping of the ball against ground and wall and bodies would echo through the halls of the Underworld. One day, the brothers and the twins played a very hard game of ball. The thudding and thumping were even louder than usual as they tried to defeat one another. It was so loud and so distracting that the Lords of Xibalba, One Death and Seven Death, said to one another, "What is all the racket they make up there? This is so disrespectful. They should not make such noise. We'll show them what it means to respect the Lords of Xibalba. We will invite them to play that noisy game down here. We will show them who the best ballplayers in the whole world are, and when we do, they won't be able to play anymore, and our realm will be peaceful and quiet once again."

First One Death and Seven Death called to themselves all the judges and demons of Xibalba, and these are their names and duties:

Flying Scab and Gathered Blood make people ill in their blood.

Pus Demon and Jaundice Demon make the skin turn yellow and cause the body to swell and ooze pus.

Bone Staff and Skull Staff bear staffs made of bone. Their duty is to cause people to waste away until they are nothing but skin and bones.

Trash Demon and Stab Demon attacked people who did not clean the trash from around their houses, those who did not sweep their thresholds and keep the space around their homes clean and tidy. These demons would descend upon those people and stab them until they died.

The last two judges of Xibalba were called Wing and Packstrap. They afflicted those who traveled the roads, and those who walked the roads carrying heavy burdens. Wing and Packstrap made these people die vomiting blood.

And so, the Lords of Xibalba told the judges and demons what they were going to do. They said, "One Hunahpu and Seven Hunahpu do not respect us. They play their ballgame very noisily. We are going to challenge them to a ballgame to make them stop. What say you?"

The judges and demons replied, "This is a good thought. These are good words. We also are weary of the noise they make. Also, we desire to have their ballgame equipment, their pads and masks, and their ball. Yes, let us play the ballgame with them and show them who the true champions are. We can win from them their gaming things. Then they will not be able to play, and perhaps we shall have some peace and quiet."

When the judges and demons had agreed to the plan, the Lords of Xibalba next called to themselves their messenger Owls. They sent the Owls to One Hunahpu and Seven Hunahpu, commanding them to come to Xibalba to play the ballgame there and to bring with them all their gaming equipment. One Hunahpu and Seven Hunahpu accepted the summons, but before they left, they told One Monkey and One Artisan to stay with their Grandmother, Xmucane, to look after her. They also told the boys to continue practicing their arts.

Xmucane was very frightened when she heard what One Hunahpu and Seven Hunahpu had been called upon to do. She wept most bitterly. "O my sons," she said, "surely I will never see you again. Surely the Lords of Xibalba will never let you go. Please don't leave me here alone."

"Never fear, Mother," said the brothers. "We will return. This we promise you. And while we are gone, One Monkey and One Artisan will care for you as well as we have always done."

And so, One Hunahpu and Seven Hunahpu took up their gaming things to go to play the Lords of Death. But they left behind their rubber ball, which they tied to the top of their house. Then taking their leave of their mother and the twins, they followed the Owls to the entrance of Xibalba.

It was a long and weary road to Xibalba. The Owls led the brothers down a long flight of stairs that went to the bottom of a canyon. Two canyons they had to pass through. The brothers also had to cross many dangerous rivers. One river was full of scorpions. Another was made all of blood, and another made all of pus. But the brothers crossed them all without coming to harm.

After crossing all the rivers, the brothers came to a place where four roads met. There was a white road that led north, a yellow road that led south, a red road that led east, and a black road that led west. The brothers did not know which road to take, until they heard a strange whisper coming up from the ground. "I am the black road," said the whispering voice. "It is my path you must tread to the place you are going."

At last the brothers arrived at the council chamber of the Lords of Xibalba. There they saw two seated figures. "Greetings, O One Death," they said. "Greetings, O Seven Death."

But the figures made no reply. One Hunahpu and Seven Hunahpu were very puzzled, until they heard rasping, gargling laughter coming from inside the chamber. Then they realized that the figures in front of the chamber were nothing but wooden statues meant to fool them.

"Come in, come in!" said the Lords of Death. "Do not mind our little joke. Come in!"

The brothers went into the chamber where the Lords of Death awaited them along with all the judges and demons.

"Sit down!" said the Lords of Death, showing the brothers a bench. "You must be weary after your long journey. We will play the ballgame tomorrow. Please, sit down!"

One Hunahpu and Seven Hunahpu went to the bench and sat down, but they immediately jumped up again. The bench was made of stone, and it was red hot. The brothers could not sit on it; the stone burned their buttocks. Again, all the Xibalbans roared with laughter. They laughed and laughed until tears ran down their cheeks and their ribs hurt.

When the Lords of Death and the other Xibalbans were finally done with their merriment, they told the brothers that they would be taken to a place where they could spend the night. Now, the Land of the Dead has many Houses within it, and in each House is a different kind of trial.

The House of Darkness contains nothing but the black of night, a night without moon and without stars. It is completely dark within.

The House of Ice is a house of cold. The inside is rimed with frost, and a freezing wind continually blows through it.

The House of Jaguars is full of jaguars. The jaguars prowl about. They have sharp teeth and claws with which to rend and tear.

The House of Bats is full of bats that flitter and flutter all about. They never rest, but fly about squeaking.

The House of Knives is full of sharpened blades that slide back and forth.

The Lords of Death decided that the brothers should be placed in the House of Darkness. "Here is a torch, and here are cigars for you," said the Lords of Death. "Mind that you do not use them all up, for they do not belong to you. Mind that you give them back to us in the morning, just as you receive them now."

And so, One Hunahpu and Seven Hunahpu passed the night in the House of Darkness, watching as the torch and cigars slowly burned away until nothing was left.

In the morning, the Lords of Death came to fetch the brothers for the ballgame. They opened the door to the House of Darkness and said, "Good morning! It is time for our game, but first you must give back the torch and the cigars."

"We cannot, Lords," said the brothers, "for they have all burnt quite away during the night."

"What?" said One Death and Seven Death. "We told you to return them. You have not followed our instructions. You have destroyed our belongings. Therefore, you must die!"

The Lords of Xibalba took the brothers away and sacrificed them. They cut off the head of One Hunahpu, and then buried the rest of his body together with his brother. One Death and Seven Death commanded that One Hunahpu's head be placed in the branches of a tree that stood near the road. As soon as the head was placed there, the tree suddenly began to bear fruit, even though it had never done so before, and the head of One Hunahpu changed to look so much like the fruit that no one could tell where the head was any longer. This is how the calabash tree began to bear fruit, and it is why its fruit is like a human head.

The Xibalbans gathered around the tree, amazed that it had begun to bear fruit so suddenly, simply because One Hunahpu's head had been placed there. And so, the Xibalbans made a law that no one was to take the fruit of that tree, and no one was to take shelter in its shade, on account of the power of One Hunahpu's head.

Lady Blood and the Tree of One Hunahpu

Once there was a maiden named Lady Blood, and she was the daughter of a lord named Gathered Blood. One day, her father came home with a strange tale to tell: it was the story of the calabash tree in Xibalba, and how it had begun to bear fruit on account of One Hunahpu's head having been placed in it. After Lady Blood had heard the story, she could think of nothing else but the calabash tree. She longed to see it and to taste of its fruit, and no matter how hard her father tried, no matter how much he warned her about the law against touching the tree or standing in its shade, he could not change his daughter's mind, nor distract her from her desire for the fruit of the calabash tree.

Finally, Lady Blood's desire became so strong she could stand it no longer. She went down the road to the place where the calabash tree was. She stood before the tree and looked longingly upon its fruit. "That fruit seems very good indeed," she said. "I should pick one and eat it. No harm will come to me, I am sure."

A voice replied from the midst of the branches, the voice of the skull of One Hunahpu. "Why should you desire a skull that has been placed in the branches of a tree? That is not something desirable."

"Maybe not, but I wish to have one all the same," said the maiden.

"Very well," said the skull. "Put out your right hand. Put it among the branches of the tree where I can see it."

Lady Blood did as the skull instructed, but instead of receiving a calabash fruit, she felt something wet dripping into her palm: the skull had dribbled some saliva onto her hand. The maiden pulled back her hand to see what had dripped there, but when she looked, she saw nothing at all.

"Have no fear," said the skull, "it is only my spittle that I have given to you, and in the spittle of kings are the descendants of kings. When a man is alive, he has beauty because his bones are covered in flesh, but the bones of the dead are frightening. The essence of the man, especially if he be a great lord, is in his spittle, and thus is his essence passed on to his children. The essence of the lord, and his face, and his speech, continue in the bodies of his sons and daughters. And so shall it be for me, for I have given you my spittle. It is time now for you to return to your home. You will come to no harm, and you will see that I have spoken the truth to you."

And thus was the will of Heart of Sky accomplished in the meeting of Lady Blood and the skull of One Hunahpu.

After giving Lady Blood other instructions, One Hunahpu bade her return home. She did so, and not long afterward, she found that she was with child. This had been accomplished when the skull spit into her hand, and this was how the Hero Twins Hunahpu and Xbalanque were conceived.

Lady Blood was able to hide her condition for six months, but after that time she began to show. Gathered Blood noticed his daughter was with child, and he became angry. He went before One Death and Seven Death and the other lords of Xibalba and told them that his daughter had lain with a man and now was with child.

"Go and ask her what happened," said the lords of Xibalba. "Get the truth from her. And if she is not truthful, she will be sacrificed."

Gathered Blood agreed that this was a good plan. He returned home and asked his daughter how it was that she was with child. He asked her who the father was, which man she had lain with.

"I have never lain with a man, Father," said Lady Blood. "I don't know what you are talking about."

"So it is true, then," said Gathered Blood. "You are nothing but a common whore."

Gathered Blood summoned the four Owls of Xibalba. When they arrived, Gathered Blood said, "Take that common whore away and sacrifice her. Bring back her heart in a bowl."

The Owls grasped the young woman in their talons. Taking also with them a bowl and a flint knife, they carried Lady Blood through the skies of Xibalba to the place of sacrifice.

"You cannot kill me," said Lady Blood. "I am with child, but not because I have lain with a man. This is the child that was given to me by the skull of One Hunahpu, which rests in the calabash tree, the one that stands next to the road near the ballcourt. I do not deserve to be sacrificed."

"We do not want to sacrifice you," said the Owls, "but we must bring something back in the bowl. What should we do?"

"Go to the croton tree," said Lady Blood. "Gather its sap, for it looks like blood. Gather its sap, and it will look like a heart when it is placed in the bowl."

The Owls did what the young woman told them. They went to the tree. Lady Blood stabbed it with the Owls' sacred flint knife. Red sap oozed out. The Owls caught the sap in the bowl, and there it formed a lump. The sap came together, and it became a rounded shape that looked like a heart.

"Wait here," said the Owls. "Wait here for us. We will go show this to the Lords of Xibalba, and when they are satisfied that you have been sacrificed, we will return to guide you away from here. We will guide you to a place of safety."

And so, the Owls flew back to the Lords of Xibalba with the bowl full of sap. When they arrived, One Death said, "Is that the heart of the young woman in that bowl?"

"It is," said the Owls. "It most truly is."

"Bring it here that I may examine it," said One Death.

The Owls brought the bowl to One Death. He put his fingers into the red sap. He stirred the sap with his fingers, then held them up and looked at them. His fingers seemed to drip with blood.

"Build up the fire," said One Death. "Build it up to burn more hotly. Then we shall burn the heart upon it."

The Owls poked the fire and added wood to it. When it was blazing well, One Death put the sap into it. The sap smoked up with a sweet fragrance. All the Xibalbans gathered around the fire to smell the fragrance of the burning sap, which they all thought was blood. And this is how Lady Blood tricked the Lords of Xibalba.

Now, while the Lords of Xibalba were smelling the fragrance of the tree sap, the Owls returned to Lady Blood and guided her to the world above. Then the Owls went back to Xibalba.

Lady Blood went to the home of Xmucane, the Grandmother of Light, who was the mother of One Hunahpu and Seven Hunahpu and the grandmother of One Monkey and One Artisan. Lady Blood went before Xmucane and said, "I greet you, O Mother, for I am your daughter-in-law."

Xmucane was astonished. "How can this be? My sons descended into Xibalba and never returned, and I am sure that they must be dead. I have only my grandsons, One Monkey and One Artisan. They are all that I have left of my own beloved sons. What you say cannot be true. Go away. Go back to where you came from."

"I speak truth," said Lady Blood. "I am with child, I carry twins, and they are the sons of One Hunahpu. One Hunahpu and Seven Hunahpu are not dead. You will see them again. You will see them when my two children are born."

"No, you lie," said Xmucane. "You lie. My sons are dead. Those cannot be their children. You lay with some man, and now you come to me thinking I will believe you. I do not. Go away."

"I speak truth," said Lady Blood. "Truly these are the sons of One Hunahpu."

"If you really are my daughter-in-law," said Xmucane, "you must prove it. Take this net, and fill it with maize. Do that task successfully, and I will accept that you are my daughter-in-law."

"I will do as you ask," said Lady Blood.

Lady Blood took the net. She went to the field where the maize grew, the field that belonged to One Monkey and One Artisan. Lady Blood went into the field and started looking for maize to fill her net. She looked and looked, and although the maize was growing well, she could only find one ear to take home. No matter how she searched, she could find no more than one ear of maize that was ready to eat. "Oh, no!" cried Lady Blood. "What shall I do? Surely I have done wrong, for I cannot bring back a netful of maize to my mother-in-law. There is no maize. What shall I do?"

Then Lady Blood began to sing. She sang a song calling on the goddesses of the maize field. "Come, O Lady Thunder!" she sang. "Come, O Yellow Lady! Come, Lady of Cacao! Come, Lady of Cornmeal! Come to my aid, O guardians of the field of One Monkey and One Artisan."

Lady Blood took the corn silk at the top of the ear between her fingers. She pulled gently at the corn silk, without opening the husk, without taking the ear off the stalk. Gently and gently she pulled, and as she pulled, ripe ears of maize tumbled down from the silk into her net. The maize multiplied and multiplied, and still the single ear of maize was untouched upon the stalk. Finally, the young woman had enough maize to fill her net, but how to carry it? It was very full and very heavy, and Grandmother Xmucane's house was a long walk away. But soon the problem was solved: animals came from out of the trees to help her. They took up the net and the pack frame, and they carried it back along the path. But when they came within sight of Xmucane, they handed it back to Lady Blood, who took it up and pretended she had carried it the whole way herself.

When Xmucane saw Lady Blood carrying the heavy net full of maize, she was astonished. "Where did you find all that maize? Did you steal it from some other field? I am going to the field of One Monkey and One Artisan. I will see whether you truly got the maize from there or from some other field."

Xmucane went down the path to the maize field, and there she saw the plant with only one ear upon it, and the other plants with no ripened ears at all. She looked down at the ground underneath the plant with one ear. There she saw the grooves of the strings of the net that were pushed into the soil as the maize came tumbling down from the corn silk, the depression in the soil from the heaviness of the great pile of maize. Then Xmucane understood what had happened, and she returned home.

Xmucane went to Lady Blood and said, "I see now that you have spoken truly. You are my daughter-in-law, and those are my grandsons that you carry."

The Boyhood Deeds of Hunahpu and Xbalanque

When the time came for the twins to be born, Lady Blood went into the mountains. It was there the twins were born. They came suddenly; their grandmother did not have time to arrive to see them born. Lady Blood named the boys Hunahpu and Xbalanque, and she took them down the mountain to live in Grandmother Xmucane's house with their older brothers One Monkey and One Artisan. But this was not easy for anyone, for the twins wailed constantly, and no one was able to get any sleep.

Finally, Xmucane had had enough. "Take those two babies away! Take them someplace else! No one in this house gets any sleep with them here."

Lady Blood took the boys to an anthill. The ants scurried to and fro, in and out of their anthill. Lady Blood put the twins on the anthill, and they instantly stopped crying and went to sleep.

Another time when the twins were wailing, One Monkey and One Artisan took them and put them in a thorn bush. Again, the baby twins went right to sleep. "We should leave them there," said One Monkey and One Artisan. "We should leave them in the thorns, or on the anthill. Maybe they will die there, and we will have some peace."

They said this because they were seers and knew all that would happen to Hunahpu and Xbalanque, and all they would accomplish. One Monkey and One Artisan wished their brothers would die because they were sorely jealous, despite all their own great skills and gifts.

And so it was that Hunahpu and Xbalanque grew up outdoors in the mountains, and not in their grandmother's house. The twins grew well and strong, and soon they were able to go hunting. Every day they went into the forest to hunt birds for their family to eat, and they always came back with something good. One Monkey and One Artisan, however, sat around the house and played their flutes. They did not help with the hunting. They practiced their writing and carving, and they sang. They were very wise, for they had become the face of their father, One Hunahpu, who had been defeated by the Lords of Death in Xibalba. But nothing ever came of their great skills, because their hearts were eaten up with envy, their hearts burned hot with jealousy of Hunahpu and Xbalanque.

When Xmucane would prepare food, One Monkey and One Artisan would eat first. Hunahpu and Xbalanque waited in the doorway for the leftovers. When Hunahpu and Xbalanque brought birds from the forest, One Monkey and One Artisan would snatch them away and eat them, and give nothing to their younger brothers. The twins received no love from their older brothers, nor did they receive any from their grandmother. But Hunahpu and Xbalanque did not become angry. They understood how things were in their grandmother's house. Instead they bided their time, waiting for an opportunity for justice.

One day, Hunahpu and Xbalanque returned from a day in the forest without any birds. Xmucane was very angry with them. "Where are the birds? Why have you returned empty-handed?" she said.

"The birds flew up into the top branches of the tree, Grandmother," said the twins. "They flew so high we could not catch them. We need help to catch them. We want One Monkey and One Artisan to help us." They said this because Hunahpu and Xbalanque had come up with a plan to defeat their envious brothers.

They did not plan to kill One Monkey or One Artisan, but rather to transform them, as a punishment for their envy and the poor treatment they dealt to Hunahpu and Xbalanque. "They did not treat us as brothers," said the twins. "They treated us as slaves, and so we will have justice for that."

And so it was that One Monkey and One Artisan went into the forest with their brothers to hunt birds. They came to a big tree that was full of birds. The birds sat in the branches of the tree and sang. Hunahpu and Xbalanque pointed their blowguns into the trees and shot at the birds, but none of the birds they shot fell to the ground.

"See? This is the problem," said Hunahpu and Xbalanque. "We shoot the birds, but the tree is so large that they get stuck in the branches. We need you to climb the tree and bring the dead birds down to us."

"Very well," said One Monkey and One Artisan, and they began to climb the tree.

Up, up, up they climbed, high among the branches. Then something strange happened. The higher they climbed, the larger the tree became, until the tree was so big that when One Monkey and One Artisan were ready to descend, they could not get down.

"Help us!" cried One Monkey and One Artisan. "Help us, brothers! This tree is frighteningly tall! We cannot get down!"

"Take off your loincloths," said Hunahpu and Xbalanque. "Tie them around your waists, and let the long part dangle behind you. Pull on that loose part. Then you will find that you can climb the trees very well indeed."

One Monkey and One Artisan did as their brothers said. They retied their loincloths, and pulled on the loose end that was dangling behind. As they pulled, the end of their loincloth turned into a tail. Fur began to grow all over their bodies. Their hands and feet became long and slender. Their toes became long and grasping-like fingers. Their arms became long, and their bodies and heads shrank. One Monkey and One Artisan had become spider monkeys!

One Monkey and One Artisan screamed and chattered, as they no longer had human speech. But climbing trees was not difficult for them: they darted up and down the great tree, climbing with quickness and skill, and swinging from the branches on their tails. They went into the forest, where they climbed about in the trees, screeching at one another.

Hunahpu and Xbalanque went home. When Xmucane saw that their brothers were not with them, she asked what had become of them.

"Never fear, Grandmother," said the twins. "Our brothers are quite safe. In fact, you will see them very soon, but you must promise not to laugh at them. We will call them now. Remember: you must not laugh!"

Hunahpu and Xbalanque took up the flute and the drum. They started playing a song, and the name of the song was "Hunahpu Spider Monkey." One Monkey and One Artisan heard the song where they were out in the forest. They could not resist its call. They came ambling into Grandmother Xmucane's house, chattering and gesturing in the way monkeys do. When Xmucane saw them, she immediately began to laugh. This frightened the monkeys, and they ran back into the forest.

Hunahpu and Xbalanque said, "Shall we try again, Grandmother? We can call them again, but we can only do it four times. We can call them three more times, but you must promise not to laugh."

Xmucane promised not to laugh, so once again Hunahpu and Xbalanque played their song. Once again, One Monkey and One Artisan came into Xmucane's house. They danced about, and they were completely naked in the way of monkeys. Xmucane looked upon their nakedness and their silly dancing. She tried very hard not to laugh, but she could not contain herself. Soon she was laughing very hard indeed, and the two monkeys ran away back into the forest.

The twins tried once more to call their brothers back from the forest. Again, they warned their grandmother not to laugh. Again, the monkeys came when they heard the call of the song, and they danced about in Xmucane's house. This time Xmucane tried even harder not to laugh, but so amusing were the antics of her grandsons that she could not help herself. Yet again she burst out laughing, and the monkeys ran away back into the forest.

"We will try once more, Grandmother," said the twins. And so, they began playing their song, but this time the monkeys did not come. They stayed in the forest instead.

"Do not grieve, Grandmother," said Hunahpu and Xbalanque. "We cannot bring One Monkey and One Artisan back, but we are here. We are here, and we also are your grandsons, and we ask that you love our mother. Know also that we never will forget our brothers. Always will their names be spoken. Always shall we remember their deeds."

And so it came to pass that whenever musicians or writers or carvers began a piece of work, they called upon One Monkey and One Artisan to bless their art. But even though these brothers were revered, they were not considered gods. They did not have that honor, for although their deeds as musicians and writers were good and worthy of memory, they had too much pride and envy, and for those sins they were changed into monkeys.

Now that One Monkey and One Artisan lived in the forest as monkeys, they could not help their family by working in the maize field any longer. "Never fear," said Hunahpu and Xbalanque to their mother and grandmother. "We will do that work now. We will take the place of One Monkey and One Artisan."

The twins took up their farming tools and their blowguns and made ready to go to the maize field. "Bring us a meal at midday please, Grandmother," they said.

"I will bring it," said Xmucane.

The twins arrived at the maize field. They took the hoe and swung it with great strength into the soil. The hoe began to dig furrows in the soil by itself. They took the ax and swung it with great strength into a tree. Then the axe cut down the tree by itself. And so, the hoe plowed the field and dug out the briars from it by itself, and the axe cut down trees.

Hunahpu and Xbalanque saw Turtle Dove at the edge of the field. "Turtle Dove," they said to the bird, "you must be our lookout. When you see Grandmother Xmucane coming, call out to us so that we may take up our tools in our own hands."

Turtle Dove agreed, and went to a place where she could watch for Xmucane. Meanwhile, the twins took their blowguns and went hunting for birds to eat instead of working in the maize field. Soon enough, Turtle Dove called out to the twins. They rubbed dirt all over their bodies. They picked up the hoe and the ax. They pretended to be exhausted from all their hard work. Grandmother came and saw all the work that had been done. She gave the boys their meal, but they had not earned it, for they had not done the work themselves.

Every evening, the twins would return home and pretend to be sore and exhausted from all their work. "Oh!" they said, "Oh, how our backs ache! Oh, how tired our limbs are! Truly we worked very hard today."

Every morning, Hunahpu and Xbalanque went back to the maize field. But when they arrived there, they stopped and stared in wonder. For in the night, all the furrows had been flattened out. All the briars and bushes that had been dug out were back in their places. All the trees that had been chopped down were whole again.

"How has this happened?" cried the twins. "Someone is playing tricks on us."

Now, this is what had happened: in the night, the animals came. They smoothed over the furrows. They replanted the briars and bushes. They made the chopped trees whole. And so it was that when Hunahpu and Xbalanque arrived the next morning, all their work had been undone.

Again, Hunahpu and Xbalanque plowed furrows and dug out briars and cut down trees. But when the day's work was done, they swore to watch over their field in the night to see who it was that was undoing all their labor. They went home and told their grandmother what had happened and what they planned to do, and so they returned to the maize field to keep watch.

Night fell. Hunahpu and Xbalanque concealed themselves in a place where they could see the field but not be seen themselves. Soon there was a rustling from the forest. Out of the forest poured all manner of animals: jaguars and coyotes, rabbits and deer, tapirs and coatis, and all manner of birds. The animals went to the briars and bushes and bid them replant themselves, and once again the briars and bushes grew in their places. They did the same to the trees, and the trees once again were whole and growing in their places.

Hunahpu and Xbalanque saw the animals undoing all their work. They came out of their concealment and tried to catch the animals. First, they tried to catch jaguar and coyote, but those animals were too quick. Then they tried to catch rabbit and deer. They caught rabbit and deer by their long tails, but the tails broke off, and the animals got away. This is why rabbits and deer have short tails today.

The twins tried and tried to catch the animals, but they had no success. Finally, they were able to catch a rat. They took out their fury on the rat. They held it over the fire and burned the fur off its tail, and this is why rats have naked tails today.

"Stop!" said the rat. "You must not kill me. I have a message for you, and it is this: you are not meant to be maize farmers. But I do know what it is you are meant to do."

"Tell us," said the twins.

"I will tell you if you let me go, and if you give me a little food." said the rat. "I swear that I will not run away and that I will tell you the truth."

"We will give you food after you give us your message," said the twins.

"As you wish," said the rat. "This is my tale: I know where the gaming equipment is, the pads and helmets and ball that belonged to your fathers, One Hunahpu and Seven Hunahpu, who went to Xibalba and died there. If you look in the roof loft of your grandmother's house, there you will find all their equipment for the ballgame. Your grandmother hid these things from you, because your fathers died after accepting a challenge to a ballgame from the Lords of Xibalba."

The twins rejoiced to hear what the rat told them. Then they gave the rat much good food, as they had promised. They gave it maize and chiles and cacao, and many other good things besides. They told the rat that from then on it would have the right to take any morsels of food that had been swept outside the house.

"Now we will take you home with us so you can show us where the ballgame equipment is," said the twins.

"Gladly," said the rat, "but what if your grandmother catches us? What shall we do then?"

"Never fear," said the twins. "We know what to do. We will put you up among the rafters, and you will show us where the things are. We will be able to see what you do reflected in the chile sauce grandmother will make for us."

Then the twins and the rat passed the rest of the night making their plans, and at the noontide they returned home. They hid the rat so that it could not be seen. When they arrived at Grandmother Xmucane's house, one twin went inside while the other went around the outside of the house to put the rat in a place where it could get into the roof loft, and then that twin went inside as well.

"Will you make us some food, Mother?" asked the twins.

"Yes, gladly," said their mother. "What would you like?"

"Oh, make something with that chile sauce that is so very good," they said.

Soon the food was set before them, along with a bowl of chile sauce. The twins pretended to be very thirsty. They drank up all the water in the water jug.

"Will you fetch us some more water, O Grandmother?" they asked. But they were not truly thirsty; this was but a ruse to get the grandmother to leave the room.

While this was going on, the rat waited in the rafters of the house. When the grandmother had left, the rat went to where the ballgame things were. It stood beside the ballgame things, and the twins saw its reflection in the bowl of chile sauce. In this way, Hunahpu and Xbalanque learned where the ballgame equipment had been hidden.

In order to get the equipment down secretly, they also had to send their mother from the house. They told a small biting fly to find the grandmother and to pierce a hole in the water jug so that it would leak. The grandmother did not see the fly, but she did see the leak. She tried and tried to fix it, but she could not.

Back at the house, the twins began to complain about how thirsty they were. "What is taking Grandmother so long? Something surely must have gone wrong. O Mother, go find Grandmother and see whether she needs help."

And so, the mother also left the house, and once she was gone, the rat gnawed through the ropes that were tying the ballgame things in place up in the roof loft. The boys caught the things as they fell, and then went to hide them on the road near the ballcourt. Carrying their blowguns, they next went to the river, where they found the women struggling with the pierced jug.

"What has been taking so long?" asked the twins. "We became impatient with waiting."

"The jug has a hole in it," said the grandmother. "We have been trying to fix it so that we could bring back the water."

Hunahpu and Xbalanque fixed the hole in the jug. And so, the twins and their mother and grandmother returned to the house together.

Ballgames in Xibalba

Now that Hunahpu and Xbalanque had the gaming equipment of their fathers, they went to the ballcourt to play. First, they had to clear the field, for it had become overgrown with brush in the time since One Hunahpu and Seven Hunahpu had gone to Xibalba. When the field was clear, they put on their pads and helmets. They took up the ball and began to play. They ran about happily, hitting the ball back and forth and shouting to one another.

The sound of their play resounded below in the halls of Xibalba. The Lords of Death said, "Who is this, making all that racket? Did we not kill One Hunahpu and Seven Hunahpu already? Who could it be, bumping and thumping about?"

The Lords of Death called to the Owl messengers. "Go to those noisy people up there. Tell them that if they wish to play the ballgame, they must come and do it down here. They must come here, with their gaming equipment, in seven days' time, and play the game with us. The Lords of Xibalba command it."

The Owl messengers flew to the house of Xmucane. The Owls told her that in seven days, Hunahpu and Xbalanque must go to Xibalba with their gaming things to play against the Lords of Death.

"I will give them this message," said Xmucane.

When the Owls had left, Xmucane began to weep. She remembered how her sons had been summoned in the same way, and how they had never returned. She did not want to lose her grandsons also. As she wept, a louse fell onto her head. She scratched at it, and then picked it up.

"Little louse," said Xmucane, "I have a message to be taken to my grandsons, who are playing at the ballcourt. Will you take it for me?"

The louse agreed, and scuttled off on its errand. On the road to the ballcourt, there was a toad. The toad saw the louse scuttling along and said, "Where are you going?"

"I am going to the ballcourt," said the louse. "I have a message for the twins."

"Hm," said the toad. "You do not move very quickly. Perhaps it would be better if I swallowed you. I can hop faster than you can scuttle. I will help you take the message."

The louse agreed to this. The toad stuck out its long, sticky tongue. It swallowed the louse, and then went hopping along the road. Presently the toad hopped past a snake.

"Where are you going?" said the snake.

"I am taking a message to the boys who are playing ball at the ballcourt."

"Hm," said the snake. "You do not hop very quickly. Perhaps it would be better if I swallowed you. I can slither faster than you can hop. I will help you take the message."

The toad agreed to this, and presently the snake was slithering along the road, with the toad in its belly. Presently the snake met a falcon, who swallowed the snake. Then the falcon flew swiftly to the ballcourt and alighted on the wall. Hunahpu and Xbalanque were playing ball, but they stopped when they heard the falcon's cry.

"Look! There is a falcon there!" they said. "Let's get our blowguns."

The twins fetched their blowguns. They shot the falcon, hitting him in the eye. The falcon fell from the wall, and the twins picked him up.

"What were you doing there on the wall?" asked the twins.

"I came with a message for you, but I won't tell it until you cure my eye," said the falcon.

The boys agreed to this. They took a small piece of their rubber ball and put it into the eye socket of the falcon. Then the falcon was cured.

"Tell us the message!" said the twins to the falcon, so the falcon vomited up the snake.

"Tell us the message!" said the twins to the snake, so the snake vomited up the toad.

"Tell us the message!" said the twins to the toad, but no matter how he tried, the toad could not vomit up the louse.

"We think you are a liar," said Hunahpu and Xbalanque. They tried to force the toad to vomit, but still he could not vomit up the louse.

Then the boys pried the mouth of the toad open, and there they found the louse. The louse had not been swallowed by the toad. It was just sitting there inside the toad's mouth.

"Tell us the message!" the twins said to the louse.

The louse said, "The Lords of Death bid you come to Xibalba to play the ballgame in seven days' time. You must bring all your own gaming equipment. Your grandmother bade me bring you this message, and because of it, she weeps very sorely."

Hunahpu and Xbalanque let the louse go on its way, and they returned home. There they found Xmucane and their mother, weeping.

"Never fear, Grandmother. Never fear, Mother. We know what we must do," said the twins.

Hunahpu and Xbalanque each planted an ear of maize in the center of the house. They told Xmucane and Lady Blood that if the ears withered, that meant they had died. But if the ears flourished, that meant they were alive.

Then the twins took up their gaming things. They took up their blowguns. Together they took the road that leads to Xibalba. They crossed all the evil rivers, but they did not come to harm. When they arrived at the crossroads, Hunahpu took a hair from his leg and turned it into a mosquito.

"Go to the Lords of Xibalba," the twins said to the mosquito. "Bite them, and listen to what they have to say. Then come and tell us what you heard."

The mosquito buzzed away to the chamber where the Lords of Xibalba were seated. There he found the two wooden figures. He tried biting each of them, but they were only wood. Then he went into the chamber, where he bit One Death.

"Ouch!" said One Death.

"What is it, One Death?" said the others.

"Something bit me!" said One Death.

Then the mosquito went to Seven Death, and bit him too.

"Ouch!" said Seven Death.

"What is it, Seven Death?" said the others.

"Something bit me, too!" said Seven Death.

And in this way, the mosquito bit all the Lords of Death, and thus he learned all their names. But this was no ordinary mosquito, for it had been made from a hair from Hunahpu's leg, and thus the twins heard everything the mosquito had heard. Now the twins knew the names of all the Lords of Xibalba.

Hunahpu and Xbalanque went along the black road. They came to the doorway where the effigies were.

"Greet these lords correctly," said a voice.

But Hunahpu and Xbalanque merely laughed. "These are not lords. They are only wooden figures," they said.

Then the twins went into the chamber where the Lords of Xibalba were seated. Hunahpu and Xbalanque greeted each one of them by name.

The Lords of Xibalba said, "Sit there on that bench."

But Hunahpu and Xbalanque did not sit. They saw that the stone of the bench was heated.

"Go into that house," said the Lords of Xibalba. "Spend the night there, and in the morning, we will play the ballgame."

Messengers guided Hunahpu and Xbalanque to the house, which was the House of Darkness. The messenger of One Death gave each of them an unlit torch and a lit cigar.

"Take these things into the house with you," said the messenger. "Light the torches so that you can see, but be sure to give everything back in the morning, exactly as it is now."

Hunahpu and Xbalanque did not light the torches. Instead, they put some bright red feathers on the ends, to make it look like flames. Then they put out the cigars, but not before they summoned some fireflies. They put the fireflies on the ends of the cigars. And thus it was that the Xibalbans thought that the twins had lit the torches and were smoking the cigars. The Xibalbans watched them all night, and they rejoiced because they were sure that the twins had been defeated.

In the morning, Hunahpu and Xbalanque returned the torches to the lords, unburnt, and the cigars, unsmoked. The Xibalbans were amazed. "Who are they? Who are their parents? Where do they come from? This seems unlikely to end well for us," they said.

Then the boys were summoned before the Lords of Xibalba. "Who are you, and where do you come from?" asked One Death and Seven Death.

"Oh, we have no idea where we are from," said the twins.

Then the Xibalbans said, "Let us go to the ballcourt and play ball. We will use our ball for the game."

"No," said Hunahpu and Xbalanque. "We will use our ball."

"Our ball is better," said the Xibalbans. "We will use this one."

"That isn't a ball," said the twins. "It is a skull."

"No, it isn't," said the Xibalbans. "It only looks that way. It's a ball with a skull drawn on it."

"All right, we'll use your ball," said the twins.

And so, the ballgame began. But when the ball made its first bounce a dagger came out of it. The ball bounced around the court, trying to slash the twins with the dagger.

"Is that any way to treat your guests?" said the twins. "You invited us here to play the ballgame, but now you are trying to kill us. Very well; we will just go home now. We will not play."

"No, please don't leave," said the Xibalbans. "Stay and play. We will use your ball."

Hunahpu and Xbalanque agreed to stay. "What shall we have as our wager?" they asked.

"If we win, you must bring us four bowls of flowers," said the Lords of Death, "some with whole blossoms and some with just the petals."

"That is a fair wager," said the twins. "Let us play."

And so, the game began. Up and down the court the players ran. It was a hard-fought game, and the twins played well, but in the end the Xibalbans won.

"You will bring us the wager in the morning," said the Lords of Death. "And then we will play ball again."

Messengers took Hunahpu and Xbalanque to the House of Knives, where they were to spend the night. The twins could hear the blades of the knives clashing against one another. When they entered the house, the twins said, "Do not cut us. Cut the flesh of animals instead."

When they said that, the knives ceased their clashing. The knives did not cut Hunahpu and Xbalanque. Then the twins called to the ants. "Ants! Leaf-cutters! Come to our aid! Come and help us! Collect up flower petals and flower blossoms, four bowls full."

The ants agreed to help the twins. They went into the garden, and began to collect flower petals.

Now, the Lords of Xibalba had set some birds to act as watchmen. They told the birds, "Allow no one into the garden! No one at all!"

The birds agreed to watch the garden, but they did not see the ants. They just flitted about in the trees and bushes, singing their night songs. The ants climbed up into the plants and cut down flower petals. They cut down blossoms. They even climbed up onto the birds and clipped off some of their feathers, but the birds did not notice. The ants worked all night, collecting flower petals and whole blossoms, and soon they had filled four bowls.

In the morning, a messenger was sent to the House of Knives to bring Hunahpu and Xbalanque before the Lords of Xibalba. The twins went into the chamber where the Lords sat, bearing the four bowls of flower petals and whole blossoms. The Lords of Xibalba saw the bowls full of flower petals and whole blossoms, and they knew they had been defeated. They called to themselves the bird guardians and said, "Explain yourselves! We told you to guard our flowers, but here we have four bowls full of flower petals and whole blossoms."

"We do not know what happened," said the birds, "but even we were attacked. Look at our tails!" And they showed their tails to the Lords, their tails with the feathers the ants had plucked out.

The Lords of Xibalba were very angry with the bird guardians, and as punishment, they split the birds' mouths wide open.

Then the Lords went to play ball again with the twins, but nobody won that match.

"We will play again in the morning," said the Lords.

"Yes," said the twins, "we will gladly play again tomorrow."

That night the Xibalbans put Hunahpu and Xbalanque in the House of Ice. It was incredibly cold inside the house. The twins' breath misted thickly before their faces. Hail rained down on them. Hail covered the floor of the house, and the walls and rafters were thick with ice. Hunahpu and Xbalanque worked quickly. They built a fire of good logs and stood before it all night.

When the Xibalbans went to fetch the twins in the morning they said to themselves, "Ha! There is no way they could have survived the House of Ice! When we open the door, we will see their dead bodies, and we will have victory!"

But when they opened the door, they did not see the dead bodies of the twins. Instead, they saw Hunahpu and Xbalanque standing there, perfectly well and alive. "Good morning," said the twins. "Shall we go to the ballcourt and play?"

At the end of that day, the Xibalbans put the twins in the House of Jaguars. "Surely they will never survive this night," said the Xibalbans to themselves.

The House of Jaguars was full of hungry jaguars. The fierce cats surrounded the twins, growling and prowling. Hunahpu and Xbalanque said, "Do not bite us, O Jaguars! Here are bones for you to gnaw!"

And so, the twins threw bones to the jaguars, and the cats gnawed on those instead.

Outside the house, the Xibalbans heard the noise of crunching bones. "Ha!" they said to themselves. "The jaguars are eating those two for sure. We will find nothing left of them at all when we open the door in the morning."

Again, the Xibalbans were disappointed, for when they opened the door of the House of Jaguars, they found Hunahpu and Xbalanque perfectly well and alive.

The next night, the Lords of Xibalba put the twins in the House of Fire, but they were not burned at all. In the morning, Hunahpu and Xbalanque came out of the house perfectly well and alive.

The night after that, the twins were put in the House of Bats. But these were no ordinary bats: they were great Death Bats, and anyone who went near them was instantly killed. Hunahpu and Xbalanque crawled inside their blowguns to escape the Death Bats, and there they were safe.

All night long, the twins listened to the cries of the bats and to the flapping of their great wings. The bats made a great din, all night long. But after a time, the noise died down.

"Is it morning yet?" asked Xbalanque. "Are the bats asleep?"

"I don't know," said Hunahpu. "I'll go look."

Hunahpu crawled to the end of his blowgun. He stuck his head out the end to see whether it was morning. Suddenly, a great Death Bat swooped down and cut off Hunahpu's head.

Xbalanque waited inside his blowgun, but when no word came after a time, he said, "Hunahpu? Is it morning yet?"

But no answer came.

Xbalanque asked again, "Is it morning? What do you see?"

But no answer came save some light fluttering of bats' wings. And it was then that Xbalanque knew that they had been defeated, and that his brother was dead.

The Xibalbans celebrated the death of Hunahpu. One Death and Seven Death said, "Let his head be put atop the ballcourt!" And so that was done.

Meanwhile, from inside his blowgun, Xbalanque called to the animals. "Animals! O Animals great and small! Come to me; come and get your food."

And so, the animals came to where Xbalanque was, looking for their food. Last of all came a turtle. He came slowly and calmly, as is the way of turtles. The turtle walked over to the body of Hunahpu. It attached itself to Hunahpu's neck, and so a new head began to be fashioned. Heart of Sky came down into the House of Bats to help make a new head for Hunahpu.

All night long they worked to make a new head, but soon dawn was approaching, and the only thing that had been finished was the outside. Xbalanque called to the vulture. "Old One!" cried Xbalanque. "Make it dark again."

"I will do this," said the vulture, and immediately it became dark.

And so, the darkness lasted until Hunahpu's new head was completely finished, and then the dawn broke in the eastern sky. Then Hunahpu and Xbalanque took counsel together. They planned what they were going to do. "The Lords will want to play ball again," said Xbalanque. "You hang back; let me do all the playing." Then Xbalanque called to himself a rabbit. "O Rabbit," he said, "go and hide over there near the ballcourt. When I hit the ball toward you, bound across the ballcourt."

The rabbit went to the place he was to hide. Xbalanque and Hunahpu went to the ballcourt. When the Xibalbans saw Hunahpu, they said, "Ha! We have already defeated you. We don't know why you have even bothered coming here. Maybe we should hit your head with the ball!"

This made Hunahpu very angry, but he gave them no answer. And so, they began their ballgame. They played up and down the court, but Hunahpu hung back and did very little. Xbalanque played for both of them instead. After a time, the Xibalbans hit the ball toward the hoop. Xbalanque blocked the shot, and sent the ball bouncing toward the place where the rabbit was hiding. When the ball arrived there, the rabbit came bounding across the ballcourt as Xbalanque had asked him to do. The rabbit bounded and bounced just like the ball, and so the Xibalbans went running after the rabbit.

While the Xibalbans were chasing the rabbit, the twins ran over to the place where Hunahpu's real head was. They took that head down and replaced it with the head that had been made out of the turtle. They put Hunahpu's real head back on his body, and he was made whole. Laughing for joy, the twins went to the place where the real ball was. They brought it back to the ballcourt. They called to the Lords of Xibalba saying, "Look! We have the ball here. Let us finish our game."

The Lords came back, and they played ball with the twins. Now that Hunahpu had his own head back, he could play properly again. Back and forth and up and down the court the twins went, playing hard against the Xibalbans. No matter how hard the Xibalbans tried, they could not defeat the twins. The game ended in a tie. At the very end, Xbalanque threw the ball at the false head of Hunahpu where it sat atop the ballcourt. The head toppled from the wall, and split apart when it hit the ground.

"What is that?" said the Lords of Xibalba. "Who put that there?"

And so it was that Hunahpu and Xbalanque defeated the Lords of Xibalba. The Lords put the twins through many trials, but every time Hunahpu and Xbalanque defeated them and did not die.

The Deaths and Resurrections of Hunahpu and Xbalanque

Even though Hunahpu and Xbalanque had been through many trials, they knew there was no way the Xibalbans would let them leave alive. And so, the twins called to themselves two wise soothsayers, to give instructions about what to do with their bodies.

The twins said, "The Xibalbans will surely kill us; we will not leave here alive. We think that they will burn us. This is what you are to say when they ask what to do with our bones. Tell them not to throw the bones into the canyon; we will come back to life if they do that. Tell them not to hang our bones in the trees; that will merely remind them of all the times we defeated them. Tell them to scatter our bones in the river, but that first they should grind the bones into powder. They should grind our bones well, like the finest maize flour, and then pour that into the river."

"We will do as you say," said the soothsayers.

While the twins were speaking with the soothsayers, the Lords of Xibalba were making a huge bonfire. They were making it to kill Hunahpu and Xbalanque. When the fire was all made and very hot, the Xibalbans came to fetch the twins. "Let us play a game with the fire!" said One Death and Seven Death. "Let us fly across it, and see who comes out alive!"

But the twins were not fooled by this. "We know you mean to kill us," they said, "so let us finish that task right now."

And so, the twins embraced one another, and then jumped into the bonfire, where they died. The Xibalbans celebrated the deaths of Hunahpu and Xbalanque. They sang and danced. They jumped and shouted. And when their celebration was done, they sent for the soothsayers.

"What shall we do with their bones?" asked the Xibalbans.

"Grind them into powder, grind them like the finest maize flour, and then pour that into the river," said the soothsayers.

The Xibalbans ground the bones into powder. They poured the powder into the river. The powder floated away down the river, but soon it began to sink to the bottom. There on the bottom of the river the powder gathered up. It gathered itself, and made itself into two boys. It made itself into two beautiful boys, and Hunahpu and Xbalanque were alive again.

After five days, they came out of the river and began to show themselves to the people, but to the people they did not look like beautiful boys: they looked like fish people. When the Xibalbans learned that the twins were alive again, they began to search for them in all the rivers, but they did not find them.

Then the twins dressed themselves in rags. They went about pretending to be orphans. Wherever they went, they performed dances and worked miracles. They burned down houses and then made them whole, as though nothing had ever happened. One of them would kill the other, and then bring him back to life. The Xibalbans watched all of this, marveling at the deeds of these strange orphans. The Xibalbans watched, not knowing that in this way the twins were planting the seeds of their victory over the Lords of Death.

Soon enough, word of their skillful dancing came to the ears of One Death and Seven Death. They called to themselves their messengers. "Go and fetch these orphans," said One Death and Seven Death. "Tell them we command them to come before us and perform their dances and work their miracles. We have heard of their skill and wish to see it for ourselves."

The messengers went to Hunahpu and Xbalanque. They delivered the message of One Death and Seven Death. But the twins refused to go. "We do not wish to dance before the Lords of Death," they said. "We are but poor orphans. We do not belong in a stately house such as theirs. It is better if we do not go."

The messengers insisted that the twins should go. The messengers bullied them and threatened them. Finally, the twins agreed to go, but they went very, very slowly, with a great show of reluctance.

Finally, Hunahpu and Xbalanque arrived in the chamber of One Death and Seven Death, where they sat with the other Lords of Xibalba. The twins prostrated themselves in front of the Lords. They bowed low, they behaved in the most humblest of ways.

"Who are your people?" asked the Lords. "Where do you come from?"

"We are just poor orphans," replied the twins. "We have never known our parents. We don't know where we come from."

"It does not matter, then," said the Lords. "Perform your dances and miracles now. We will pay you when you are done."

"Oh, we require no payment, Lords," said the twins. "This place is very frightening. We are frightened indeed."

"Never fear," said One Death and Seven Death. "Perform your dances and miracles. Do the dances. Work the miracle where you make a sacrifice and then bring him back to life. Burn down our house and then restore it. Show us all the wonders you can do, and you will be handsomely rewarded."

And so, the twins began their dancing. They did the Armadillo Dance. They did the Weasel Dance. They did the Owl Dance, and many other dances. The Xibalbans watched them with great wonder and delight, for Hunahpu and Xbalanque were skilled dancers indeed.

"Now do the sacrifice trick," said One Death. "Cut up my dog and bring him back to life again."

The twins sacrificed the dog. They cut the dog into pieces, and then brought it back to life again. When the dog came back to life, it was very happy and went about wagging its tail.

"Now burn down my house," said One Death. "Burn down my house and restore it again."

Hunahpu and Xbalanque burned the house down. They burned it down with all the Lords inside it, but no one was harmed. They burned the house down and then restored it, as though nothing had ever happened. The Xibalbans marveled at this. They were much delighted by the miracle of the burning house that was restored.

Next the Lords demanded that the twins sacrifice a person and revive him. The twins took a person and cut out his heart. They took the heart and showed it to the Lords. Then they brought the person back to life again, and he was very happy to have his life restored to him.

"That is most marvelous!" cried the Lords. "Now sacrifice each other. Do that one, where you sacrifice each other and come back to life again."

"Very well," said the twins, and so Xbalanque sacrificed Hunahpu. Xbalanque cut his brother's body into pieces. The Lords of Xibalba watched this with great delight. Then Xbalanque brought Hunahpu back to life, and the Lords were even more happy and amazed.

"Oh!" said One Death and Seven Death. "That is a wonder indeed! Now do that to us! Sacrifice us, and bring us back to life!"

"Very well," said the twins. And so, they sacrificed One Death and Seven Death. The twins tore out the hearts of the Lords of Death, but they did not restore them to life. The twins let them stay dead, as punishment for their misdeeds.

A third Lord cowered before Hunahpu and Xbalanque. "Do not kill me!" he cried. "Have mercy!"

But when the other Xibalbans saw what had happened to One Death and Seven Death, they fled, because they were afraid that Hunahpu and Xbalanque would sacrifice them next. They ran and ran. They ran to the lip of a canyon and threw themselves over the edge, thinking that they could hide there. But there were so many of them, that soon the canyon was completely filled with the bodies of the Xibalbans.

Soon the ants discovered the canyon full of bodies. The ants ran into the canyon. They climbed all over the Xibalbans. This drove the Xibalbans out of the canyon. They went before the twins and begged them for mercy.

It was then that Hunahpu and Xbalanque revealed who they truly were. They said their names before the assembled Xibalbans. "We are Hunahpu and Xbalanque," they said, "and we are the sons of One Hunahpu and Seven Hunahpu, who came here to your realm and who were killed by you. We came here to avenge their deaths. We came here, and you put us through many sore trials. For those misdeeds, we shall surely kill you all!"

When the Xibalbans heard this, they all fell to their knees before the twins. "No, no!" they cried. "Do not kill us! Have mercy! Our deeds against your fathers surely were wrong; we confess it. We confess that our deeds against them were evil and that we killed them and buried them near the ballcourt. We are very sorry for that. Have mercy!"

Hunahpu and Xbalanque heard the pleas of the Xibalbans. They heard their cries for mercy and said, "Very well. We will not kill you. But still you must be punished. Never again will you receive good offerings. Yours will be croton sap, not fresh blood. Never shall you have offerings of sound goods, but only those that are cracked and worn. Never again will you be able to take good people. Only those who have truly done wrong will be for you."

And so it was that the Lords of Xibalba lost their status. They became lowered in their rank. They had never been gods, but still people had honored them. But after the coming of Hunahpu and Xbalanque to Xibalba, they were made unworthy of honor or worship. They were unworthy because they were untruthful and unfaithful, because they had bad hearts. Hunahpu and Xbalanque humbled the Lords of Xibalba. They took away their rank and status from them.

Now, while Hunahpu and Xbalanque were in Xibalba, their grandmother Xmucane had watched the ears of maize the twins had planted within the house. For many days, the maize was green and growing, but when Hunahpu and Xbalanque jumped into the bonfire, the maize withered and died. Xmucane saw that the twins had died, and she mourned greatly. She shed many bitter tears and burned incense before the maize, in memory of her grandsons. But then the boys came back to life, and so did the maize. Xmucane saw this and rejoiced. She celebrated when the maize came back to life.

Xmucane worshiped the reborn maize plants. She gave them a new name. She called them "Center of the House" and "Green Reeds." Thus did Xmucane honor her grandsons. Thus did she honor their memory.

After Hunahpu and Xbalanque defeated the Lords of Xibalba, they sought out the place where One Hunahpu and Seven Hunahpu had been buried. They went looking for the pieces of One Hunahpu's body. They found many of the pieces, but they could not make him whole. They found One Hunahpu's head, but when asked to say its name, it could not.

When the twins found that they could not restore their father to life, they said, "Be comforted, father. Be comforted, uncle. Your name shall not be forgotten. The name of Hunahpu will belong always to this place.

"We have avenged your deaths. We have avenged all the misdeeds committed against you by the Lords of Xibalba. May your hearts be at peace."

Then Hunahpu and Xbalanque rose into the heavens. Up, up, up they rose, high in the sky. One became the sun, and the other became the moon. They dwelled together in the sky ever after.

With them arose the four hundred boys who had been killed by Zipacna. The four hundred boys rose up into the sky with Hunahpu and Xbalanque, and there they became a constellation.

And this is the end of the tale of Hunahpu and Xbalanque, and of all their deeds, and of their transformation when their deeds were accomplished.

PART III: THREE MAYA FOLKTALES

The Man Who Became a Buzzard

This story of a lazy man who is changed into a buzzard exists in multiple variants throughout Central America. In some stories, the man is permanently changed, while in others he is allowed to resume his human form. Whatever their ending, each of these stories is a cautionary tale about the value of hard work and of accepting one's place in the world. In this retelling, I am following the ending related by Martha Schmitt in her collection of Central American legends.

Once there was a farmer who lived together with his wife, and they were very poor indeed. The reason they were so poor was that the husband was extremely lazy. Every day he would go out to his fields, but instead of working hard caring for his crops and clearing land, he would do only a little work in the morning and then for the rest of the day he would sit under a shady tree and take a nap, or he would go to the river and paddle about in the water, or he would lie on his back and watch the clouds floating by in the sky. And so, his crops never grew well, and he never had space to plant more, because he did not do his work.

One day, as the man lay on his back gazing at the sky, he saw a buzzard sailing in slow circles in the air above him. "What a life!" said the man to himself. "What a life it must be, to just sail through the air like that, and to never have to work. I wish I could be like that buzzard. Then I would be content indeed."

Then the man had an idea.

"Hey!" he shouted at the buzzard. "Hey! Come down here and talk to me!"

The buzzard flew in slow circles above the man. He flew, circling and circling, and the man began to think that maybe the buzzard hadn't heard him. But then the buzzard began to descend, ever circling, until finally he landed in the field next to the man.

"What do you want?" croaked the buzzard.

"I have an idea for you," said the man. "I've watched you circling up there in the sky, without a care in the world, while meanwhile I have to work so hard down here on the ground. And so, I have an idea for you. How about we change places? I could put on your feathers and fly about, and you could put on my clothes and work my farm."

"Well," said the bird, "being a buzzard might not be as good as you think it is. Yes, we fly about, but that's because we're looking for food. We eat dead animals, you know. Ones that are dead and rotting. The more rotten the better. That's what you'd have to eat."

"Yes, I know that," said the man. "I know buzzards eat rotten meat. I think I could do that, if it meant I didn't have to work anymore. If you changed places with me, you could eat the good food my wife cooks. Our food is very simple, and we don't have much, but she cooks it well."

The buzzard thought for a moment, then he said, "All right. I will change places with you. Give me your clothes and skin and I will give you my feathers."

The man took off his clothes and skin and gave them to the buzzard. The buzzard took off his feathers and gave them to the man. And soon there in the field stood a buzzard and a man, but they had changed places. The man in the buzzard's feathers flapped away up into the sky and flew in two circles above the field, then he returned to the ground.

"Right!" said the man, who had become a buzzard. "I am a buzzard now. I like my wings. Thank you for trading with me! Now, let me show you where my house is, so that you can meet my wife. I'll alight on the roof, and you will know that that is my house."

The man flapped his new wings and went flying into the sky. The buzzard moved his new legs and walked. Together they went to the man's house, where the man who had become a buzzard alighted on the roof. Once the buzzard who had become a man knew which house it was, the man flew away. The buzzard in the man's skin went into the man's house. He went to the man's wife to greet her, but she pushed him away. "Oh!" she cried. "Oh, you smell so very, very bad! What have you been doing, that you smell that way?"

"I have been working in the fields," said the buzzard. "It is very hard work, and I am sweating a lot. That's why I smell bad."

"Wait here," said the wife. "I will go and prepare a bath for you."

The wife prepared a sweat bath for the buzzard. The buzzard took off the man's clothes and went into the sweat bath, but he didn't like it much. It was so hot and so damp. He became truly uncomfortable, and so he left the bath and went back into the house, even though he still smelled bad and wasn't clean at all.

Meanwhile, the man in the buzzard's feathers decided to enjoy his new wings. He went up, up, up into the sky and began flying in circles. He was very pleased with being a buzzard. "This is the life!" he said. "This is the way to be, flying in circles, up here in the sky!"

After a time, he began to be hungry. He thought about what he would have to eat as a buzzard, and it made him sick to his stomach. Even being able to fly about in the sky was not enough to make him want to remain a buzzard if he had to eat dead, rotting animals. He decided to go home. He flew over his house and circled above the roof a few times before landing on the ground outside the door. Then he went into the house. Hop, hop, hop he went, as buzzards do, because he still wore the buzzard's feathers.

He saw the buzzard who was wearing his skin inside the house arguing with his wife.

"You still smell so bad! Didn't you finish your bath?" said the wife.

"No, I didn't. I don't like that bath at all," said the buzzard. "It is too hot and too damp. Anyway, I can't help the way I smell, can I? I've always smelled like this."

Then the wife caught sight of the man who had turned into a buzzard. She screamed when she saw the large, ugly bird standing there in the house.

"Rawk, rawk!" croaked the bird. It was the man, trying to tell his wife that he was her husband, but she didn't understand. Instead, she grabbed a broom and started trying to hit the huge bird.

"Rawk!" croaked the bird, as it tried to hop out of the way of the broom.

"Wait!" said the buzzard who had turned into a man. "Wait! Don't hurt that bird! That is your husband. He and I changed places. He wanted to try being a buzzard, and I wanted to try being a man. That's why I smell so bad."

"Well, change back!" said the woman. "Give him back his skin and clothes, and he'll give you back your feathers."

"We can't change back," said the buzzard. "We have to stay the way we are."

The wife began to cry, because although her husband was very lazy indeed, she still loved him. The man who had become a buzzard was also very sad, because he loved his wife, and although he could still fly about in the sky, now he could only eat rotten meat instead of his wife's good cooking. And although the buzzard who had become a man got to eat the good cooking, he now had to work very, very hard, and take baths whenever his wife told him to.

How the Sun and Moon Became Man and Wife

The tropes of the old man who doesn't wish his daughter to marry and of the young couple who must go through a sore trial before they can wed is common to many cultures. In this tale from Guatemala, these tropes are woven into a just-so story that explains the creation of the moon, snakes, and many kinds of insects.

Long, long ago, when the world was new, there was an old man who lived alone with his only daughter. The daughter was very beautiful, and she was very skilled and industrious. She knew how to spin and weave, she knew how to sew, she knew how to keep a good garden, and how to cook delicious food. She looked after her father very well, and he looked after her, and together they were very happy.

One day, the Sun happened to see the old man's daughter, who was sitting outside spinning some new thread. The Sun looked at her, and fell in love. She was so very beautiful! Her long black hair shone in the light, her dark eyes twinkled with merriment, and her strong fingers worked quickly and well with her spindle and thread. That very moment, the Sun decided that he must have the young woman for his bride.

The Sun decided that he would turn himself into a hunter and impress the young woman with his strength and prowess at the hunt.

Surely that way he would win her heart, and they could be wed and live together in great happiness. But there was not much game to be found in the part of the forest where the old man lived with his daughter, so the Sun thought of a way he might trick the young woman into thinking him a fine hunter. He found the skin of a deer, then filled it with ashes and dried grass and sewed it up so that it looked like he had caught a fine, fat animal that would feed a family well. Then he put the false deer on his shoulders, and strode past the old man's house where the daughter sat working at her spindle.

And so, for many days, the Sun took the form of a handsome, strong young man. In the mornings he would walk past the old man's house with his bow and arrows, and in the afternoons, he would return with the fat, false deer on his shoulders, as though he had just killed it and was going home to cook and eat it. Now, the young woman noticed the young man striding by—although she gave no hint to him that she was looking—for he was indeed well to look upon, with his thick, black hair and his warm, brown eyes, and his broad shoulders and his fine, strong legs. Surely he would make a good husband for some lucky woman, as handsome as he was, and as skilled at the hunt, for he never failed to return home with a fat deer.

One morning, after the young man had passed by the old man's house, the daughter went to her father and said, "Father, I think that young hunter would make a good husband for me. He is so very handsome, and he always comes home with a fat deer."

"Hm," said the old man. "I am not sure of that. There is not much game in this part of the forest. He could be tricking you. Young men do that sort of thing, sometimes. Next time he goes past, throw some water onto the ground in front of him. That might tell you something about him."

That afternoon, the young woman sat in front of her father's house washing some maize in a bowl full of water. Soon enough, the young hunter came into view, with the deer on his shoulders. Remembering what her father had said, the young woman put the maize into a different bowl and then threw the water onto the ground in the hunter's path. When his foot touched the wet earth, the hunter slipped and fell. He landed right on top of the false deer, splitting the seams and sending a great cloud of ash into the air. The woman saw this, and gasped. The Sun felt very ashamed, because now his trick was made plain before her, so he changed himself into a hummingbird and flew away.

But even though his trick with the deerskin had gone awry, the Sun still was in love with the beautiful young woman, and he could not stay away from her. In the form of a hummingbird, he would go into the old man's garden and flit amongst the flowers there, and in that way, he would watch the young woman at her work. One day, the young woman noticed the hummingbird flying in the garden and sipping nectar. The bird was such a pretty thing, with bright, shining feathers, that she wanted to have it for her own, and she did not know that this little bird was the Sun in disguise.

The young woman went to her father and said, "Father, will you get your blowgun and catch that hummingbird for me?"

"Certainly, my dear," said the old man, and he went out into the garden and PHUT! he blew a shot at the hummingbird and knocked it to the ground, stunned. The young woman ran to pick up the little-feathered thing. She cradled it carefully in her hands, then took it into the house, where she put it in her room.

That night, while the young woman slept, the Sun turned himself back into the form of a young man. The young woman woke up and found him standing there in her room.

"What are you doing here?" she said. "Who are you? If my father finds you here, he will kill us both!"

"Have no fear," said the man. "I am the young hunter who tried to trick you with the deer, but you were too clever for me. And I am the hummingbird who drank nectar from the flowers in your garden, but your father captured me with his blowgun. I saw you sitting in your father's garden many, many days ago, and I fell in love with you. Come away with me, and be my wife! We will live together most happily, that I promise you."

"Oh!" said the young woman. "I should very much like to go with you, but it is not safe. My father has a magic stone, in which he can see anything he chooses, both far and near. And he has a magic blowgun that he could use to kill us. We would never be able to get away from him."

"Never mind that," said the Sun. "I will make it safe for us; you will see."

Creeping through the house as quietly as two mice, the young man and young woman went to the place where the old man kept his magic stone and his magic blowgun. The Sun took some ash and poured it all over the stone, so that the old man would not be able to see anything in it. Then he took some ground chili powder and put it inside the blowgun. That done, the pair slipped out the door and into the forest.

In the morning, the old man woke and called to his daughter, but she did not answer. He went through the house and garden looking for her, but did not find her. Angry that his daughter had run away, the old man went to the place where he kept his magic stone. He picked it up, and tried to see where the young woman had gone, but he couldn't see through the ash the Sun had poured on it. Suddenly, he saw that there was one spot where there was no ash, because the Sun had not been careful enough in covering the whole stone. In that small spot on the stone, the old man saw his daughter with a young man on the river in a canoe.

The old man trembled with rage. How dare his daughter leave with a young man without his permission! He took up his blowgun and went out after the young couple. He put the blowgun to his lips and drew in a breath so that he could take a shot, but instead of air, he breathed in the ground chili powder. How the old man coughed, and how his eyes watered! How his throat and his mouth burned! The old man was furious. He called to the lightning to go and strike down the young man and his daughter.

The Sun and the young woman were in the canoe, paddling as fast as they could to get away from the old man. The Sun realized that a lightning bolt was coming. "Jump into the water!" he said, and then threw himself into the river, where he turned into a turtle and swam as fast as he could toward the river bottom. The young woman also jumped into the water, where she became a crab. But she couldn't swim as fast as the turtle, so when the lightning bolt struck the water, it hit her.

The young woman's blood slowly spread out over the surface of the water. The Sun swam up from the depths of the river, where he saw the blood of his beloved floating on the surface. The Sun wept with grief. He called to the dragonflies for help, asking them to collect up the blood for him. The dragonflies did as the Sun bid them. They collected up all the blood, putting it into little bottles. When they were finished, they gave the bottles to the Sun, who hid them away in a safe place.

After a certain time, the Sun returned to the place where he had hidden the bottles. He opened the first one, and a great many snakes came pouring out. He opened the second one, and a cloud of wasps buzzed out of it and into the sky. The Sun opened bottle after bottle, and from each one poured a different kind of small creature, that then flew or crawled away. And that is how snakes and many kinds of insects came to be in the world.

Finally, the Sun opened the very last bottle. In that bottle was the young woman, as beautiful as ever, with her long, shining, dark hair, and merry eyes, and skillful fingers. The Sun took her hand and drew her up into the heavens with him, where he could gaze on her beauty and where she could delight in his strength, for when she went up with him, she was transformed into the Moon. And there in the heavens the Sun and the Moon have lived happily as husband and wife ever since.

Rabbit Gets His Drink

*The rabbit is a trickster in the Maya culture, as he is in many others.
In this story from Nicaragua, Rabbit needs to find a way to get to the
waterhole safely which, of course, he does by means of a trick.*

As everyone knows, Rabbit is a clever animal. He lives by his wits,
always getting into trouble and then getting out of it again. One
village had constant problems with Rabbit. He was forever getting
into their gardens and stealing their vegetables, and doing other
naughty things. The villagers went to the king and said, "We cannot
abide Rabbit's tricks any longer. You must rid us of him."

Now, the king was a wise man, and he knew how clever Rabbit was.
He also had many other important things to do besides deal with
naughty Rabbits. He told the villagers, "Very well. If you catch him
and bring him here to me, I will deal with him."

The villagers thought this a fair bargain, so they went home and
called a meeting to decide how to catch Rabbit. They thought of
traps they might set, but then they remembered that every trap they
had tried in the past had failed. Then someone said, "Why don't we
lie in wait for him at the waterhole? All the animals go there to
drink. Eventually Rabbit will become thirsty, and he will go to the
waterhole, too. Then we can grab him while he is taking his drink,
and bring him to the king."

The others thought this a splendid plan. They went to the waterhole
and hid themselves among the trees and bushes, waiting for Rabbit
to come and get his drink. They waited and waited, not knowing that
when they had their meeting, Rabbit had been hiding nearby. Rabbit
heard everything the villagers said. He knew that the waterhole was
not a safe place for him anymore, but he also knew that soon he
would be thirsty. Rabbit set to thinking, and soon he had a plan. He
would trick the villagers. Then he would be able to drink all the

water he wanted. And the villagers would be able to do nothing about it.

First Rabbit went to another village, one where the people did not know him. He went along the street until he came to a shoemaker's shop. The shoemaker was sitting outside his shop, working on a lovely new pair of shoes.

"Good morning!" said Rabbit to the shoemaker. "A fine, hot day, is it not?"

"Good morning!" said the shoemaker. "Yes, it is indeed both fine and very hot."

"Maybe you should go inside," said Rabbit. "I can see that you are a hard worker. You have made so many lovely shoes already today. Why don't you go inside, and get yourself a nice cool drink? You deserve it."

"Why, I do believe I am thirsty," said the shoemaker. "I will do as you suggest."

As soon as the shoemaker was inside, Rabbit selected a pretty pair of red shoes and hopped away with them. Rabbit went down the road for some time. Then he saw a man coming toward him. The man was carrying a heavy gourd on his back, the kind of gourd that people often fill with golden, sweet honey.

"Oh!" said Rabbit to himself. "That gourd is probably full of honey. Sweet honey would be a tasty treat right now, and it's just the thing I need for my trick!"

Rabbit dropped one of the shoes in the middle of the road, then hopped off to the side and hid in some bushes. Soon enough, the man came along and found the single shoe.

"What is this?" said the man, stooping to pick up the shoe. "Why, this is a very pretty shoe, and just the right size for my daughter. Alas, it's only a single shoe, so it does us no good."

The man dropped the shoe in the road where he had found it, and carried on with his journey.

Rabbit was delighted. That was exactly what he wanted the man to do. Rabbit took the remaining shoe and ran with it up the road, ahead of the man. Rabbit put the other shoe in the road where the man would find it, and then hid himself in the bushes again. Sure enough, when the man came upon the shoe, he picked it up and said, "Oh! This matches the one I saw back there. I shall have a fine pair of shoes to give my daughter now. But first I'll put down my gourd; it's heavy, and there's no reason to carry it back and forth."

And so, the man set his gourd down in the road, and went to get the first shoe.

As soon as the man's back was turned, Rabbit hopped out into the road. He picked up the gourd, and hurried back into the forest. Rabbit ran along, carrying the gourd, until he came to a clearing. The floor of the clearing was covered with fallen leaves.

"Oh!" said Rabbit. "This is a fine place to sit and eat my honey."

Rabbit opened the gourd and began to eat the honey. It was golden, and sweet, and very good. Rabbit ate and ate and ate until he thought he would burst. Even so, there was still quite a bit of honey left, for it was a very large gourd. Rabbit took the remaining honey and poured it all over his body. He poured it into his fur, and down his legs, and up his ears, and even made sure there was some on the puff of his white, fluffy tail. Rabbit was soon covered all over with golden, sticky honey.

Then Rabbit hopped into the middle of the clearing. He flopped down onto the fallen leaves and began to roll, back and forth, back and forth, until he was all covered with fallen leaves. When the leaves touched the honey, there they stuck, and did not fall off. Soon Rabbit looked nothing at all like a rabbit. Not a bit of his fur was visible, not even the puff of his white, fluffy tail. He looked like some kind of odd leaf-creature that hopped out of a dark corner of the forest.

Covered in his leaf disguise, Rabbit went back to his home village. He hopped right down the middle of the main street, but no one recognized him. In fact, the people were a little bit frightened, because they had never seen a creature quite like that before. Piles of leaves and twigs were not supposed to have legs! Piles of leaves and twigs were not supposed to hop down the middle of the street! The people were frightened enough that they did not go near Rabbit at all.

Rabbit hopped down the middle of the main street, right down to the waterhole. The villagers who were lying in wait for Rabbit saw him coming toward them, but they did not recognize him, either. All they saw was a strange leaf-creature, hopping, hopping, hopping toward the water, so they stayed in their hiding places.

Rabbit chuckled to himself as he hopped up to the edge of the water. He knew the villagers were watching him, but they did not recognize him! This was a fine trick he had played, for sure.

Rabbit was thirsty after playing tricks and eating so much honey. He took a long, long drink of water, as much as he liked. Then he hopped away.

The villagers never did catch Rabbit, and they never did bring him before the king.

Section 2: Aztec Mythology

Captivating Aztec Myths of Gods, Goddesses, and Legendary Creatures

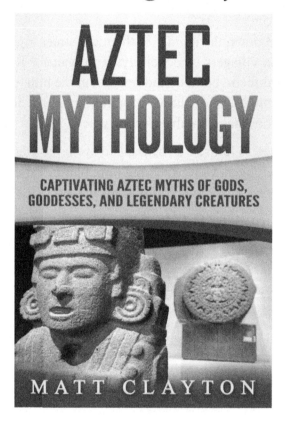

Introduction

Between the ninth and the late eleventh centuries, a great migration began where tribes, including one who called themselves "Mexica," moved from places "far to the north" into what is now Central Mexico. The myths that describe this migration call the place of origin "Aztlan," which is sometimes translated as "Place of the White Heron," and it is from this name that we get the word "Aztecs," or "People from Aztlan."

The Aztec civilization of Central Mexico was not a single unitary culture but was rather made up of different peoples who spoke the Nahuatl language and who traced their origins to that far-off northern home. Over the centuries that followed the start of the migration from Aztlan, Aztec peoples established city-states and empires in Central Mexico, the largest of which was centered in the great city of Tenochtitlan, the capital of Mexica culture and political power, which had been built on the waters of Lake Texcoco. Today, that ancient capital has been overbuilt by Mexico City, the lake bed long ago having been drained of water.

By the time the Spanish arrived in 1519, the Aztec Empire was well established and had been consolidated under the umbrella of the

Triple Alliance since 1428. This alliance of city-states included Mexico-Tenochtitlan, centered in the city of Tenochtitlan; the city-state of Texcoco, based on the eastern shore of the lake; and Tlacopan, a city-state on the western shore. The empire was orderly and prosperous; indeed, Spanish witnesses from the time of the conquest describe cities and markets that were larger, better built, and better organized than anything they had seen before. But only two years later, through a combination of war, conquest, and disease, the Aztec Empire was no more, and Mesoamerican culture and religion had been irrevocably damaged by the imposition of Spanish rule and the forced introduction of Christianity.

One of the primary difficulties in reconstructing the original mythological traditions of the Aztecs is the paucity of sources. In an act of iconoclasm born of efforts at Christianization, Spanish missionaries and government officials tracked down and burned Aztec books and government records. Of the many thousands of books and documents that must have once existed, only twelve are left today. Further, much else of what we know of Aztec myth and culture comes through the filter of early modern Spanish witnesses, whose cultural and religious biases undoubtedly skew much of what they reported.

However, invaders from across the sea were not the only iconoclasts: the Mexica emperor Itzcoatl (r. 1427 or 1428 to 1440 AD) consolidated his own power in part by revising history and myth in order to bolster claims of Mexica ascendancy in the region. Itzcoatl ordered the destruction of earlier codices and the creation of new ones that emphasized the legitimacy both of Mexica power and the supremacy of the Mexica war god Huitzilopochtli.

As a result of these instances of destruction, we therefore have only a partial view of what must have been the original Aztec mythos. However, what does exist shows a rich and complex tradition of origin myths, trickster tales, and mythologized pseudo-history that gives us a glimpse into the cosmology, religion, and world-view of this once-vibrant Mesoamerican culture.

The present book is divided into two sections. The first contains myths of the gods and goddesses, including the "Legend of the Suns," which is a complex of origin myths describing the creation of the world, followed by a tale that explains the origins of the Aztec practices of blood offerings and ritual warfare. Three other myths in this section relate the advent of other things important to Aztec life and culture: maize, pulque (an alcoholic beverage made from the sap of the maguey cactus), and music. A final story describes the Aztec concept of the afterlife.

The second section of the book contains Aztec political myths, all of which were intended to paint the Aztecs as a heroic people favored by the gods and worthy of conquering the civilizations they encountered. The first of these tales is the myth describing the Mexica journey from Aztlan to Central Mexico and the founding of the city of Tenochtitlan, all under the aegis of the god Huitzilopochtli. The second involves a mythical embassy to Aztlan commanded by the emperor Motecuhzoma I, who wishes to reconnect with the ancestral people there and with the mother of Huitzilopochtli, to let them know how great the Aztec Empire has become.

The remaining political stories in this section are a complex that create a mythical pseudo-history of the downfall of the Toltecs. Toltec civilization flourished in Central Mexico between the early tenth and late twelfth centuries and was one of the cultures that was displaced by the arrival of the Mexica and the imposition of Aztec rule in that region. In the third and fourth stories in this section, Huemac, the legendary last king of the Toltecs, is subjected to various misadventures and humiliations at the hands of Tezcatlipoca, the Aztec god of night, enmity, and discord, who presents himself in various disguises in order to play tricks on the king and destroy the Toltec people, while Huemac's own insolence towards the servants of Tlaloc, the god of rain, brings drought, famine, and a final prophecy of the end of Toltec culture.

One practice of the Toltec kings, who also functioned as priests in Toltec religion, was to claim the title of "Quetzalcoatl." In the final legend presented here, the priest-king is the god himself. Once again, Tezcatlipoca works his cunning against the Toltec ruler, this time turning him out of the city once and for all. The myth of how Quetzalcoatl exiled himself in shame from the Toltec capital, Tula, and then was transformed into the Morning Star is an episodic tale along the lines of the classic hero's journey.

In many of these myths, we see repeatedly the Aztec belief that offerings of human blood and human lives were necessary to the continued running of the universe. Indeed, in these myths the gods themselves make sacrifices of their own blood and even of their entire bodies in order to create a universe humans can live in and, in one story, to create humans themselves; humans therefore must make blood sacrifices in turn to feed the gods and to keep the universe in existence. To the ancient Aztecs, these practices seemed fitting, necessary, and honorable, helping to connect the world of humans to the divine world of the gods, a universe that in Aztec myth took shape in cycles of creation, destruction, and rebirth.

Note on the Aztec Calendar

A prominent feature of many ancient Mesoamerican civilizations is the use of well-constructed calendars and timekeeping systems. The Aztecs used two separate but interlocking yearly calendars: one was a 360-day solar year calendar, the other a 260-day ritual calendar. In addition, the Aztecs kept careful track of much longer spans of time, in particular the 52-year *xiuhmolpilli* (Bundle of Years) cycle.

The solar year was called "xihuitl" in Nahuatl, while the calendar for that year was known as *xiuhpohualli* (year count). This calendar was composed of eighteen months having twenty days each, for a total of 360 days. Each month was named after a specific religious festival, and days in this calendar were designated in much the same way as in the modern Western calendar. So, for example, days in the month called "Teotleco" (Return of the Gods) would be designated 1 Teotleco, 2 Teotleco, 3 Teotleco, and so on until 20 Teotleco was reached, at which point the new month would begin.

Because this 18-month calendar did not completely match the actual solar year, an additional five intercalary days were added at the end of the eighteenth month in order to keep the calendar aligned with the seasons. These five days were called "nemontemi" (nameless) and were considered to be very unlucky. The Aztecs were aware that the solar year is actually 365.25 days, but we do not know how they might have adjusted their calendars in order to account for the extra partial days.

The ritual calendar was called *tonalpohualli*, which means "count of day signs." The tonalpohualli was used to determine when specific rituals ought to be performed, as well as for astrology and auspice-taking, and was further connected to the world of the divine by having various gods preside over certain units of time as well as over specific days.

The Aztec sacred calendar was composed of a set of 20 "day signs," such as "Alligator," "Death," or "Flint Knife," that occurred and repeated in a fixed order. Alongside these signs was a count of 13 days that is known in Spanish as a *trecena* (the original Nahuatl word is unknown), such that a particular day could be called "3 Monkey" or "11 Reed," for example. The number count would restart when the thirteenth day was reached and continue numerically when the 20-day count ran out. Thus, the day-sign "Calli" (House) might be "1 Calli" in one cycle, but "8 Calli" in another. The table below shows all the day signs and the way they interact with the 13-day number count:

Day Name	Translation	Day Counts		
Cipactli	Alligator	1	8	2
Ehecatl	Wind	2	9	3
Calli	House	3	10	4
Cuetzpallin	Lizard	4	11	5
Coatl	Snake	5	12	6
Miquiztli	Death	6	13	7
Mazatl	Deer	7	1	8
Tochtli	Rabbit	8	2	9
Atl	Water	9	3	10
Itzcuintli	Dog	10	4	11
Ozomatli	Monkey	11	5	12
Malinalli	Grass	12	6	13
Acatl	Reed	13	7	1
Ocelotl	Jaguar	1	8	2
Cuauhtli	Eagle	2	9	3
Cozcacuauhtli	Vulture	3	10	4
Ollin	Movement	4	11	5

Tecpatl	Flint Knife	5	12	6
Quiahuitl	Rain	6	13	7
Xochitl	Flower	7	1	8 *etc.*

After Michael E. Smith, The Aztecs, *3ʳᵈ ed. (Chicester: Wiley-Blackwell, 2011), 252.*

As we see in the table, when a trecena runs out, a new one starts again with the next day sign. So, a trecena that starts on 1 Cipactli ends on 13 Acatl, and the new trecena begins on 1 Ocelotl and continues to the end of the day-sign list on 7 Xochitl. The day-sign list then restarts in the middle of the trecena, on 8 Calli, and this second trecena ends on 13 Miquiztli. The next trecena then starts on 1 Mazatl, and so on. This interlocking combination of 20 day signs and 13 numbers means that it takes 260 days to run through a complete cycle, which contains 260 unique combinations of day signs and numbers. Additionally, each trecena in the cycle was associated with a particular deity.

The solar calendar and ritual calendar when combined form a cycle that begins and ends in a space of 52 years. This cycle is known as *xiuhmolpilli* (Bundle of Years) in Nahuatl, although English-speaking scholars sometimes refer to it as the "calendar round." Similar to the ritual calendar, the count of the calendar round was based on the number 13, working within a cycle of 13 years, except with only four year signs instead of 20 day signs. These four years were called, in order, Tochtli, Acatl, Tecpatl, and Calli. Therefore, the year-cycle went 1 Tochtli, 2 Acatl, 3 Tecpatl, 4 Calli, 5 Tochtli, 6 Acatl, and so on until 13 years had passed and the next cycle would start on 1 Acatl. After 52 years, the cycle would return to its starting place on 1 Tochtli.

Within this cycle, days are described by their position in the solar calendar, the ritual calendar, and the four-name, 13-year cycle of counts within the calendar round. Because each day designation recurs every 52 years, Western scholars must make some calculations and research events in order to align the Aztec calendar to the Western one. If we take as our example the date of the arrival of the Spanish in Tenochtitlan, 8 November 1519, we would see that the designation for that day in the ritual calendar would be 8 Ehecatl; in the solar calendar it was 9 Quecholli; and the year was 1 Acatl. (Note: some alignments of the Western and Aztec calendars place this as 7 Cipactli, 8 Quecholli, 1 Acatl.)

We therefore see that the number 52 and its factors 4, 13, and 26 were central to the Aztec concept of time and practice of timekeeping, and that the 52-year xiuhmolpilli cycle was central to Aztec cosmology, since 52 was a number associated with completion and fullness of time. Every 52 years, the Aztecs celebrated the New Fire Ceremony, the successful performance of which they believed to be necessary to the continuation of the universe. The ceremony involved extinguishing all fires in the city, after which a man would be sacrificed by having his heart torn out; in his chest cavity, the new fire would be kindled. From this new flame, fires would be lit first in the temples, then in other important spaces, and then distributed to private homes. If the ceremony was not properly carried out, or if the fire failed to kindle, then the "tzitzimime," the spirits of the stars, would come to earth and devour the people. For the Aztecs, therefore, proper timekeeping and proper use of the calendar were more than just a way to keep track of days and years; it was a means by which to time the cycles of the universe itself, which human beings were responsible for keeping in motion through blood sacrifice.

PART I: AZTEC GODS, GODDESSES, AND COSMOLOGY

The Legend of the Suns

There is no unitary Aztec creation myth, but rather several variant tales of how the world came to be. One of the primary myths is the "Legend of the Suns," which explains the repeated creation, destruction, and recreation of the world until finally it assumes the form that we know it as today. These myths also explain why blood sacrifice was such an integral part of Aztec religious practice; it was this blood that kept the earth and the sun in existence because the gods who were the earth and sun demanded sustenance in that form.

We see here important connections between the Aztec concept of time as it was laid out in their calendrical system and their understanding of the phases of creation. Within Aztec culture and timekeeping practices, the number 13 was sacred and taken to represent a form of completeness, as was the number 52. Therefore, the first two "suns" represent a full and complete space of time, since their spans of 676 years are equal to 13 times 52. The second two "suns," however, are not full and complete in and of themselves, since they represent 7 times 52 and 6 times 52, respectively.

The number 4 likewise had associations with completeness through its function within the Aztec year count and in its reference to the four cardinal directions. We see these connections play out in the creation myth retold below with regard to the number of the first major gods created by the union of Tonacatecuhtli and Tonacacihuatl, the male and female aspects of the creator-god Ometeotl.

Long, long ago, before even time had come to be, there was Ometeotl, the Dual God. Ometeotl was made by the union of the god Tonacatecuhtli and the goddess Tonacacihuatl, the Lord and Lady of Our Sustenance. And so Ometeotl was both one and two at the same time. They came to be out of nothing, and for a time they were all that was in the whole of the universe, for nothing else had yet been made.

Tonacatecuhtli and Tonacacihuatl had four children. There was red Xipe Totec (the Flayed God), god of the seasons and the things that grow upon the earth; black Tezcatlipoca (Smoking Mirror), god of the earth; white Quetzalcoatl (Plumed Serpent), god of air; and blue Huitzilopochtli (Hummingbird of the South), god of war. The god-children lived in the thirteenth heaven with their parents. Of these children, Tezcatlipoca was the most powerful. Together the four children of the Dual God decided that they would like to create a world and some people to live in it. It took them several tries before the world became the way we know it today because the gods fought over who should be the sun and rule the earth.

The first attempt at creation was made by Quetzalcoatl and Huitzilopochtli. First, they made a fire, which was the sun. But it wasn't big or strong enough to give much light or heat, as it was only half of a sun.

After they made the sun, Quetzalcoatl and Huitzilopochtli made a man and a woman. They called the woman Oxomoco, and the man

Cipactonal. The gods told the man and the woman what work they were to do. The man was to be a farmer, while the woman's duty was to spin thread and weave cloth. The gods gave the woman the gift of maize. Some of the grains were magical and could cure illnesses or help foretell the future. Together Oxomoco and Cipactonal had many children, who became the macehuales, the farmers who worked the land.

Even though there was already a half-sun, and even though there were already a man and a woman, the gods had not yet created time. This they did by making days and months. Each month had twenty-one days. And when eighteen months had gone by, this made three hundred and sixty days, and that span the gods called a year.

After there was a sun, a man and a woman, and time, the gods created the underworld, which was called Mictlan. Then Quetzalcoatl and Huitzilopochtli made two other gods to rule over this place. They were called Mictlantecuhtli and Mictecacihuatl, the Lord and Lady of Mictlan.

When all this was done, Quetzalcoatl and Huitzilopochtli created some water, and in it they placed a giant fish. The fish was called Cipactli, and the earth was made out of the body of the fish.

Oxomoco and Cipactonal had a son named Piltzintecuhtli. The gods looked upon him and saw that he had no wife. At that time, there was a goddess of beauty and young women called Xochiquetzal (Flower Quetzal Feather). The gods took some of Xochiquetzal's hair and from it they made a woman to be Piltzintecuhtli's wife.

The gods looked at all the things they had created, and they were not satisfied with them, especially with the sun, which was too weak to give much light. Tezcatlipoca thought about how to make the old sun brighter, but then he thought of a better idea: he turned himself into the sun. This new sun was much better than the old one. It was a whole sun, and it gave enough light to the world the gods had made. This was the beginning of the first age of the world, the age of the First Sun.

The gods also wanted more beings in their new world. They made a race of giants who ate nothing but pine nuts. The giants were very large and very strong. So strong were these giants that they could uproot trees with their bare hands.

So, for a time, Tezcatlipoca shone brightly over the world the gods had made. But after this world had existed for 13 times 52 years, or 676 years, Quetzalcoatl thought his brother had reigned as the sun for long enough. He took his club and struck Tezcatlipoca with it, sending him plummeting down, down, down into the waters that encircled the world. Tezcatlipoca was very angry that Quetzalcoatl had done this. He rose up out of the water in the shape of a giant jaguar, and in this shape, he roamed about the whole earth. The jaguar hunted all the giants and devoured every one of them. Once all the giants had been eaten, Tezcatlipoca rose back up into the heavens, where he became the constellation Jaguar (Ursa Major).

The second age of the world was the age of the Second Sun. This was the age of wind. Quetzalcoatl made this world, and Quetzalcoatl was the sun during this age. The macehuales lived in this age eating nothing but pine nuts. The second age also lasted for 676 years, until Tezcatlipoca took his revenge on his brother. Tezcatlipoca came to the world in a blast of wind so great that Quetzalcoatl and the macehuales were blown away, although some of the macehuales escaped the blast. These turned into monkeys, and they ran away into the jungles to live.

After the time of the Second Sun was complete, the god of rain whose name was Tlaloc (He Who Makes Things Sprout) became the sun and ruler of creation, and his age is the age of the Third Sun. This age lasted for seven times 52 years, or 364 years. During this age, the people ate the seeds of a plant that grew in the water. But again, Quetzalcoatl destroyed this world. He brought down a rain made of fire, and all the people were turned into birds.

After Quetzalcoatl ended the reign of Tlaloc, he gave the world to Tlaloc's wife, Chalchiuhtlicue (Jade Skirt Woman) to rule.

Chalchiuhtlicue was the goddess of rivers, streams, and all manner of waters. She was the sun for six times 52 years, or 312 years. This Fourth Sun age was a time of great rain. It rained so long and so hard that there was a great flood that covered the earth. The flood washed away the macehuales, turning them into fish. After the flood was over, the sky fell down and covered the earth so that nothing could live on it.

The gods looked upon the world they had made and saw how it had been destroyed by their quarreling. Quetzalcoatl and Tezcatlipoca made peace with one another and went down to rebuild the world. The gods each went to one end of the world, where they transformed themselves into great trees. With their mighty tree-limbs, they pushed the sky back up into its place, and they hold it there still.

The god Tonacatecuhtli, father of Quetzalcoatl and Tezcatlipoca, looked down and saw that the brothers had ceased their fighting and had worked together to mend what their anger had broken. Tonacatecuhtli therefore gave the brothers the starry heavens to rule, and he made a highway of stars for them to use as they traveled; this highway is the Milky Way.

Then the gods created new people to walk upon the earth. Once the sky had been put back in its place, Tezcatlipoca took flint and used it to make fires. These fires lit the world, for the old sun had been destroyed in the flood and a new one had not yet been made. Also, there were no people, for the giants had all been devoured, and the people had all been turned into monkeys, birds, and fish. So, Tezcatlipoca met with his brothers to take counsel about what to do. Together they decided that a new sun would have to be created, but this would be a new kind of sun, one that ate human hearts and drank human blood. Without sacrifices to feed it, this sun would cease to shine, and the world would return to darkness once more. So, the gods made four hundred men and five women, and these were to be food for the new sun.

Some say that Quetzalcoatl and Tlaloc each wanted their sons to become the Fifth Sun, and that these gods each took their sons to one of the great fires that had been kindled. Quetzalcoatl's son had been born without a mother. The god threw his son into the fire first, and he became the new sun. His son rose out of the fire and went into the sky where he still is to this day. Tlaloc waited until the fire had nearly burned itself out. He took his son, whose mother was Chalchiuhtlicue, and threw him into the glowing embers and ashes. Tlaloc's son rose out of the fire and went into the sky as the moon. Because Quetzalcoatl's son went into the blazing fire, he became a creature of fire and glows with a light that is too bright to look at. But because Tlaloc's son went into the embers and ashes, his light is dimmer and his face is splattered with ashes. And this is how night became divided from day, and why the moon and the sun cross the sky in different ways and along different paths.

But another tale tells how the sickly god Nanahuatzin willingly sacrificed himself to become the Fifth Sun. The gods had gathered at the great city of Teotihuacan to discuss how they might make a new sun to replace the old one that had been destroyed in the flood. One of them needed to jump into a bright bonfire and then rise into the sky. Nanahuatzin, god of disease, whose name means "Full of Sores," came forward. "I will do this thing," he said, "even though my body is diseased and bent, and even though my skin is covered with leprosy."

The other gods laughed at Nanahuatzin. They said, "You silly fellow. You are sickly and weak. You will not have the courage to jump into the fire. Let someone else become the sun."

Then Tecuciztecatl (The One from the Place of the Conch), came forward. He was a most wealthy god, well made in his body and well dressed with all manner of gold and feather ornaments. "I will do this thing," he said, "for it would be better that a healthy god make this sacrifice than a sickly one."

The other gods agreed that it should be so and caused a great fire to be kindled. While this was being done, Tecuciztecatl and Nanahuatzin retired to places where they might fast and prepare offerings to purify themselves so that they would be worthy to become the new sun. Tecuciztecatl prepared offerings that were made of the finest things, of jade and quetzal feathers, and balls of gold. Nanahuatzin's offerings were humble reeds and the spines of the maguey cactus.

At the appointed time, Tecuciztecatl and the other gods gathered around the fire. The wealthy god, dressed in his best finery, strode up to the great blaze with its searing heat. He made as though to throw himself in, but at the last minute he balked and walked away. Again, he tried, but he could not bring himself to jump into the flames. He tried again, and yet again, but each time his courage failed him. After the fourth time, he walked away from the bonfire and from the other gods, ashamed that he had not been able to turn himself into the sun as he had boasted he would do.

The other gods wondered how they would make a new sun, since Tecuciztecatl had failed to jump into the fire. But all was not lost; Nanahuatzin had not forgotten his offer to become the new sun, and he had also fasted and purified himself so that he might be a fitting sacrifice. The sickly god stepped forward, dressed in garments made of paper, and walked straight up to the raging fire. He stared into the heart of the blaze for just a moment, then threw himself into the very heart of the flames.

Nanahuatzin's hair was ablaze. His clothing was ablaze. His skin crackled with the heat of the flames that licked all around his body. Tecuciztecatl saw the courage of the sickly Nanahuatzin and was deeply ashamed. So, he also stepped forward and jumped into the flames with Nanahuatzin. An eagle and a jaguar had been watching the sacrifice too. They saw the courage of Nanahuatzin and of Tecuciztecatl, and so they joined the gods, throwing themselves among the flames. This is why the eagle's feathers are tipped with black, and why the jaguar is covered with black spots. This is also why the Aztecs created the orders of the eagle and the jaguar to honor their bravest warriors.

After the eagle and jaguar had thrown themselves into the fire, the other gods waited to see what would become of Nanahuatzin and Tecuciztecatl. Slowly, slowly, light began to rim the world. The gods looked all around, wondering where the source of the light was. Then suddenly Nanahuatzin burst forth over the eastern horizon, covering the world with the brightest light. His sacrifice transformed him from the lowly, sickly leper-god into a new sun-god: Ollin Tonatiuh, whose name means "Movement of the Sun."

But Tecuciztecatl also had been transformed by his sacrifice, and shortly after Nanahuatzin rose into the sky, so did Tecuciztecatl. And now the gods had a new problem, for there was not one but two suns in the sky, and the light they made together was too bright for anyone to see anything. One of the gods snatched up a rabbit that was nearby and flung it into the face of Tecuciztecatl. The rabbit hit Tecuciztecatl so hard that his light was dimmed. That was how the moon was created, and the shape of a rabbit was now permanently marked on his face.

Then the gods rejoiced for now they had both a sun and a moon. But their joy was short-lived for Tonatiuh refused to move from his place in the sky until all the gods had sacrificed themselves to him. The other gods grew angry and refused to do this thing, but Tonatiuh was steadfast. He would not move until he had drunk the blood of the other gods.

Tlahuizcalpantecuhtli (Lord of Dawn), who is the Morning Star, said, "I will stop Tonatiuh. I will save you from having to be sacrificed." Tlahuizcalpantecuhtli threw a dart at Tonatiuh with all his might, but it missed. Tonatiuh threw a dart of his own back at the Morning Star, hitting him in the head. This changed Tlahuizcalpantecuhtli into Itztlacoliuhqui (Curved Obsidian), the god of coldness, frost, and obsidian, and this is why it is always cold right before the sun rises.

The other gods realized they could no longer refuse what Tonatiuh demanded. They came before him with bare breasts, and Quetzalcoatl cut out their hearts with a sacrificial knife. Once the gods had been sacrificed, Quetzalcoatl took their clothing and ornaments and wrapped them into sacrificial bundles. These sacred bundles were then worshipped by the people.

Sated with the blood of the gods, Tonatiuh began to move across the sky, and he has done so ever since. And this was the birth of the Fifth Sun, the Sun under which all life lives to this day. But still the people offer blood and hearts to the sun, to ensure that he is satisfied and to keep him on his sacred path across the sky.

Now, another legend says that the remaking of the earth after the great flood happened in a different way. This tale says that Quetzalcoatl and Tezcatlipoca looked down and saw that there was nothing but water, but in this water swam a great monster. The monster's name was Tlaltecuhtli, which means "Earth Lord," even though the creature itself was female. It was a giant thing, with mouths all over its body and a ravenous desire to eat flesh. The gods thought it likely that the monster would devour anything they managed to create, so they devised a plan to be rid of Tlaltecuhtli and make a new earth at the same time. Quetzalcoatl and Tezcatlipoca therefore transformed themselves into monstrous serpents. In these forms, they dove into the water and attacked Tlaltecuhtli. The gods wrapped themselves around the body of the monster and began to pull. No matter how hard Tlaltecuhtli thrashed, she could not escape the grip of the gods. Slowly, the body of the monster began to tear apart, until finally it was torn in two. The top half of Tlaltecuhtli became the new earth, and the bottom half was flung up into the sky to become the heavens.

Tlaltecuhtli screamed in pain as she was torn asunder. The other gods heard her in her agony and were angry at what Quetzalcoatl and Tezcatlipoca had done to her, but they could not heal her wounds. Instead, they transformed her body. Her hair became flowers, shrubs, and trees, and from her skin grew the grasses. Fresh water sprang from her eyes in the form of rivers, wells, and streams, and her mouths became the caves of the world. Mountains and valleys were made from her nose. But even though she was no longer a monster, Tlaltecuhtli still had a need for fresh blood and flesh, and so once the people had been created, they made sacrifices to feed her. In this way, the earth continues to provide all the things that people and animals need to live.

But the gods first needed to create the new people since all the people who had lived under the previous four Suns had been turned into monkeys, birds, and fish, and that the bones of those who had died were kept in Mictlan. So, the gods sent Quetzalcoatl to Mictlan to see whether he might fetch the bones of the ones who had been turned into fish.

"O Mictlantecuhtli," said Quetzalcoatl, "I have come seeking the bones of the people who were turned into fish."

"Why do you want them?" asked the Lord of Mictlan.

"The earth was destroyed in the great flood," said Quetzalcoatl, the Plumed Serpent, "and we have rebuilt it and made a new sun and moon and a new sky, but there are no people. We wish to use the bones to make new people, for it is good that the earth be inhabited."

But Mictlantecuhtli was jealous of all the things that he kept within his realm. He did not care whether the earth had people on it or not, and he did not want Quetzalcoatl to have the bones. So, he gave Quetzalcoatl a test.

Mictlantecuhtli handed a conch shell to Quetzalcoatl and said, "You may have the bones if you walk four times around all of Mictlan while blowing blasts on this conch shell."

Quetzalcoatl thought that this was an easy challenge to pass, until he looked closely at the shell. It had not yet been made into a trumpet, and there was no way for him to make any sounds on it. But Quetzalcoatl was friends with the worms. He called the worms to come and make holes in the shell. Quetzalcoatl also was friends with the bees. He called the bees to come and buzz inside the shell to make a great noise. And so, Quetzalcoatl was able to pass the test that the Lord of Mictlan had set for him.

Mictlantecuhtli gave the bones to Quetzalcoatl, as he had promised, but he had no intention of allowing them to leave Mictlan. Mictlantecuhtli ordered his servants to dig a deep pit along the path that Quetzalcoatl was taking. Now, Quetzalcoatl knew that Mictlantecuhtli was not trustworthy, and so he was hurrying to leave Mictlan before the bones were taken away from him. As Quetzalcoatl ran along the path, Mictlantecuhtli sent a bird to fly in the Plumed Serpent's face and frighten him just as he approached the pit. When the bird flew at Quetzalcoatl, he lost his footing and tumbled down into the pit. His fall broke the fish bones into many pieces, and this is why people are of all different sizes.

After a time, Quetzalcoatl recovered from his fall. He gathered up all the pieces of the bones and climbed out of the pit. He was able to safely leave Mictlan, and by and by he came to a place called Tamoanchan, Land of the Misty Sky, a holy and blessed place. Quetzalcoatl gave the bones to the goddess Cihuacoatl, Woman Serpent. Cihuacoatl put the bones in her quern and ground them into a fine flour. She put the bone flour into a special jar, and all the gods gathered around it. One by one, the gods pierced their flesh and let drops of their blood drip onto the bones. When the bones and blood were all mixed into dough, the gods shaped it into the forms of people. The gods gave the dough forms life and put them upon the earth to live.

And these are the tales of how creation came to be, and why we live under the Fifth Sun, and why the earth and the sun demand sacrifices from the people who live upon the earth under the light of the sun.

The Deeds of Mixcoatl

One surviving original work by sixteenth-century Spanish friar Andrés de Olmos is the Historia de los Mexicanos por sus pinturas (History of the Mexicans as Told by Their Pictures). *In this work, which is also known as the* Codex Ramirez, *de Olmos gives accounts of Aztec myths. One section of the codex is devoted to the god Camaxtli, who was also known as Mixcoatl (Cloud Serpent). De Olmos understood Mixcoatl as an aspect of Tezcatlipoca rather than as a separate figure. In this brief tale, Mixcoatl, god of hunting and the Milky Way, is said to have originated both ritual warfare and the Aztec practice of piercing the tongue and ears to bring forth a blood offering.*

Ritual warfare was an important aspect of Aztec life. Sacrifices for the gods had to be acquired in some manner and in some quantity, so Aztec city-states would challenge one another to battles on a regular basis. The purpose of this warfare was not conquest, and neither was it the point to kill as many of the enemy as possible. Rather, the warriors were expected to capture as many of the enemy as they could. These captives were then brought back to the victors' home city where they became sacrificial victims. The Aztecs believed that the noblest deaths a man could hope for were either to perish in battle or to be offered in sacrifice to the gods, after which the soul would be transformed into a hummingbird.

The name "Chichimecs" referred to the various peoples who lived outside the Valley of Mexico and sometimes had connotations similar to that of our English word "barbarian." Here we see that Mixcoatl creates these people precisely so that they can be slaughtered, and he also turns them into drunkards, a state that was anathema to the Aztecs and could be punished by death.

And so, it came to pass that one year after the new sun had been created and fed by the blood of the gods that Mixcoatl thought to himself that it would be a good thing to ensure that the sun never lacked for blood or hearts. Therefore, he went up into the eighth heaven and there he made four men and a woman.

"Go down to earth," said Mixcoatl to the new people. "Go there and learn the art of war, for the sun has need of blood to drink and hearts to eat."

Mixcoatl then cast the new people down to the earth, where they landed in the water. But they immediately returned to the heavens, and so Mixcoatl's wish that they should make war did not come to pass. So, the next year Mixcoatl again bethought himself how to create new people so that there could be war and sacrifices, and this time he went to the earth and found a great stone, which he struck heavily with his club. The stone split open, and from it came forth 400 Chichimecs, who were the first people to live in Mexico before the Aztecs came.

Mixcoatl saw that his efforts had thus far come to naught because the Chichimecs did not yet know the art of war for they had no enemies, and they did not make war amongst themselves since they were kin to one another, and the original five people he had created to make war to provide blood and hearts to the sun had returned to the heavens. So, for eleven years Mixcoatl did penance. He took the sharp spines of the maguey cactus, and with these, he pierced his tongue and his ears. He pierced them so that the blood dripped down as an offering and a penance, so that the four men and one woman he had created would come back to earth and make war upon the Chichimecs. And in this way Mixcoatl began the practice of these small blood offerings using the spines of the maguey on the tongue and ears, which the people then also did in reverence and supplication to the gods.

When Mixcoatl's penance was done, the four sons and one daughter he created came down from the heavens. They went to the earth, where they made homes in trees, and in the trees, they fed the eagles who also made their nests there.

Now, while the five first children of Mixcoatl were making their new homes in the trees, Mixcoatl bethought himself of ways to make the Chichimecs and his five children make war upon one another to provide blood and hearts for the sun. Therefore, Mixcoatl took the sap of the maguey and showed the Chichimecs how to make pulque and other wines from it. Once the Chichimecs learned how good this wine was, they spent all their time making it and drinking it, and thus spent their days in drunkenness. And so, it came to pass that one day the Chichimecs saw the five children of Mixcoatl where they sat in their trees, and the children saw that the Chichimecs were drunken and worthless. Therefore, the children came down from the trees and slew all the Chichimecs except for three who escaped, one of these being Mixcoatl, who had turned himself into a Chichimec.

And so, this was how Mixcoatl taught the people the art of warfare and the proper way to do penance, that there might always be blood and hearts with which to feed the sun.

The Origin of Maize and the Creation of Pulque

Two of the most important staples in Aztec agriculture were maize and maguey, which is a type of agave cactus. Maize was—and still is—a staple food for many Central American traditional cultures and had an important place in their mythology and their concepts of themselves as peoples. Pulque was an intoxicating beverage used primarily for ritual purposes, but the maguey plant had uses beyond providing the sap from which pulque was fermented. The leaves were edible and were used to make paper; the thorns were used as ritual objects and as needles; and rope and cloth could be made from its fibers. In the stories about maize and pulque, as in the above tale of the creation of new people from fish bones and gods' blood, we see the vital function of Quetzalcoatl as a trickster who uses his shapeshifting abilities to find things that will benefit human beings.

Oxomoco and Cipactonal, the first man and woman ever created, play a role in bringing maize to the people. Here we see that Aztec myth is divided as to which of these mythical personages is male and which female. In the "Legend of the Suns," told above, Oxomoco is female and Cipactonal male, but in the story of the origin of maize, these genders are reversed.

Once the gods had recreated people out of their own blood and the bones of the fish that Quetzalcoatl brought out of Mictlan, they saw that these new beings had no food to eat, so they went looking for a source of food for the people. Quetzalcoatl looked and looked, and finally he saw a little ant carrying a kernel of maize in its jaws.

"Where did you get that?" said Quetzalcoatl to the ant.

"I'm not going to tell you," said the ant, and it continued its march back to its hive.

Quetzalcoatl followed the ant. "That looks like a fine kind of food," said the god. "Where did you get it?"

But the ant wouldn't answer. It kept walking along with the maize in its jaws. Quetzalcoatl wouldn't give up. "Where did you get that?" he said to the ant.

The ant saw that the god would not leave it alone until it answered his question, so the ant took Quetzalcoatl to a great mountain called Tonacatepetl, the Mountain of Food. Quetzalcoatl saw long lines of ants streaming into and out of the mountain. He changed himself into an ant and followed his guide into the mountain. Inside the mountain were huge piles of maize and other good things to eat. Still in his ant-form, Quetzalcoatl picked up a kernel of maize in his jaws and brought it outside the mountain. When he had collected enough maize, he brought it back to Tamoanchan, the blessed place, where the gods were waiting with their newly-made people. Quetzalcoatl gave the grains of maize to the gods. They tasted the maize and realized that it would make the best food of all for the new people. But they did not know how to get it out of the mountain and carry it to their new people, for turning themselves into ants to remove it one kernel at a time would take too much time and labor.

"I know!" said Quetzalcoatl to the other gods. "I will go and get the mountain and bring it here, if you will help me."

So, the gods went to Mount Tonacatepetl together. They tied many strong ropes around the mountain. They pulled and pulled and pulled, but the mountain would not move. Quetzalcoatl and the other gods went back to Tamoanchan feeling very discouraged.

Then Oxomoco took some of the grains of maize that Quetzalcoatl had brought back with him. With the help of his wife, Cipactonal, Oxomoco performed a divination with the maize.

"What do the kernels of maize tell you?" asked Quetzalcoatl.

Oxomoco said, "The mountain must be broken open, but the only one who can do this thing is Nanahuatzin."

Nanahuatzin, the sickly god, agreed to open the Mountain of Food. He asked Tlaloc, the god of rain, whether he might have the help of the tlaloque, the servants of Tlaloc who are the lords of rain and lightning. Tlaloc said, "I will gladly let them go with you."

Tlaloc summoned his four servants, and these were the blue tlaloque, the white tlaloque, the yellow tlaloque, and the red tlaloque. "You will go with Nanahuatzin and help him break open the mountain of food," said Tlaloc to his servants.

And so Nanahuatzin and the tlaloque went to Mount Tonacatepetl. Nanahuatzin and the tlaloque used their powers to split the mountain open. Out of the mountain poured every good thing: maize, beans, amaranth, and many other seeds that the people could plant and eat for food. But the gods were jealous of this bounty, and so the tlaloque took it all away. Thus, it is that Tlaloc and his servants dole out rain and food to the people in season.

Quetzalcoatl and the other gods looked upon the people they had made. The people had food to eat and seeds to plant, and the land they lived in was good, but the people were not happy. So, Quetzalcoatl set out to find something that would help the new people have happiness as well as good food. The god went up into the heavens, where he found Mayahuel, the goddess of the maguey cactus. Mayahuel was the granddaughter of a tzitzimitl, which is a deity of a star that shines in the night sky. Quetzalcoatl went to Mayahuel and said, "Come with me to earth. I need your help to make a thing for the people so that they can be happy."

Mayahuel secretly went with Quetzalcoatl, for she feared the wrath of her grandmother and the other tzitzimime, who struggle every night to keep shining in the black sky but are pushed away by the sun. Together Mayahuel and Quetzalcoatl entwined their bodies, turning themselves into a tall tree. Mayahuel was one branch of the tree, and Quetzalcoatl was the other. When Mayahuel's grandmother woke from her sleep, she saw that her granddaughter was missing. She called to the tzitzimime and ordered them to find and kill Mayahuel.

The tzitzimime went down to Earth. They searched high and low for Mayahuel, until finally they came upon the tree that she and Quetzalcoatl had become. The tzitzimime attacked the tree. They knocked it down and broke the branches apart. Mayahuel's grandmother recognized the branch that was Mayahuel. She broke it into many small pieces and gave these to the other tzitzimime to eat.

Quetzalcoatl's branch was not touched by the tzitzimime, and when these star-gods had gone back to the heavens, Quetzalcoatl resumed his own form. He looked about him and saw the bones of Mayahuel scattered in pieces all around. Sorrowful, Quetzalcoatl picked up the bones. He planted them carefully in the earth, and after a time, maguey plants sprang from them. Quetzalcoatl then took the sap from the plants and fermented it into pulque. He brought the pulque to the people and gave it to them to drink. They found that when they drank it, their hearts were lighter, and it made them want to sing and dance.

And so, it was that the gods gave the people maize to be their food and pulque to be their wine.

How Quetzalcoatl Brought Music to the People

This story survives in three early modern sources, all of which originally were written in Spanish, and shows Quetzalcoatl operating in his secondary persona as Ehecatl, the wind-god. The names of Tezcatlipoca's servants are given here in only English because there is some confusion over the Nahuatl names given in the sources and what types of creatures are indicated.

The Spanish missionaries Juan de Torquemada, writing in the early seventeenth century, and Gerónimo de Mendieta, writing in the late sixteenth, list these servants as "ballena, sirena, y tortuga" (whale, mermaid, and turtle). Nahuatl names are preserved in the French version of a lost sixteenth-century treatise by Spanish missionary Andrés de Olmos. However, in his modern edition of the French translation of Olmos' treatise, Édouard de Jonghe suggests that the Nahuatl names would seem to list a mermaid (Aciuatl, literally, "fish woman"), a crocodile (Acipactli), and another creature the nature of which is uncertain. De Jonghe posits that the name for the third creature might originally have been compounded from the Nahuatl words for "reed" and "shell," but he suggests that transmission of this name appears to have been corrupt. Because of the difficulties with the original Nahuatl, I am giving English names only to these servants, while trying to hew as closely as possible to what is known of the Nahuatl originals based on de Jonghe's notes in his edition of Olmos' text.

The versions of this myth in the Spanish sources are rather laconic. Therefore, I have taken the liberty of fleshing the myth out somewhat to make it a better story.

There was a time when Quetzalcoatl tired of being the Plumed Serpent. He changed himself into Ehecatl, which means "Wind." Ehecatl flew up and down the land, blowing the clouds about. He made the treetops dance with the force of his breath. He went out to sea and made a huge storm that whirled and blew and stirred up waves as big as houses. Quetzalcoatl had a fine time being Wind.

While he was doing this, he happened to blow past his brother, Tezcatlipoca, the Smoking Mirror. "Stop blowing for a minute," said Tezcatlipoca. "I have something to ask you."

Ehecatl stood still and said, "Ask, brother."

"Have you looked upon these new people we have made? I think there might be something missing for them," said Tezcatlipoca.

"No, I have not looked upon them much lately," said Ehecatl, "for I have been Wind and have not stood still for long. But have they not good food to eat and cool water to drink? Have they not bright feathers and good woven cloth to adorn themselves? Have they not tools and skills with which to do their work? Do they not worship the gods as they ought? What could be missing for them?"

Tezcatlipoca thought for a minute. His brother had listed many good things the people had. But still there seemed to be something missing.

"I know!" said the Smoking Mirror. "I know what is missing. The people do not have music. We must find a way to give them music so that they might sing and dance, for those are joyful things that they do not have. And with songs and dances they can make their worship of the gods even better and more beautiful."

"That is a fine idea," said Ehecatl. "Let us give music to the people."

"Yes," said Tezcatlipoca, "but there is one problem. Music belongs to Tonatiuh, to the god of the Sun. Can you go up into the heavens and take it from him?"

"I think I can," said Ehecatl, "but I will need your help."

Tezcatlipoca agreed to help Ehecatl. First the two gods went to the shore of the sea together. There Tezcatlipoca called his servants, Crocodile Woman, Fish Woman, and Reed-and-Shell Woman and told them to give Ehecatl whatever aid he might need.

The first thing Ehecatl needed to do was to get up into the heavens where the Sun lived and kept his musicians. It was too high for Ehecatl to fly by himself. He needed a great bridge to get there. Ehecatl went to the servants of Tezcatlipoca and said, "Build me a bridge to the house of the Sun."

Crocodile Woman, Fish Woman, and Reed-and-Shell Woman worked together. Soon they had made a fine bridge that went all the way up to the house of the Sun. Ehecatl walked along the bridge. As he grew nearer to the house of the Sun, he began to hear the sounds of flutes, drums, and singing, but he could not yet see who was making these sounds. Closer and closer he came, and soon he could see the musicians. Some of them were wearing yellow clothing. Others wore white. And the rest were clad in blue or red.

But before Ehecatl could get close enough to speak to the musicians, Tonatiuh saw him approaching. "Why are you coming to my house, O Wind?" asked the sun-god.

"I am coming to find music and bring it to the people," said Ehecatl.

Tonatiuh did not want Ehecatl to take away his musicians. The Sun told the musicians to hide themselves and to be silent, so that Ehecatl would not be able to find them, but it was too late. Ehecatl had already heard them playing and singing. He had seen their bright clothing. Ehecatl knew that the musicians were there. He also knew that no musician could be silent for long. So, Ehecatl began to sing. "Come with me down to earth; play and sing for the people there," sang Ehecatl.

The musicians remained silent because they feared the wrath of the Sun. Tonatiuh was satisfied. He thought Ehecatl would never find his servants and that music would belong to him alone, forever. Ehecatl was not discouraged. He reached the end of the bridge and entered the house of the Sun. Ehecatl tried again, making his song even more beautiful than before. "Come with me down to earth; play and sing for the people there," sang the Wind.

 But still the musicians were silent. Tonatiuh saw that Ehecatl had entered his house and was looking for the musicians. The Sun tried to stand in the way of the Wind, but the Wind was too quick for him. Ehecatl flew around Tonatiuh. He flew through all the chambers of the house of the Sun, singing, "Come with me down to earth; play and sing for the people there," and this time the musicians answered him. They played rhythms on their drums and tunes on their flutes, and sang back, "Take us to earth to play and to sing."

Still Tonatiuh tried to catch Ehecatl, but each time Ehecatl flew nimbly out of reach. Following the sound of drums and flutes, Ehecatl went to the chamber where the musicians were hiding. "Come with me," sang Ehecatl.

"Take us to earth," sang the musicians.

And so Ehecatl wrapped the musicians in his feathered cloak. He sped through the chambers and halls of the house of the Sun, bearing the musicians with him. Tonatiuh pursued Ehecatl with all the swiftness he had, but it was not enough to catch the Wind. Ehecatl carried the musicians down the bridge that the servants of Tezcatlipoca had made. When he neared the bottom, he cried out, "Crocodile Woman! Fish Woman! Reed-and-Shell Woman! Tear down the bridge so that the Sun may not follow!"

The servants of Tezcatlipoca did as Ehecatl commanded. They tore down the bridge, stranding Tonatiuh in the heavens. Ehecatl turned himself into a gentle breeze and floated down to earth with the musicians. When they reached the ground, Ehecatl unwound his cloak and set the musicians on the ground. "This is earth," said Ehecatl. "Go to the people and teach them your music."

The musicians went straight away to the nearest village. They showed the people how to make flutes and drums and how to make horns out of conch shells. They taught the people how to play those instruments and how to sing and make new songs. They went from village to village, teaching all they knew. And then the people taught their children, and their children's children, and soon every village throughout the world was full of the sounds of flutes, drums, and singing.

And that is how the Plumed Serpent brought music to the people.

The Fall of Xochiquetzal

Xochiquetzal was a goddess of craftspeople, especially weavers and workers in precious metals. She also was a goddess of fertility, childbirth, and female sexual power, and as such was particularly associated with female beauty and with flowers. This story of her exile from the paradise of Tamoanchan has parallels with the Genesis story of Adam and Eve.

As in the biblical story of Eve and the apple, Xochiquetzal's sin involves the violation of a rule given by a supreme deity—in this case, the creator-god Ometeotl—about a sacred tree. While Aztec codices also contain representations of sacred trees, the concept of a Great Tree or World Tree may originally have been taken from the Mayans, as was the Aztec name for the paradise of the gods; "Tamoanchan" is a Mayan word, not an Aztec one.

Long, long ago, there was a place called Tamoanchan. Tamoanchan was a place of plenty, where it was always sweet summer, and the birds sang in the boughs of the trees. It was in Tamoanchan the gods and goddesses made their home.

In the center of Tamoanchan was a great tree. It had a thick trunk covered with smooth bark. It had branches reaching up to the sky, covered with green leaves and beautiful flowers and bright fruit. The tree had been planted there by Ometeotl themselves, and they told the other gods and goddesses that no one was to touch the tree or pick its flowers or fruit. And for a long time, the gods and goddesses obeyed what Ometeotl commanded.

Among the gods and goddesses who lived in Tamoanchan was Xochiquetzal (Flower Quetzal Feather). She was the most beautiful of all the goddesses and was attended at all times by entertainers who danced and sang for her. Xochiquetzal loved beautiful things and could make them with her own hands. She especially loved weaving, for in a piece of cloth she could weave all the colors of the world.

Xochiquetzal also loved the Great Tree of Ometeotl. She loved the green of its leaves, the colors of its flowers, and the scent of its bright fruit. But most of all, she loved to sit in the shade of the tree while she did her work, and while her entertainers danced and sang for her. Day after day, she gazed at the colors and smelled the scents of the Great Tree, and day after day she felt more and more tempted to pick some of these for herself.

Finally, Xochiquetzal could stand the temptation no more. "The tree has many flowers," she said to herself, "and it bears a great deal of fruit. Surely if I pick only one or two of these it will do no harm."

And so, she picked two flowers to put into her hair and one piece of fruit to eat. No sooner had Xochiquetzal plucked these things than the tree began to sway as though in a strong wind. Its branches creaked and groaned. The leaves came cascading down as though it were autumn. And then with a great *crack* the tree split open. The pieces fell to the ground, and when it struck the earth, the branches all shattered and were strewn about like so much matchwood, all the while making a great noise like thunder as it burst into fragments. Then, when silence had returned to Tamoanchan, the pieces of the Great Tree began to seep blood.

Ometeotl looked upon the ruins of the Great Tree, and they were greatly saddened. They saw that it was Xochiquetzal who had caused the death of the Tree, and so they sent Xochiquetzal out of Tamoanchan, never to return. Xochiquetzal left the home of the gods and went to live on earth. But no longer was she a goddess of joy and bright colors. Instead, she went about weeping and mourning, and her name was changed to Ixnextli, which means "Ashen Eyes," for she wept so long and so heavily that she became blinded by her tears.

The Fate of Souls

The Florentine Codex *is an important early modern record of Aztec history, religion, and culture. A twelve-volume ethnography written in Nahuatl by Fray Bernardino de Sahagún, a Franciscan missionary to Mexico, the codex was created between 1545 and de Sahagún's death in 1590 and was originally titled* Historia general de las cosas de Nueva España (General History of the Things of New Spain). *In the third volume of this ethnography, de Sahagún describes Aztec funerary customs and beliefs about the afterlife. The information he presents in his ethnography as reportage and descriptions has been reworked and presented here in story form, adopting the conceit of an elder addressing a child.*

And so, my child, you wish to know what happens to us when we die? Listen well, and I shall tell you, for the fate of our bodies and our souls is varied and is in the care of the gods themselves.

First, we shall speak of those who die of disease, for this is a fate that takes many of us from this earth. The souls of these people go first to Mictlan, to the Land of the Dead, where they are greeted by the Lord and Lady of Mictlan, Mictlantecuhtli and his consort Mictecacihuatl. To these dead the Lord of Mictlan will say, "Come into thy new abode, for here I have prepared a place for thee."

But do not think that it is easy to cross from the land of the living into Mictlan and to come before Mictlantecuhtli and his lady wife. Oh, no. It is not easy at all. Many dangers and pains must the soul endure before it is welcomed into its final home.

When the soul leaves its body, first it comes to a pass between two mountains. There is a road there that the soul must follow, and the road is watched by a great serpent. And when the road has been walked, the soul will come to a place that is watched by a great lizard. If the soul passes the serpent and lizard safely, it then must walk across eight deserts, and it is a long and lonely walk. After the soul traverses the deserts, it must climb over eight great hills, and this is a walk of great weariness and toil. Last of all, and most difficult of all, is a place where the winds are made of obsidian blades and stones, and by these the soul is slashed and buffeted. But if all is borne well, then the soul comes to Mictlan and is greeted by Mictlantecuhtli.

And it is to help the souls of our dead to pass through all these hardships in safety that we dress them in special paper clothing and burn with them the things they used in life, for these will be armor for them against the serpent, the lizard, and the obsidian wind. We put into their mouths a piece of obsidian to become a new heart for them in the land of the dead, and to our very great ones we give a piece of jade. Our brave warriors we burn with their swords and mantles and the spoils they have taken from our enemies. Our women we burn with their baskets and weaving tools, with their thread and their combs. Those who die with many goods are well protected, but alas for those who die in poverty! For they will not have the things they need to fend off the dangers on the path to Mictlan, and they will suffer much by the obsidian wind. But with all we send a small dog to act as their guide. We sacrifice the dog to the gods and burn it on the pyre with our loved ones. This is so when the soul reaches the nine rivers of Mictlan, the dog can guide it across in safety.

Once the soul passes through all the dangers and crosses the nine rivers, then it comes into the presence of the great Mictlantecuhtli. And O my child, what a thing it is to come before that god, with his blood-spattered skeleton body and necklace all made out of eyes! To him the dead offer their paper clothing, the incense, and other offerings that were burned on their pyres. To him the men give their breechcloths and the women their dresses. And thus, the soul of the dead one enters into Mictlan.

But think not that the journey of the soul is ended there! For it is not. Another great river there is to cross, and the living on earth must send more gifts to the Lord of Mictlan before their loved ones are allowed to move on. After eighty days, we burn more clothing, and again after two years, and three, and four. And when the dead have been four years waiting and when Mictlantecuhtli has received the gifts of the four years, only then does he permit the soul to go into the nine realms of the dead.

The soul goes to the bank of the last great river and there waits for a guide. For on the opposite bank there are a great many dogs, white and black and yellow, and only a dog can ferry the soul across. But the white dogs will not carry souls, for they say they have just bathed and do not wish to soil their coats. The black dogs will not carry souls, for they have made themselves unclean and must bathe first. The yellow dogs will leap into the water and ferry the souls across. And once the soul has been taken to the other side of that river, it is destroyed.

So much for the souls who die of disease.

What is that, my child? Why, yes, there are other deaths than by disease, and by and by I will tell you what happens to those souls.

Some people die when they are struck by thunderbolts. Others drown in water. Others die of leprosy or tumors or dropsy, while others die of diseases they get when men lie with women. Those who die of any of those causes go to a place called Tlalocan. O my child, Tlalocan is a pleasant place indeed. Maize and squash grow in abundance, and there one may eat one's fill of tomatoes and chilis and amaranth, for there it is always spring, and the tlaloque, the lords of thunder and rain, are there to receive the souls that come to Tlalocan.

The bodies of these dead we do not burn, but rather we bury them. But first we adorn them fittingly for their journey. We paint their faces with liquid rubber and amaranth paste. We put blue paper on their foreheads. We make a lock of hair of paper, and this we affix to the back of their heads. And thus adorned they enter Tlalocan. Also, we put into their graves images of mountains, like the ones in Tlalocan, and we dress them with capes and give them staves to help them on their journey there.

But the best home for the soul is reserved to our very bravest warriors who have died in battle and for those who are offered in sacrifice to the gods. For these have died the noblest of all deaths and they are rewarded by being given a place in the house of the sun.

And the house of the sun is not a house such as we live in, but rather it is a wide plain where there is much maguey cactus and many mesquites, and the souls who dwell there watch the sun as it rises each day. Those who died with many piercings in their shields have the honor of being able to look the sun in its face, for they died most bravely. Those whose shields were not pierced have not this honor. A further honor is bestowed on those who died in battle or in sacrifice: when the living makes offerings to them, the offerings are conveyed to the souls for their use and enjoyment.

But even these souls do not stay long in the house of the sun. For after four years have passed, they are transformed into all manner of bright birds. They become hummingbirds, with their emerald and ruby plumage. They become the coztotol bird, with its yellow head, breast, and stomach. They become butterflies of every pattern and hue, and they come back to earth to drink of the sweet nectar in the flowers.

And now, my child, you know the fates of those who die upon this earth, and how we who are left behind must honor them and the gods.

PART II: AZTEC POLITICAL MYTHS

Huitzilopochtli and the Founding of Tenochtitlan

This is the origin tale of the Aztec people which tells how they migrated from a place far to the north under the guidance of the god of war, Huitzilopochtli. As with many myths, this one likely contains grains of historical truth. Linguists argue that Nahuatl, the language spoken by the Aztecs, likely originated in the southwestern United States, since as part of the Uto-Aztecan language family, it is related to Native American languages such as Hopi, Shoshoni, and Paiute.

Some scholars posit that the figure of Huitzilopochtli may originally have been a mortal human leader who later came to be deified, and certainly the origin story of Huitzilopochtli told here is different from that found in the "Legend of the Suns." But regardless of how this god was inserted into the Aztec pantheon, it would seem that it was during the reign of Itzcoatl (c. 1427 or 1428 to 1440 AD) that his worship became foregrounded in Aztec religion, along with the idea that blood sacrifice was supremely necessary to the proper honoring of the gods. This may have been at the instigation of Itzcoatl's general, a brilliant military man named Tlacaelel. Timothy Roberts, in his book on Mayan, Inca, and Aztec myth, states that the Aztec migration myth, which relies heavily upon the power of Huitzilopochtli, was the creation of the Itzcoatl regime, as part of the emperor's program of rewriting history to favor Aztec power and ascendancy.

Long, long ago, far to the north, there was a place called Aztlan, which means "Place of the White Heron." In Aztlan there were seven tribes, and they all lived together in peace. Aztlan was a land of plenty. The soil grew fine crops of maize, and the waters teemed with fish and waterfowl. But best of all was the great mountain at the center of Aztlan. This mountain had the power to restore people their lost youth. At the base of the mountain was old age, while infancy was at the very summit. When the people felt they were becoming too old, they would climb the mountain to the age they wanted to attain and wait there until their bodies became youthful again. When they had the youth they desired, they would go back down the mountain and rejoin the people.

For many long years, the seven tribes lived together in Aztlan, enjoying the fruits of the earth and the long lives given by the sacred mountain. But word came to the ears of the people of Aztlan that to their south was a new place, one that had a great lake between the mountains, a place with rich soil for farming and plentiful obsidian for tools. One by one, the tribes left Aztlan in quest of this new place, until finally only one tribe was left, the Mexica, who later would take the name "Aztecs," meaning "People from Aztlan." The Mexica were saddened that they had been left in Aztlan all alone. They wanted to join the other tribes at the lake in the south to find a good, new life there, but there was no one among them who might lead them. And so, they remained in Aztlan, living as they had always done, but ever yearning to make the journey southwards.

Now, while six of the tribes of Aztlan were making their way to their new home in the south and while the Mexica languished in Aztlan waiting for a leader, the goddess Coatlicue (Serpent-Skirt), was busy about her home on Coatepec, the sacred Serpent Mountain. Dressed in the skirt of living serpents that gave her her name and a necklace made of severed human hearts, severed heads, and severed hands, the goddess went about her work. She took her broom in her clawed hands and went outside to sweep her patio. While she was sweeping, a beautiful ball of feathers came floating down through the air towards her. The feathers glinted and shone in brilliant greens, reds, and yellows. Coatlicue had never seen something so colorful, and she desired to keep it. The goddess put out her hand to catch the pretty thing, and when she had caught it, she tucked it away into her clothing.

Finally, Coatlicue finished all her work. She put her cleaning tools away and went to take the ball of feathers out so that she could look at it more closely. But no matter how she searched, she could not find it; the ball had disappeared. Not long afterward, Coatlicue found that she was with child. This was puzzling; she had not lain with a man in a very long time, certainly not recently enough that she would find herself in this state. She thought about how this might have come about and realized that somehow the feathered ball had entered her, making a new child grow in her womb.

As the months went on, Coatlicue's belly swelled. Soon all could see that she was with child. This greatly angered her four hundred sons, the Centzon Huitznahua (Four Hundred Southerners), and her daughters Coyolxauhqui (Precious Bells) and Malinalxochitl (Wild Grass Flower). They knew that their father, the hunter-god Mixcoatl (Cloud Serpent), had been away for a very long time, and so they thought that their mother had been unfaithful to him. They gathered outside Coatlicue's house, threatening to kill her if she did not tell them who she had lain with. But Coatlicue did not know who the father of her baby was, only that she had gotten the child from the ball of feathers, and so she did not answer her children.

"What shall I do?" said Coatlicue. "I am not a warrior. My children are many, and I am alone."

Coatlicue began to weep. Then from her womb she heard the voice of her unborn child. "Do not fear, Mother," he said. "It is I, your child, the god Huitzilopochtli, the Hummingbird of the South, and I will protect you from all dangers."

At this, Coatlicue felt greatly comforted. Meanwhile, the Centzon Huitznahua and their sisters paced outside their mother's house, shouting that they would surely kill her for dishonoring their family. But before they could enter the house, the baby leaped from Coatlicue's womb. Huitzilopochtli came forth fully grown and armed as a warrior. He descended upon his brothers and sisters, slashing with his weapon. The young god slew many of his brothers. Huitzilopochtli also slew his sister, Coyolxauhqui, cutting off her head and chopping her body into pieces and throwing them about the base of the sacred Serpent Mountain. Only a few of his brothers and his sister, Malinalxochitl, escaped, running away southwards.

Coatlicue was grateful that Huitzilopochtli had saved her from the wrath of her sons, but she grieved at the death of her daughter. Huitzilopochtli went to his mother and said, "Do not mourn, Mother. See? I will make it so that you can see your daughter's face every night." Then he took the head of his sister Coyolxauhqui and threw it with all his might into the heavens, and this is how the moon was made.

Word of Huitzilopochtli's great deeds came to the ears of the Mexica in Aztlan. They took counsel among themselves and decided that they would ask the god to be their leader and to take them to the lake in the south where the other tribes of Aztlan had already gone. Huitzilopochtli readily agreed to do this thing, and so when preparations were complete, the Mexica left their home in Aztlan and began the long journey to the good place by the lake.

After a time, the Mexica came to a place called Patzcuaro. Patzcuaro was a very pleasant place in the land of Michoacán. It had many lakes and much good land, and so the Mexica stopped there to rest a while. Some of the people, both men and women, went down to the edge of one of the lakes. On the shore of the lake, they undressed, and then went to bathe in the cool water, for the day was hot and their journey had been long. "Surely this is a very good place," they said to one another, "and we should make this our home."

But this was not the home to which Huitzilopochtli was leading the Mexica, although he agreed it was a good place and worthy of settlement. And so, he told the others who had stayed out of the water to go and steal the clothing of the ones who were bathing, so that they might not be able to follow when Huitzilopochtli led the rest on the next part of the journey.

Onwards the Mexica journeyed with Huitzilopochtli, looking for their new home at the good place by the lake. Now, among the people who were journeying southwards was Malinalxochitl, the sister of Huitzilopochtli, who had survived the day of his wrath against his half-siblings. Malinalxochitl was a beautiful sorceress who had the power to command all manner of venomous creatures such as snakes, scorpions, and spiders. She was jealous of the honor her brother had from the people and thought that she also should have the reverence due a divine being. She used her powers to threaten the people and to torment them. Soon the people begged Huitzilopochtli to rid them of her, for they were frightened and tired of her tricks and abuse. Huitzilopochtli told the people that they would make camp and then in the middle of the night they would depart while Malinalxochitl was sleeping, so that she would not know where they had gone. The people agreed this was a good plan, and so they did as Huitzilopochtli said.

Malinalxochitl slept soundly through the night, not realizing that everyone else had left. In the morning, she woke and found herself completely alone. She raged at her brother's betrayal and vowed revenge against him. But instead of trying to find where he and the Mexica had gone, she decided to stay in that place and found her own city, which she called Malinalco.

The Mexica continued walking southwards, until they came to the sacred Serpent Mountain, Coatepec, where Huitzilopochtli was born. A river flowed through the place, and so Huitzilopochtli instructed the Mexica to build a dam so that a lake might form in the low parts of the place. The Mexica did as the god commanded, and soon the place had a fine lake, full of fish and wildfowl, with rushes growing all around it. Thus, the place was named Tula, which means "Place of the Rushes."

Now, Huitzilopochtli had never intended the Mexica to stay there forever, for the good place by the lake was still a long way away. The god had told them to build the dam and make the lake so that they might see what awaited them when they finished their journey and so that they might have a good place to rest, for they had come a long way and had further yet to go. But the people saw how lovely Tula was, how plentiful the game was, and how beautiful the trees, and soon some of them began saying that they would rather stay there than continue on their journey, and they tried to convince the others that they should settle here and make it their home forever. This angered Huitzilopochtli, for it was not the place to which he was leading them, and it was not the place that was their destiny.

That night, the people's rest was disturbed by the sound of anguished cries. In the morning, they went to investigate, and in the place where the cries had come from, they found the bodies of those who had been urging the people to stay at Tula. Each one of the bodies had been ripped open and their hearts torn out by Huitzilopochtli.

The god then called the people to him and ordered them to take down the dam they had built. The pent-up waters rushed forth at first, but soon the river returned to its bed. No longer was Tula a place of shade and plenty. The rushes and reeds dried up. The fish died flopping and gasping on the desert sand. The waterfowl flew away. And so, the Mexica had to leave and continue their journey to the good place by the lake that Huitzilopochtli had promised to them.

Long and long the Mexica journeyed. There had been marriages among them and babies born. And the babies had grown into children and the children into men and women who made marriages and had their own children in turn. And so, there came a time when there were very few who remembered their old home in Aztlan and those were most aged, and still the Mexica had not reached the end of their journey to the good place by the lake.

Eventually they came to a place called Chapultepec, which means "Hill of the Locusts." Chapultepec was on the shores of Lake Texcoco. The Mexica made camp there, but they were afraid for the people of that region were hostile and unwelcoming. The people of Chapultepec were led by Copil, the son of Malinalxochitl, who had been raised to manhood on the story of Huitzilopochtli's betrayal and abandonment of his mother and who therefore had a hatred of the Mexica and their god. But Huitzilopochtli told his people to be of stout heart, for he did not mean for them to stay there long. The god also told them that if they were to be the truly great people he wanted them to become, they would have to face enemies and defeat them, for in this way they would show their own strength and courage not only to others but to themselves.

Copil, meanwhile, went to all the peoples in the nearby land. He told them that the Mexica were not honorable, that they were not trustworthy, that their customs were disgusting and reprehensible, and that they were warlike and meant to attack at any moment. Soon he had aroused all of the people in the district to hate the Mexica. The people of Chapultepec and their allies raised an army. They attacked the Mexica, and a fierce battle ensued. Copil's army was victorious, but Copil himself was captured. Huitzilopochtli cut open Copil's chest and tore out his beating heart, then threw it far out into the lake, where it came to rest on a small island.

Although Copil's army left the Mexica alone after the death of their leader, the Mexica saw that they could not stay in Chapultepec. Huitzilopochtli led them next to a place farther south on the other side of the lake. This place was called Culhuacan, a prosperous city ruled by a mighty king. When the Mexica arrived, they asked Huitzilopochtli what they ought to do, for they had not forgotten the battle at Chapultepec and they did not want to make enemies in this new place. Huitzilopochtli answered them, saying, "Make an embassy to the king of this place. Ask him for some land where our people might settle and thrive. Whatever he gives to you, take it, whether it is good or bad."

The Mexica therefore chose an embassy from among their elders and brave men and sent them to meet with the king of Culhuacan. The king himself received them graciously and listened to their plea for land where they might settle. But his advisers did not look kindly on the Mexica, and they told the king to send them away. When the king refused to do this inhospitable thing, his advisers told him to give the Mexica land in a place called Tizapan. The king agreed to this and told the Mexica embassy where the place was and how they might get there. The ambassadors thanked him for his kindness and went back to their own people, where they told Huitzilopochtli what had passed between them and the king of Culhuacan. Huitzilopochtli then told the people to gather up their belongings and make ready to go to Tizapan.

When the Mexica arrived there, they were much saddened for the land the king gave them was poor. What is more, it was on the edge of a swamp and infested with great swarms of insects and a multitude of venomous serpents. But Huitzilopochtli told his people to be of good courage for he would show them a way to make Tizapan a goodly place to live. First, he showed them how to capture the insects and cook them for food, and soon there were so few insects that the Mexica were hardly troubled by them at all. Then the god showed the people how to do the same with the serpents, and in a short time all of them had been eaten as well. Once all the vermin had been consumed, the Mexica set about building a settlement, with farms and homes and a temple.

After a time, it came to the ears of the king that the Mexica had made a settlement in Tizapan and appeared to be prospering. The king would not credit these stories for he knew that Tizapan was a most inhospitable place. But he wanted to see whether the stories were indeed true, so he sent messengers to Tizapan to give the Mexica his greetings and ask how they did. The messengers came back to the king saying that they had seen fertile fields and a well-ordered town, and that the Mexica thanked the king for his generosity in giving them the land for their settlement. They also asked whether they might be allowed to enter Culhuacan to trade with the people there and to make marriages with the inhabitants.

The king listened well to all the messengers told him. He took careful thought about the requests the Mexica had made. Then he agreed to allow them to trade and to marry, for he saw that they were indeed a hardy people and he deemed it most unwise to make enemies of them. Indeed, the king went so far as to ask the aid of the Mexica in his fight against a nearby people called the Xochimilco. The Mexica sent their warriors willingly, and so they helped the king of Culhuacan to victory. And so it was that the Mexica and the people of Culhuacan lived peaceably together for a time.

Huitzilopochtli saw that the Mexica had made a good home for themselves in Tizapan. He saw that they had begun to think of their settlement as a permanent home. But Tizapan was not the good place by the lake that he had promised them. And the Mexica needed to face yet more hardship before they could become the rulers of the land as Huitzilopochtli intended. They needed to find some reason to fight with the people of Culhuacan, to get themselves expelled from that land, before they truly thought of it as their home and could not be persuaded to leave. So, the god called to himself his priests and told them that they were to go to the king of Culhuacan and ask him for one of his daughters, that he might marry her. The priests did what Huitzilopochtli asked of them, and when the king heard that his daughter was to be the bride of a god, he readily agreed and sent his daughter to Tizapan.

When the young woman arrived, Huitzilopochtli told his priests to bring her to the temple and make her a sacrifice. Then they were to flay the girl and place her skin on one of the priests, who was to pretend to be the young woman as if she were still alive. After all that had been done, Huitzilopochtli sent messengers to Culhuacan to invite the king and his court to attend the wedding ceremony between himself and the king's daughter. The king rejoiced at this invitation. He collected many fine gifts to give the god and his wife. But when he arrived at Culhuacan, he was horrified to see one of the priests of Huitzilopochtli doing ritual dances dressed in the skin of his daughter.

The king of Culhuacan and his nobles ran back to their city, where the king summoned to him all his army. Then he led them on an attack against the Mexica. The Mexica fought so well and so bravely that the king and his army were forced to retreat. But the Mexica knew that they could no longer stay in Tizapan, so they went further along the lakeshore to a place called Ixtapalapan, where they made camp. Even though they had been victorious against the army from Culhuacan, the Mexica were in great distress, for yet again had they been driven out of a place that they had settled and begun to think of as home.

Huitzilopochtli saw the distress of his people, so he said to them, "Be of good cheer. Your long journey is nearly ended. You will know where your final home is when you see this sign: on an island in the lake, the one where I threw the heart of your enemy, Copil, you will see a nopal cactus. Atop the cactus there will be a great eagle, holding a white serpent in its talons. That island is to be your home. On that island, you will build a great city, and you will call it Tenochtitlan, the Place of the Nopal Cactus."

Then Huitzilopochtli told the Mexica to take their rest and that in the morning they would go in search of the island with its cactus. When the sun rose, the people ate a hurried meal and then began searching along the lakeshore for the island the god had told them of. After many hours, one of the priests cried out and pointed towards the middle of the lake. There on an island not far from shore was a nopal cactus, and atop the cactus was a great eagle, holding a white serpent in its talons, just as Huitzilopochtli had said. The people rejoiced greatly and fell down in homage to the great bird. The eagle saw the people doing it honor, and it bowed to them in turn. This increased the joy of the Mexica, for it told them that they had finally come to the end of their journey and that their future was surely to be a prosperous and blessed one.

And this is the tale of how the god Huitzilopochtli was born and how he led the Mexica to their new home in Tenochtitlan, which became the center of the mighty Aztec Empire.

Motecuhzoma I and the Search for Chicomoztoc

One place where history and myth collide is in this tale of the search for Chicomoztoc, which means "Place of the Seven Caves." Chicomoztoc is one of the mythical places of origin for the Aztec people, and according to this legend the search was undertaken at the command of Motecuhzoma I (r. 1440-1469 AD), the successor to Itzcoatl. This search may never have actually happened, and even if it did, it is certain that Motecuhzoma's emissaries did not find the mystical mountain of youth or the goddess Coatlicue, mother of Huitzilopochtli. It seems likely that this myth, like that of the Aztec migration and those about the fall of the Toltecs, was constructed as part of the effort to elevate Aztec culture and legitimize Aztec rule in the years following the creation of the Triple Alliance under Itzcoatl.

In this story, we also see the central place of cacao beans (Nahuatl cacahuatl, *but the word originally was Mayan) and chocolate (Nahuatl* chocolatl*) as a luxury item in Aztec culture. So valuable were cacao beans that they even were used as a form of currency and demanded as tribute. Although today we tend to eat or drink chocolate as a sweetened food, early Mesoamerican cultures including the Aztecs and Mayans usually drank chocolate bitter, often flavored with chilis, vanilla, or spices, and sometimes thickened with maize.*

One day, the Emperor Motecuhzoma (Angry Like a Lord) bethought himself of the ancestors of the Aztecs and of the great tale of their journey from Aztlan to Lake Texcoco and all the deeds they had done. He bethought himself also of the great god Huitzilopochtli who, like the Aztecs, had left his own home and his own mother behind in order to guide the Aztecs and help them achieve greatness in their new home of Tenochtitlan. Motecuhzoma remembered that Huitzilopochtli had promised his mother, the goddess Coatlicue, that he would return, but he had not done so; rather, he had stayed in Tenochtitlan to look after the Aztecs and to receive the worship he was due as a mighty god and protector of his people. Motecuhzoma wondered whether Coatlicue was still alive and whether she had received any news of her son.

The emperor therefore sought the advice of his chief general, a man named Tlacaelel, who besides being the bravest warrior and best strategist the Aztecs had ever known was also a pious man and learned in the history of his people. Motecuhzoma called Tlacaelel before him and said, "I have in mind a great deed to be done by our bravest men. I want them to go in search of Chicomoztoc, the Place of the Seven Caves, where our people first lived many ages ago. I want to send many warriors, well equipped, to find Aztlan and its sacred mountain and to see whether Coatlicue the Serpent-Skirted is still alive and to bring her tidings of our people and of her mighty son, Huitzilopochtli. I wish that these men bring with them many fine gifts to be given to Coatlicue, to show her our gratitude and the strength and prosperity of the Aztec people and that she may know the true might and worth of her son."

"O Mighty One," said Tlacaelel, "surely this is a great and blessed deed that you propose and will bring much honor to you, to our people, and to the god Huitzilopochtli. But if you ask for my advice on how this might be accomplished, I say this: do not send warriors, for they will not be able to find Aztlan, nor will they be able to find Coatlicue the Serpent-Skirted. Our warriors are worthy and courageous, but all their skills will not avail them in this venture. No, if you would follow my advice, I would tell you to send sorcerers and wise men, for only they know the way to find such a place as Aztlan.

"For as our scholars tell us, this place was most delightful and a land of plenty when our people dwelled there, even though it was in a marshy land; but then it became wild and overgrown with reeds, brambles, and trees with long thorns, and the ground was stony and infertile when our people departed it to seek a new home elsewhere. Aztlan will not be easily found, even by our doughtiest men, and even should they find it, the trees themselves will turn against them and keep them away.

"Also, by sending soldiers armed for battle we may frighten the people of Aztlan, which is not desirable. Neither would we want to make Coatlicue fear your emissaries. Rather we should send men who are wise and learned, those who will know how to speak to the people of Aztlan and to Coatlicue in a manner befitting an embassy from one great nation to another. These also should be sorcerers with much knowledge of how such a place as Aztlan might be reached by magic."

Motecuhzoma listened carefully to all Tlacaelel said, and he agreed that this was sage advice. The emperor therefore called to him Cuauhcoatl (Eagle Serpent), who was the royal historian and a very aged and learned man. Motecuhzoma asked Cuauhcoatl to tell him the story of Chicomoztoc and all he knew about Aztlan and the place where Huitzilopochtli dwelt before he led the Aztecs on their great journey.

"O Mighty One," said Cuauhcoatl, "I will do my best to tell you all I know, that your royal purpose might be accomplished with great success. The place our ancestors dwelt was called 'Aztlan,' which means 'Place of the White Heron.' As our scholars tell us, in Aztlan there is a great lake, and in the midst of this lake is a great hill called Colhuacan, which means 'Twisted Hill,' because its summit is twisted all round. This hill is where the Seven Caves are located, and it was from these caves that our ancestors first emerged into the world, and it was in these caves where they first lived. Our ancestors called themselves 'Mexica' and 'Aztecs,' which are names we still use proudly today.

"We know that Aztlan was a place of plenty and ease. The people ate freely of the many kinds of waterfowl that dwelt there along with a great multitude of fish. Beautiful trees grew all about the place, giving shade to all who sought it. The gardens of our ancestors were fertile and easily worked, yielding maize, amaranth, tomatoes, beans, and all kinds of chilis; we know these still today, for those who departed Aztlan on the great journey brought seeds with them, and we, their descendants, still farm those good plants in our own gardens.

"As we do today, our ancestors went about in canoes upon the water. They delighted in the songs and colored feathers of many birds. They drew cool, refreshing water from many springs. Their life in Aztlan was altogether delightful.

"But once our ancestors left Aztlan, they found that the land was not so easily worked and that food was not so easily found. The ground was stony, dry, and overgrown with brambles. There were many venomous serpents and dangerous animals that did the people harm. It was a long and hard road that brought our people from Aztlan to the prosperous place we live in today."

When Cuauhcoatl finished his tale, Motecuhzoma thanked him for his wisdom and then said, "I think what you have told me must be true, for it is the same tale that Tlacaelel has told me. I now command that messengers be sent through our lands that they might find sixty sorcerers who have the skill and knowledge to accomplish the task I will set them. The sorcerers are to be brought here, that I may give them their instructions."

And so, it was done as Motecuhzoma commanded. Not long thereafter, the sixty sorcerers were found and assembled before the emperor to hear his will. Motecuhzoma said to the sorcerers, "I welcome you here, honored elders, for I have a mighty task for you. I wish that you go forth to find Aztlan, the land from which our ancestors came, to see whether it still exists. I also wish that you find Coatlicue the Serpent-Skirted to see whether she yet lives and to bring her news of her mighty son, Huitzilopochtli. I have heard from my wise advisers that finding this place will be difficult and that your skills are what is needed to carry out my commands. Therefore, prepare yourselves in whatever way necessary, so that you may meet with success on your road."

Motecuhzoma then commanded that many rich gifts be prepared for the sorcerers to take with them: mantles made of many colored feathers or woven from the finest cotton, beautiful women's clothing sewn with the greatest of care, gold, jewels; cacao, cotton, vanilla, and the brightest and most colorful feathers in the whole kingdom. These were to be given to Coatlicue and the people of Aztlan as tokens of goodwill from the Aztecs. To the sorcerers themselves Motecuhzoma gave colorful mantles and many other good things, along with enough food to nourish them during their journey.

Taking all these things from the emperor, the sorcerers promised to do their utmost to carry out his commands. They then departed the fair city of Tenochtitlan and went to the hill called Coatepec that stands near the city of Tula. When they arrived at Coatepec, they climbed the hill, and there on its summit they began to work their magic, for they knew it was by magic alone that they might find Chicomoztoc and Aztlan. They covered their bodies with magical ointments. They drew magical symbols upon the ground. They called to the many spirits they knew who could give them the power to go to Aztlan. The spirits replied by turning the sorcerers into birds and beasts, such as jaguars and ocelots, and then whisked them away to the place of Aztlan.

The sorcerers arrived at the shores of the lake Cuauhcoatl had described, and there they were turned back into their human forms by the spirits. Looking out over the lake, the sorcerers saw the hill of Colhuacan. They also saw many people in canoes. Some were fishing. Others tended their chinampas, the floating garden plots that the Aztecs of Tenochtitlan also used to grow their food. All seemed happy and prosperous. Then one of the people looked up from her work and cried out, "Look! There are strangers on the shore."

The people paddled their canoes to the place where the sorcerers stood. They heard the sorcerers speaking quietly amongst themselves of all the wonders they were seeing and of what they should say, and the people were astonished that the strangers spoke their own language.

When the people were close enough to the sorcerers to speak without shouting, one of them said, "Who are you? Where do you come from, and what is your business here?"

The sorcerers said, "We are Aztecs. We are ambassadors of our emperor, and we are looking for the place our people came from."

The people asked, "Which god is yours?"

"We honor the great Huitzilopochtli," said the sorcerers, "and we are ambassadors sent by the Emperor Motecuhzoma, bearing gifts for Coatlicue the Serpent-Skirted and to bring her news of her son if she yet lives, and to find Chicomoztoc, the ancient home of our people."

Upon hearing this, one of the people was dispatched to find the one who cared for Coatlicue, mother of Huitzilopochtli. They explained the errand of the sorcerers to the guardian, who was a very aged man. "Let them come here," said the guardian, "and make them most welcome, for they are our kin."

And so, the people took the sorcerers into their canoes and paddled them across the lake to the hill of Colhuacan. At the foot of the hill was the house of the guardian. The sorcerers went to him and said, "Honorable Father, we are ambassadors from our emperor, and we humbly ask your permission to speak to her who is the mother of our god."

"You are very welcome here," said the guardian. "Tell me, who was it that sent you here? What is the name of your emperor?"

The sorcerers told the guardian that Motecuhzoma was their emperor, and that he and his trusted adviser, Tlacaelel, had commanded them to undertake the journey to Aztlan.

When the guardian heard this, his brow furrowed. "Motecuhzoma and Tlacaelel? I know not those names. Tell me, are there still among you Tezacatetl or Acacitli? Ocelopan or Ahuatl? Xomimitl, Ahuexotl, or Huicton? Is Tenoch still alive? For these were the leaders of those who departed this land long ago, and we have heard nothing of them since then. Nor have we heard anything of the four who bore the god Huitzilopochtli away from here."

"Venerable One," said the sorcerers, "We have heard those names, but we do not know any of those men for they died long ago."

"Oh!" said the guardian. "Oh, what sad news you bring! How did they die? How is it that they are dead while we yet live? Who leads you now that they are gone? And who is it that cares for Huitzilopochtli?"

"The grandsons of your friends are our leaders," said the sorcerers, "and the priest of Huitzilopochtli is a very wise and holy man named Cuauhcoatl, who serves the god well and lets us know his will."

"Ah, that is good that the god is well looked after by a devout man," said the guardian. "Did you see him yourselves before you came here? Did he send a message?"

The sorcerers told the guardian that Motecuhzoma and Tlacaelel were the ones who had sent them on their mission. Then they had to admit that they had not spoken to Huitzilopochtli themselves, nor had the god given them any messages.

"That is vexing," said the guardian, "for when Huitzilopochtli left us, he said that he would be returning, and we have had no word as to when that will be. His mother has been waiting all this time, and she weeps daily because she has had no news. You should go and speak to her, for maybe you can bring her comfort."

"Indeed, we would be honored to speak with the Serpent-Skirted One," said the sorcerers, "for that is part of our mission, and we have many fine gifts to offer her."

The old man then told the sorcerers to take up their bundles of gifts and to follow him to the house of Coatlicue, which was near the top of the hill. Now, the upper part of the hill was made of very soft sand, and the old guardian walked up with great ease. But the sorcerers foundered under the weight of their burdens, their feet sinking down into the sand. The guardian noticed that the sorcerers were lagging behind him. He looked back and saw them struggling through the sand. "Why is this difficult?" he said. "Try to go faster."

The sorcerers tried and tried to do as the guardian said, but the only result was that they sank up to their waists in the sand and could not go any farther. The guardian went back to where the sorcerers were and said, "What have you been eating that you are too heavy to walk this hill?"

"We eat the food that grows in our gardens," replied the sorcerers, "and we drink chocolate."

"Ah, that is what is wrong," said the guardian. "Your food is too rich and too heavy. You should live more simply, as we do here. Then you would be able to walk this hill. But since you cannot, you must give me your bundles and wait here while I go see whether Coatlicue will come down to speak with you."

And so, the old man picked up a bundle of gifts the sorcerers had brought, and carrying it on his back as though it weighed less than a handful of feathers, he walked up the hill to the house of Coatlicue. There he set down the bundle, and then he went back to fetch the rest. The old man carried each of bundle up the hill on his back with the greatest of ease.

When all the gifts had been brought to the house, Coatlicue herself came down the hill to meet with the sorcerers. She was old, old, old and not one speck of beauty was in her face or her body. Her hair was matted, her skin and clothing were covered with filth, and she wept many sorrowful tears.

"I bid you welcome, O my sons," said the goddess, "and I beg your pardon for my appearance. But it is grief for my son that makes me like this, for I have neither bathed nor combed my hair nor changed my clothing since he departed, and I have spent my days in weeping, awaiting his return. Tell me, is it true that you have been sent here by the seven elders who went with the people that my beloved Huitzilopochtli led away from here all those long years ago?"

The ambassadors looked upon Coatlicue and her hideous aspect, and they were greatly afraid. They all bowed before her as best they could despite the sand and said, "O Great Lady, of the seven elders we know but the names, for they died long ago. The ones who sent us were Motecuhzoma, our king and your humble servant, and his trusted adviser, Tlacaelel, a man both wise and brave. They wished us to come here to give you their greetings and to see the place that our ancestors once called home.

"It has been many, many long years since our ancestors departed this place. Motecuhzoma is himself the fifth king of our people. The four who came before him were Acamapichtli, the first king, then Huitzilihuitl, then Chimalpopoca, and then Itzcoatl. Motecuhzoma bids us to say to you, 'I greet thee, O mother of our god, and I bow before thee as thy humble servant. My name is Huehue Motecuhzoma (Motecuhzoma the Elder), and anything thou biddest of me, so shall I do.'

"And our king also bids of us to tell you of the fate of our peoples, and what befell them after they left this place. They traveled long and far through many hardships. The people were often hungry and very poor, and for a long time they were vassals of others and forced to pay heavy tribute. But now we are masters of our own city, a beautiful and prosperous place. We have built many roads on which all may travel in safety. What is more, the Aztecs are the rulers of the land, our city is the principal capital, and others now pay us tribute. To show how prosperous our people have become, Motecuhzoma bids us give you these gifts, for they were won with great toil and with the aid of your mighty son, Huitzilopochtli, who now dwells among us in very great honor. And this is all the message we have been commanded to give to you."

When Coatlicue heard the message of the sorcerers, she ceased her weeping. "My sons, I bid you most welcome and give you all my thanks for these gifts and for the message you have given me. But I am greatly saddened to hear that the seven elders have passed from this world, and I wish to understand how that befell them for all their friends here are yet living.

"Also, I wish to know more of some of these gifts." She held up a bundle of cacao and asked, "What is this thing? Is it something to eat?"

"O Great Lady," replied the sorcerers, "that is cacao, and from it we make a delicious drink. We also mix it with other foods, and it is very good to eat that way."

"Ah, I see," said Coatlicue. "This is what has prevented you climbing the hill, for it is very heavy food." Then the goddess looked upon the mantles that Motecuhzoma had given the sorcerers and she said, "That is very fine raiment you wear. Does my son Huitzilopochtli wear anything like it? Does he also have clothing well woven and adorned with bright feathers?"

"Yes, indeed," said the sorcerers. "He is dressed this way and with even richer things than these mantles for he is much honored, and it is with his aid that we have won the wealth we now bring to you."

Coatlicue then said, "My children, my heart is much gladdened by your words and by the tale you tell of my son and of those who left this place long ago. It pleases me that the people now live in prosperity. But in return, I ask you to bear a message to Huitzilopochtli. Tell him to take pity on his mother, for I am lonely here now that he is gone. Tell him that he should remember his words to me when he left, that he said he would come back after he had led the seven tribes to a place of safety and prosperity, that he would go out and conquer many peoples and then come home to me when his own people were conquered in their turn.

"But it seems to me that my son has made a good home among you and that he is so content there and so well cared for that he forgets his obligation to his mother." The goddess then gave to the sorcerers a simple mantle and breechcloth woven from maguey fibers, saying, "I bid you to take this mantle and this breechcloth and to give it to Huitzilopochtli as a gift from me and as a reminder that he promised to come back."

The sorcerers bowed to the goddess. They took the clothing with the promise that they would give it and her message to Huitzilopochtli as soon as they returned home. But before they went far, the goddess called to them. "Wait!" she said. "I will show you how it is that the people live so long and never grow old here. Look at my guardian. He is very old. But when he comes down to you, he will change into a young man."

And so, the old guardian began to walk down the mountain. As he walked, he gradually became younger and younger. When he reached the sorcerers, he said, "Now I appear to be about twenty years old. But when I go back up, I will become older."

The man started walking up the hill. When he was about halfway up, he seemed to be forty years old. Further up the hill, he became very old. Then he turned to the sorcerers and said, "See, O children, what this hill does for us. If an old person wants to be younger, he climbs to the point of the hill that will give him the age he wants to be. If he wants to be a boy again, he can climb to the very top. To be a young man, he need only climb a bit more than halfway. Climbing halfway makes one middle-aged. This is how we live a very long time, and I now understand that this is why the seven leaders who left with the people are no longer living; you have no such hill in your land, and they could not restore their youth.

"I think also it must be the way that you live in your land. You drink much cacao, you eat rich foods, and you wear fine clothing. All of this has made you heavy and slow, and it causes you to age. You show this in your bodies and in the gifts that you bore hither. However, you should not go back home without gifts. We will give you many of the things that we value to take back to your king."

The guardian then ordered gifts to be prepared for the sorcerers. The people of Aztlan gave them all kinds of waterfowl that lived around the lake that surrounded the hill, ducks and geese and herons. They gave many types of plants and flowers. The people of Aztlan prepared garlands of colorful flowers, good mantles, and breechcloths of maguey fiber, clothing of the type they wore, to be given to Motecuhzoma and Tlacaelel.

"Go now with good fortune," said the guardian, "and beg the pardon of your king and his noble adviser for the humble nature of the gifts you bear. They are nothing so fine as what you brought, but they are the very best that we have."

The sorcerers thanked the guardian and the people for their gifts and their hospitality. Then they began to make the magic that would take them back to their home. They painted their bodies with the magic ointments. They drew the mystical symbols on the ground. They summoned the spirits to take them back home.

The spirits came and turned them back into the animal forms in which the sorcerers came to Aztlan and whisked them away to the hill of Coatepec. When the sorcerers regained their human forms, they looked about them and were dismayed for some twenty of their number were missing. What became of those twenty was never discovered, but some say that they must have fallen prey to wild beasts on the journey back to Coatepec.

The sorcerers shouldered their bundles of gifts and set out for Tenochtitlan. When they arrived, they were given an audience with Motecuhzoma. They told the emperor what had happened in Aztlan and gave to him the many gifts that the guardian of Coatlicue and the people of Aztlan had given them. The sorcerers reported everything that had been said between them and the goddess and between them and her guardian. They told the emperor about the magical hill that could restore lost youth and that the people who lived in Aztlan today were the same ones who had stayed behind when the seven tribes left their homes on their great journey south so very long ago. Also, they told the emperor what the goddess had said of her son, that she felt very lonely without him and wanted him to come home to her, and that she had said that one day he would do so because the kingdom of Tenochtitlan would be conquered, just as the Mexica had conquered the people who had lived there before they came.

Motecuhzoma thanked the sorcerers for their messages and their gifts. Then he summoned Tlacaelel to hear the sorcerers' report. They told him about all they had seen, the plants and the trees, the waterfowl and the fish, and the floating gardens that yielded every good thing in great plenty. They told Tlacaelel how the people navigated the lake in their canoes. They told him also that there seemed never to be only one growing season but many overlapping, so that while some maize was still sprouting, other fields were ready for harvest, and in this way, food was always very plentiful.

When all of that had been related, the sorcerers described their adventure on the hill of youth and how they could not climb it because they sank into the soft sand, but that the guardian could climb it with ease even though he was heavily burdened with the gifts they had brought for the goddess. They explained that they sank into the sand because they had been made heavy by their rich living and by drinking so much chocolate. The sorcerers also told the emperor and Tlacaelel how Coatlicue and the guardian had wept to hear that their friends who had left on the great journey south were now dead.

Motecuhzoma and Tlacaelel listened in wonder to the tale of the sorcerers. They were greatly moved to hear of all the beautiful things of the land of Aztlan and how their ancestors dwelt there still with the mother of their own god, and they sorrowed a little that they had not been able to see these things with their own eyes. Then the emperor and his adviser gravely thanked the sorcerers for the gifts and for having undertaken such a perilous journey. They ordered the sorcerers to be rewarded with many fine gifts. And when that had been done, they told the sorcerers to go to the temple of Huitzilopochtli and to clothe him in the mantle and breechcloth they bore with them, for these were the gifts his own mother had made and had sent just for him.

Huemac and the Sorcerer

Among the contents of the Florentine Codex, *Fray Bernardino de Sahagún's sixteenth-century ethnography of the Aztecs, are stories about Huemac, the mythical last king of the Toltecs and of Quetzalcoatl's exile from Tula. These are tales de Sahagún learned from his Aztec informants.*

One series of stories in the Florentine Codex *tells of the misfortunes of Huemac and of his people at the hands of the Aztec god, Tezcatlipoca. Although the primary characters in these stories are Toltecs, the stories themselves are Aztec creations intended to legitimize Aztec supremacy by providing mythical explanations for the fall of Toltec culture. In these legends, Tezcatlipoca comes in disguise to Tula, the capital city of the Toltecs, where he insinuates himself into Toltec society and then wreaks havoc, first by ensorcelling the people into destroying themselves and then finally by slaying them himself.*

Once there was a king of the Toltecs named Huemac. He had a daughter who was the most beautiful woman in all the land. Many men desired to marry her, but her father always forbade the match.

The great enemy of Huemac and of the Toltecs was the god of the Smoking Mirror, Tezcatlipoca. Tezcatlipoca was always looking for ways to cause trouble for the Toltecs, so he went to Tula disguised as the sorcerer Titlacauan. He changed himself into the form of a young man selling green chilis. He went about in this form without a breechcloth, so that his manhood was visible for all to see. Naked as he was, he went into the marketplace near the palace to sell his chilis.

While Titlacauan was selling chilis in the market, the daughter of Huemac happened to see him there. She saw him in his nakedness, along with the virility of his manhood, and was inflamed with a passion to have Titlacauan as her lover. So much in desire was she that she began to act as though she were ill, refusing food, sighing and groaning, and looking sad and unwell.

Huemac saw that his daughter was unwell, so he went to her maidservants to ask what was the matter. The maidservants told the king, "Your daughter saw that seller of green chilis in the marketplace. He goes about without a breechcloth, and she is now burning with desire for him."

Huemac therefore ordered that the seller of green chilis be brought before him to account for his behavior. Messengers went all through the city of Tula announcing that the man was wanted by the king. They looked high and low for him, but nowhere was the man to be found, until one day he reappeared in the marketplace in the very same spot where the king's daughter had first seen him. Word was sent to the king that the seller of chilis had returned, and the king commanded that the man be brought before him immediately. Not long afterward, the messengers returned with the man.

"Who are you, and where are you from?" asked Huemac.

"Oh, I'm just a stranger here. I sell green chilis in the marketplace," said Titlacauan.

Then Huemac said, "Where have you been before coming here? Also, it is indecent to go about with one's loins ungirt. Take a breechcloth and cover yourself."

Titlacauan replied "But in my land this is how we go about. We wear no breechcloths."

"I care not what you do in your own land," said Huemac. "You are now in my kingdom, and your nakedness has inflamed my daughter with desire. You must heal her of this ill."

Then the stranger became frightened. "Oh, no, great king. Do not force me to do this thing. I am merely a seller of green chilis."

"I care not," said the king. "You have made my daughter ill, so you shall heal her of it."

The king ordered that the man be taken away to be bathed and made comely for his daughter. And when this had been done, the king brought the man to his daughter and said, "There she is. Heal her."

And so Titlacauan lay with the king's daughter, and she was greatly satisfied thereby. When Huemac saw how happy his daughter was, he married her to Titlacauan. When word spread that the king had married his daughter to the seller of green chilis, the people began to make fun of the king because he had given his daughter to a stranger and not to one of his own people. Huemac was greatly shamed by this, so he came up with a plan to rid himself of the stranger once and for all. Huemac called to him his chief warriors. He ordered them to take the army and make war with Cacatepec and Coatepec, and while the fighting was well in hand, they would abandon Titlacauan on the field so that he would be either slain or taken prisoner. He also told the chief warriors to give Titlacauan only hunchbacks and others with unsound bodies to be his fellows in the battle.

And so, the Toltecs declared war on Coatepec and Cacatepec and set out to fight. The chief warriors set Titlacauan and the hunchbacks and others in one part of the field. Then the rest of them went to another part, thinking that the Coatepeca and Cacatepeca warriors would kill Titlacauan and his fellows. The hunchbacks and the others who were with Titlacauan were sorely afraid, for they knew they were not strong enough to fight the other warriors. But Titlacauan told them not to worry, for their enemies were sure to be defeated.

Once battle was joined, the Toltec warriors abandoned Titlacauan and went back to Tula. They told Huemac, "We left the stranger and his fellows alone on the field as you commanded. Surely they have all been killed by now."

But on the battlefield, Titlacauan cried out, "Fight fiercely! Be courageous! We will defeat them! I promise you that we will bring back many captives and slay that number over again!"

And when the Coatepeca and Cacatepeca warriors attacked Titlacauan and his fellows, they were taken captive and slain in great numbers. When the battle was done, Titlacauan and the others went back to Tula. Word had already come to Huemac of the deeds they had done, and word had also spread throughout the city. Titlacauan and his companions were met at the gates of Tula by a cheering crowd. They gave to Titlacauan bright quetzal feathers and the turquoise shield and many other trappings that are given to heroes and kings. The people danced and sang in Titlacauan's honor. They sounded their conch shell trumpets and beat their drums. And when the procession reached the gates of the palace, the people painted the faces of Titlacauan and his companions red, their bodies yellow, and placed feathers on their heads.

Huemac came forth to meet Titlacauan and his companions. "See, now the Toltecs greet you as a hero of the people and as one of them. Truly are you my son-in-law."

But Titlacauan had no thought for becoming one of the Toltecs. Even though he had defeated the Coatepeca and Cacatepeca, and even though he had been anointed with red and yellow paint and with feathers, he still planned to destroy the Toltecs. Now he turned to the crowds of people and thought to make them dance and sing. Titlacauan went to the summit of Tzatzitepetl, the Mountain That Speaks, that stood just outside the city. And from the top of that mountain, he called for everyone everywhere to come to Tula.

When everyone had assembled, Titlacauan went to a place called Texcalpan, and he told all the people to follow him. Then Titlacauan began to sing and beat his drum. Everyone began to dance together and to sing the song of Titlacauan. From sunset to midnight, Titlacauan led the singing and dancing, and no one sat apart from it.

The people were so intent on their songs and dances that they did not watch where they were going. Some of them fell into a canyon. They died when they hit the ground, and their bodies were turned into stones. Others had started crossing the bridge that went over the canyon, but Titlacauan broke the bridge, and everyone on it fell into the river below, where their bodies were turned into stones. But even as the people were falling into the canyon and into the river, still they did not understand that Titlacauan was making them sing and dance so they would destroy themselves.

There was another time when Titlacauan came to Tula and worked sorcery upon the people there. He disguised himself and came to Tula as a magician holding a small figurine in his hand. The figurine looked like a small child, but some say that this was the god Huitzilopochtli who had transformed himself. Titlacauan held the figurine up to the people, and lo! The figurine began to dance of its own accord.

The people were entranced by the dancing of this figurine. They crowded towards the magician, wanting to see more. So many people pushed forward towards the magician that some were crushed to death in the press of bodies, while others fell and were trampled underfoot and so died there. But the magician took no note of the crowds or of the cries and moans of the dying. Rather, he said to the people, "Look upon this sorcery! Surely it is by evil magic that this figurine is made to dance."

Then the people turned upon the magician. Instead of wanting to see the figurine dance, they wanted to kill Titlacauan and destroy the figurine. The people picked up stones and hurled them at the magician. Over and over again they threw stones at him, until finally he fell down, dead, and his body was left there to rot.

It did not take long before the corpse began to stink. The odor was more horrendous than any the people had encountered before. But not only that: those who smelled the stink of the magician's corpse were killed, and when the wind carried the stench about the land, the people died who smelled it.

But Titlacauan was not yet finished with his mischief, for still he purposed to destroy the Toltecs. And so, he took upon himself a new form and went to Tula, where he said to the people, "Why do you let such a noisome thing sit in your marketplace? Surely it should be removed."

The Toltecs listened to the words of Titlacauan and said, "Yes, this man is quite correct. We should not let this thing stay in our marketplace. Let us get ropes and tie its feet and drag it out of the city."

And so, the men of Tula went and fetched ropes, and they made them fast about the corpse. Then they pulled on the ropes to drag the dead thing away. But the corpse was too heavy; no matter how they pulled, the body would not move. The men of Tula called for aid. They called for others to come and help them pull, and when a great multitude had gathered and taken hold of the ropes, the order was given for all to pull. But still the corpse did not move. Instead, the ropes binding it broke, and the men tumbled down on top of each other, and many were killed in the press of bodies.

Titlacauan went to the men of Tula and said, "Oh, I see that you are not strong enough to pull away a simple corpse. Perhaps you should use my magic song. You should sing, 'Drag, drag, drag away this dead log! Drag him away! Help us drag him, O sorcerer Titlacauan!'"

The men of Tula listened to the song of the magician. They put new ropes about the corpse and began to pull, singing the song the sorcerer taught them. They pulled and pulled, and again the ropes broke, and again many were killed in the tumbling press of bodies.

Over and over this happened. The men would try to pull away the corpse, and many would die when the ropes snapped. But yet they would go back and try again, for they had been ensorcelled by Titlacauan, who wanted them to destroy their selves.

A last sorcery that Titlacauan practiced on the Toltecs he did in the guise of an old woman. First, he made it so that the food of the Toltecs went bad. It tasted so bitter that none could bear to eat it. No matter what food was prepared, or how it was prepared, it was unfit to eat. And so, the Toltecs became very hungry, and the other peoples in the lands laughed at them.

After taking on the guise of an old woman, Titlacauan went to Xochitlan (Place of the Flower), where there were gardens floating upon the water as well as gardens of many flowers upon the land. There Titlacauan sat in his guise as an old woman, toasting maize. The aroma of toasting maize floated up from her cookfire. It wafted away on the wind. It went along the fields and over the hills. It went into the temples and into the houses of the people. And everywhere the Toltecs said, "What is this aroma of toasting maize? Where does it come from? Surely now we shall have good food to eat, if we can find who is toasting this maize."

And so, the Toltecs set out in great numbers to find where this good maize was. They left their homes in Tula and went to Xochitlan, and they arrived quickly, for the Toltecs had the gift of moving from place to place very swiftly.

When the Toltecs arrived at the place where Titlacauan was, the sorcerer took up a great sword and slew them all as they came. Titlacauan cut them down one after another in his guise of an old woman. And so, the peoples of the lands around made sport of the Toltecs, for the old woman had slain so many of them.

Huemac Plays the Ball Game

An important early modern source of Aztec myths is the now-missing Codex Chimalpopoca, *a manuscript written in 1558 in Nahuatl and Spanish. The telling of the "Legend of the Suns" in this codex contains a story about Huemac, the mythical last king of the Toltecs, who learns a hard lesson about courtesy and the honor due to divine beings. As with the stories about Huemac from the contemporary* Florentine Codex, *this tale was created in an attempt to legitimize Aztec rule.*

In this section of the legend, Huemac plays tlachtli, *the sacred ball game, with the tlaloque, servants of the rain-god, Tlaloc. Tlachtli was played by many Mesoamerican cultures. The rules required players to use only their hips and knees to strike a solid rubber ball that was about six inches in diameter. Because of the heavy ball and the rough play of the game, athletes wore protective gear made out of deerskin. Although there is some variation in the size and shape of extant courts, playing spaces often were in the shape of a capital letter "I" flanked by stone walls. At the midpoint of the walls on the long sides of these courts were stone hoops with barely enough space for the ball to pass through. Hitting the ball through the hoop ended the game, and the team who had scored that goal was the winner. However, these goals were rare, and there were other means of keeping score in order to determine who won or lost.*

In this story, Huemac and his opponents wager jade and quetzal feathers on the outcome of their game. Mesoamerican cultures used feathers of the quetzal and other birds as an important agricultural product and trade item. Quetzal feathers, especially, were prized for their beauty and brilliant colors, but not just anyone could wear these; they were a symbol of nobility and power, and as such were given as prizes to the bravest warriors, or were worn as tokens of authority by the king and holders of government office.

One day, Huemac, king of the Toltecs, was of a mind to play the ball game. He thought about whom he might invite to play with him, but could think of no one who would give him a true challenge, for Huemac was the best player of tlachtli that had ever lived. And so, the king was vexed and invited no one, and he walked about in a sour mood grumbling to himself. Word came to the tlaloque, the lords of rain who serve Tlaloc, the god of rain, that Huemac wanted to play tlachtli but could find no one good enough to face him, so the tlaloque went to Tula and said that they would play with Huemac. Huemac was delighted by this, for here surely were players who would present a challenge to his skills.

The tlaloque asked Huemac, "Shall we have a wager on our game?"

Huemac answered, "Yes, indeed we shall! I wager my jade and my quetzal feathers."

The tlaloque said, "It is well. We also wager our jade and quetzal feathers."

Then the tlaloque and Huemac went down to the ball court and they played the game. No matter how swiftly the tlaloque ran, no matter how hard they hit the ball with their hips and knees, they were no match for the skill of Huemac. Finally, the king gave the ball a mighty stroke, it went through the hoop at the side of the court, and the tlaloque had to admit defeat.

The tlaloque brought their wager to Huemac. They gave him ears of maize in their green husks, for this to them was jade and quetzal plumes. But Huemac was insulted by this, for he had expected precious stones and bright feathers. "What is this?" said Huemac. "This is not precious jade, nor beautiful quetzal feathers. It is only maize. Take it away!"

And so, the tlaloque took away the maize and gave to Huemac jade as a precious stone and quetzal plumes as bright feathers, and when this was done, they said to the king, "Because of your insolence and greed, we will take away our own jade from you and your people. We will keep it from you and the people for four years."

Soon Huemac learned the great cost of his rudeness. The tlaloque made a great storm of hail fall on the land of the Toltecs. The hail fell out of the sky in a great shower, and when it was done, there was hail up to a man's knee all over the whole land. All the crops were buried and died from the cold and the striking of the hail. Then the sun came out. It came out and it shone mercilessly down on Tula. It shone on the maguey and nopal cacti, the trees, and the grass, drying them all up. The sun shone so much and so hotly that even the stones began to crack from the heat and dryness, for the tlaloque held back the rain as well. And so, it was that the Toltecs could not grow enough food to eat, and many of them died from hunger.

Finally, at the end of the four years, the tlaloque brought back the rain. One day, as it rained, a Toltec man walked along next to a pool of water, and out of the pool rose a ripe ear of corn that someone had already begun to eat. The man plucked the ear out of the water and began to eat it himself. Suddenly, a priest of Tlaloc, the rain-god, also emerged from the pool of water.

"Have you learned your lesson?" said the priest.

"Most assuredly I have, O Holy One," said the man, "and so have all my brothers and sisters."

"That is well," said the priest. "Wait for me here, for I go to speak to the lord of rain."

The priest went back under the water, and when he reappeared his arms were full of ripe ears of maize. "Take these to Huemac," said the priest. "Tell him that if he wishes the rain to come back, he will give the gods the daughter of Tozcuecuex the Mexica, for surely the Mexica will eat the Toltecs just as you eat the maize."

The man did as the priest commanded. When Huemac heard the message of the gods, he wept, for he understood that although the rains would come again, the kingdom of the Toltecs was at an end. Huemac sent messengers to the Mexica to demand the young woman be brought to him. The messengers told the Mexica that the young woman was demanded by the gods. And so, the Mexica prepared for a sacrifice by fasting for four days. And when the time of fasting and preparation was over, they gave the young woman to the gods, sacrificing her in Pantitlan. When the sacrifice was complete, the tlaloque appeared to Tozcuecuex, the father of the girl, saying, "Grieve not for your daughter, for she will be with you."

Then they put the girl's heart and many different kinds of food into Tozcuecuex's tobacco pouch. The tlaloque said to Tozcuecuex, "Here is food for the Mexica. Be of good courage, for surely the Toltecs will be destroyed and the Mexica will inherit their lands."

When this was done, the tlaloque brought much rain. It rained for four days and four nights, and when it was done raining, the grass, trees, and crops all began to sprout and grow, and soon there was enough food for all to eat. But in the end, what the gods had said came true: the Toltecs were destroyed. Huemac ran away to hide in a cave, and his people were scattered to many other places, and the Mexica came to rule over those lands.

How Quetzalcoatl Became the Morning Star

As with the legend of Huitzilopochtli and the migration of the Mexica, the story of Quetzalcoatl's departure from Tula, the Toltec capital, may be based in part on historical events, although it is extremely difficult to untangle facts from the web of myth. The ancient Toltec civilization in Tula gave the title "Quetzalcoatl" to their priest-kings, and at its height, the Toltec civilization appears to have been one of peace and plenty, with many fine temples. In the legend retold below, it is the Aztec god of the Smoking Mirror who tricks the Toltec Quetzalcoatl into a series of indiscretions that lead to Quetzalcoatl abandoning Tula. Like the stories of Huemac and the sorcerers, presented above, this tale also comes from the Florentine Codex.

There was a time when the god Quetzalcoatl lived upon the earth, and he was lord of Tula, the city of the Toltecs. Quetzalcoatl ruled wisely and well, and the city of Tula was a wealthy place with many palaces full of riches. The fields were always full of grain and vegetables. The markets were always busy with trade. No one in Tula ever wanted for anything.

As priest-king of Tula, Quetzalcoatl was always mindful of the things he must do. He made offerings in their seasons. He pricked his body with thorns to give blood to the gods. Nightly he prayed and went to bathe in the great river that flowed through the city. Quetzalcoatl did these things faithfully for a long time, and so Tula prospered.

Tezcatlipoca looked upon Tula and became very jealous of her good fortune. Also, Tezcatlipoca had not forgiven Quetzalcoatl the insult of having knocked him out of the sky when he was the First Sun. And so, the god of the Smoking Mirror thought how he might bring about the downfall of his brother, the Plumed Serpent. Tezcatlipoca therefore disguised himself as a young man. He brewed some pulque and put it in a jar. He wrapped the jar and his obsidian mirror in a rabbit skin and set out for Tula. When he arrived at Quetzalcoatl's palace, Tezcatlipoca walked up to his brother's servants and said, "Tell your lord that I am here to show him himself."

The servants showed Tezcatlipoca into Quetzalcoatl's palace. Still disguised as a young man, Tezcatlipoca said, "My lord, I can show you a good and rare thing. I can show you to yourself as you truly are. Very few have this knowledge. I think you should be one of them, for you are lord of a mighty city, and it is right that you should know yourself."

Quetzalcoatl said, "You may do this thing. Show to me myself."

Tezcatlipoca held up his obsidian mirror. Quetzalcoatl gazed into it. And in the mirror he saw a very old man. His hair and beard were white. His skin was wrinkled and his hands all gnarled. "Oh!" cried Quetzalcoatl. "I am so very old and ugly! How will my people see me? How will they stand to look at me? I must hide myself away and never show my face again."

"Never fear, my lord," said Tezcatlipoca. "I have here a medicine that will restore to you your youth."

Tezcatlipoca offered the jar of pulque to Quetzalcoatl. "No, I must not drink that," said Quetzalcoatl. "I am ill."

The god of the Smoking Mirror said, "Nonsense. Drink just a little taste of it. You will see how it aids you."

Over and over Quetzalcoatl refused the pulque. And over and over Tezcatlipoca urged him to drink it. Finally, Quetzalcoatl gave in. He took one sip of the pulque. It was delicious! He had never had anything quite like it. He drank the whole jar, and soon he was very drunk.

Quetzalcoatl sent for his sister, Quetzalpetlatl. He wanted her to drink pulque with him. Quetzalpetlatl came to Tula and went to her brother's palace. There she also drank much pulque, and soon she was as drunk as her brother. That night, Quetzalcoatl was so drunk he forgot to make offerings and say prayers. He forgot to bathe in the great river as a priest-king of Tula ought to do. He spent the night singing and drinking with his sister, and when they both became too weary to do anything more, they went to Quetzalcoatl's chamber where they lay together in his bed until the sun was high in the sky the next day.

When Quetzalcoatl awoke and saw his sister sleeping next to him, he recalled what he had done the night before and felt greatly ashamed. He knew that he could no longer be the king of Tula with so many sins on his soul. Quetzalcoatl decided that he must perform a penance and then leave his beloved city forever. First, he ordered his artisans to make him a fine tomb. When this was done, Quetzalcoatl had himself sealed in the tomb. He remained there for four days. After the four days were over, Quetzalcoatl came out of his tomb. He burned down his fine palace. He buried his gold and his jewels. The beautiful birds who gave him their bright feathers he sent away. The cacao trees he transformed into lowly mesquites. And when all this was done, Quetzalcoatl walked out of Tula, weeping all the while at the loss of his beautiful city.

Quetzalcoatl walked ever eastward, away from the beautiful city of Tula. After a time, he came upon a tree in a place called Quauhtitlan, the Place of the Tree. The tree was very old and gnarled. Quetzalcoatl gazed upon the tree and remembered what he had seen in Tezcatlipoca's mirror. "We are very old, you and I," he said to the tree, and from that time forth that place was known as

161

Huehuequauhtitlan, the Place of the Old Tree. Before leaving that place, Quetzalcoatl picked up many stones and hurled them at the tree. He threw them with such force that they went deep into the tree's bark, and there they remained.

The Plumed Serpent resumed his journey. Ever eastward he went, away from his beautiful city. He walked until he was very weary. Quetzalcoatl looked about him for a place to rest. Nearby there was a great stone. Quetzalcoatl rested himself on the stone, leaning on it with his hands. While he rested, he looked back towards his beautiful city, and once more he began to weep. The god's tears rolled down his face and splashed onto the rock. Soon his tears had made holes in the surface of the rock, and when the god took his hands away, the prints of his hands also were there in the stone. Ever afterward that place was called Temalpalco, the Place Marked by Hands.

Once more, Quetzalcoatl resumed his journey. He walked ever eastward until he came to a place where there was a great river. Quetzalcoatl wanted to cross the river, but there was no bridge. So, the god took many great stones and made for himself a bridge, and thus he crossed the river. And so, the place afterward became known as Tepanoayan, the Place of the Stone Bridge.

Next Quetzalcoatl came to a place where there were many sorcerers. The sorcerers came to the god and asked, "Where are you going?"

Quetzalcoatl said, "I am going east, to Tlapallan."

"Why are you going there?" asked the sorcerers.

"I go because I must," said Quetzalcoatl. "The sun calls me thither."

"Before you leave," said the sorcerers, "teach to us the crafts of metalworking and jewelsmithing. Teach us the crafts of building and of weaving with feathers, for we know that you are learned in these arts."

Quetzalcoatl did not want to part with this knowledge, but the sorcerers forced him to teach them. When Quetzalcoatl had taught them all he knew, he took a fine necklace that he was wearing and threw it into the fountain that was nearby. Thus, that place became known as Cozcaapan, the Place of Jeweled Waters.

Quetzalcoatl left Cozcaapan, walking ever eastwards. As he walked down the road, he was met by another sorcerer. "Where are you going?" asked the sorcerer.

"I am going east, to Tlapallan," said Quetzalcoatl.

"That is a good journey to make," said the sorcerer, "but you may not leave this place until you have had a drink of pulque."

Quetzalcoatl remembered his shame that came from drinking pulque. He said to the sorcerer, "I must not taste of that drink."

"Be that as it may," said the sorcerer, "I will not let you continue your journey until you have tasted of the pulque."

Quetzalcoatl saw that he had no choice. He drank the pulque the sorcerer gave him, and soon he became drunk. He lay down and fell fast asleep and began to snore. And his snores were so loud that they were heard far away, and the people far away thought to themselves, "Ah, it is thunder."

After a time, Quetzalcoatl awoke from his slumber. He looked about him and remembered where he was and what he must do. He straightened his hair and neatened his clothing. Before he resumed his journey, he named that place Cochtocan, the City of Sleepers.

On and on Quetzalcoatl traveled, until he climbed into the high mountain pass between Popocatepetl, the Smoking Mountain, and Iztac tepetl, the White Mountain. There it began to snow. White flurries came down from the sky, and the wind grew chill. There was much ice on the path. It was so cold that the servants who had come with Quetzalcoatl died of it, and the god mourned them very greatly. And when the god was done singing laments for his servants, he traveled on through the mountains. It is said that when he needed to descend a mountain, he would rest himself by sitting on the snow and ice and sliding to the bottom.

Wherever Quetzalcoatl went, he did some deed for the people of the villages and towns he passed through. In some places, he built ball courts. In others, he planted maguey cactus. Quetzalcoatl did many wonders and many useful things on his journey, and he gave names to all the places he went.

Finally, Quetzalcoatl came to the shore of the sea. And no one knows exactly what happened to him there, for there are two tales told of the fate of the Plumed Serpent. One tale says that he built himself a raft of serpents and sailed away into the east, to Tlapallan, the Red Land, and those who believe this story say that someday Quetzalcoatl will return.

The other tale says that when he arrived at the shore of the sea, he gathered much wood and kindled a huge bonfire. When the fire was big and hot enough, Quetzalcoatl threw himself upon it. In the fire, his body was transformed, and he rose into the sky where he became the Morning Star. And those who believe this tale say that ever since then Quetzalcoatl has acted as herald to the sun, leading it into the sky at each new day.

Section 3: Inca Mythology

Captivating Inca Myths of Gods, Goddesses, and Legendary Creatures

Introduction

From its inception sometime in the thirteenth century to its fall after the arrival of the Spanish in the sixteenth, the Inca Empire was a complex and well-structured political and geographical unit that encompassed a great swath of western South America, from parts of what are now Ecuador and Colombia to the north to parts of Argentina and Chile to the south, while what is now Peru and parts of western Bolivia made up the central portion. The Inca Empire was not comprised of a single unitary culture but rather was a kind of federation of many peoples under the authority of the *Sapa Inca*, the emperor who ruled from the capital in Cuzco and who was said to be the son of the sun-god, Inti. The primary language of the empire was Quechua, but Aymara and other languages were also spoken by the diverse peoples who lived in the four *suyu*, or provinces, that made up the empire.

As with other Central and South American cultures that fell victim to Spanish colonialism, the myths of the Incas have been passed down to us through a Western, Christian filter, since many of these stories were collected by Spanish writers and written down with varying degrees of accuracy, completeness, and bias toward the indigenous cultures that produced them. We are further hampered with respect to Inca myth in that the pre-colonial Inca seem not to have had a written language, as did the Maya and Aztecs; therefore, we have no indigenous Inca texts that have survived colonial rapacity as we do with Mesoamerican cultures, and therefore we have nothing with which to compare the witnesses of Spanish writers. Further, texts that were compiled by indigenous Inca writers after the conquest betray the heavy influence of Christianization.

That said, it is important to note that the Incas did have a system of strings and knots, known as *quipu*, that they used to keep track of census data and goods, but there is considerable debate whether quipu might have been used to record narrative tales as well. Scholars such as Gary Urton have argued that some quipu that remain undeciphered might in fact contain such narratives. If these could be translated, they would be a valuable check on the testimony of early colonialist ethnographers.

Official Inca religion centered around the worship of the Sun in a temple complex in Cuzco, but Inti, the sun-god, was only one of many deities revered by the Incas. There were several creator-gods, who each had their own associated myths, but there were also hundreds of *huacas*, a kind of divine spirit being who could take on a corporeal form at will and which were venerated in shrines also known as *huacas* throughout the empire. Often these shrines centered on some kind of monument made of stone, and many such shrines and holy places remain standing throughout the Andean region today.

We see the importance of stone and the mountains, which are a primary geographical feature of the west coast of South America, throughout the tales presented in this book. Many of the stories contain a scene in which a divine or mortal figure is turned into stone, thus becoming a *huaca* that subsequently is revered as a holy site, while other tales contain a scene in which a figure is transformed into an entire mountain. The myths of the Inca gods in the first section of the book explain how the world was created and also detail the adventures of various deities as they vie for supremacy or act as tricksters in the worlds of mortals and *huacas* alike. The second section contains the origin myth of the Inca Empire, which was used to justify Inca political legitimacy. This section also presents other tales involving the mythologized deeds of Inca emperors and their interactions with divine beings. The final section contains a collection of Andean folktales and a prose narrative version of the eighteenth-century drama *Apu Ollantay*, which may have been based on an ancient Inca tale and which tells the story of the forbidden love between Cusi Coyllur, daughter of the Inca Pachacuti, and the brave warrior Ollantay, whose name also graces the Inca fortress of Ollantay-tambo just north of Cuzco.

Although this book presents these tales under the umbrella designation of "Inca myths," these are in fact stories from several diverse cultures. The gods who create and destroy, play tricks and journey through the world in human guise are regional beings, revered in particular places by particular peoples within the Inca world. What ties them all together is the human desire for reasons, for explanations of why the world is the way it is, and the desire to explore love, fear, loyalty, lust for power, and the many other things that make us human.

PART I: STORIES OF THE GODS

Viracocha Creates the World

Some Inca origin myths center on the area around Lake Titicaca, which is located in the Andes mountain range on the border of southeastern Peru and central western Bolivia. Lake Titicaca is the largest lake in South America and is a striking feature of Andean geography that is easily visible from space. In Inca creation myths, Lake Titicaca and the Isla del Sol, the largest island within the lake, function as a kind of cosmic nexus from which the creator arises to make the world.

One of the primary creators in Inca mythology is a being called Viracocha, *which can be translated as "foam of the sea." In his book on Inca myth, Gary Urton points out that Viracocha was primarily an Andean highland deity, and that in the lowlands, creation was thought to be the work of a being called* Pachacamac. *The highland myth states that Viracocha is the one who initiates creation, but when it is time to people the world, he draws on the aid of two sons, Imaymana Viracocha and Tocapu Viracocha. Each of the Viracochas goes in a different direction to call people into being and give them their cultures, languages, and instructions in how to live in the places they are to call home.*

The fact that Viracocha apparently is some kind of trinity has led to speculation that the myth somehow became contaminated by Christian doctrine after Spain's conquest of Peru and the imposition of Catholic beliefs on the indigenous population. However, the concept of a triune god or of divine beings who otherwise work together in groups of three is found in many cultures throughout the world. Scholars therefore continue to debate whether the apparent threefold nature of Viracocha is a feature of native Inca belief or was something grafted onto the creation legend by the Incas in attempts to conform to the religious demands of their Christian conquerors.

Long, long ago, there was darkness. And in the darkness was a lake. The skies were dark, and the waters of the lake were dark, and the name of the lake was Titicaca.

Out of the waters of the lake came Con Tici Viracocha Pachayachachic, the Creator of All Things. Viracocha arose from the depths of Lake Titicaca, from the darkness of the waters he arose, and around him he created a world. But it was a world without light, for Viracocha did not create either a sun or a moon, nor did he create any stars. And in this lightless world, Viracocha sculpted a race of giants, huge men and women to people the earth, and he painted them with all manner of colors.

"Live!" said Viracocha to the giants. "Live, and walk, and breathe, and talk. Live without quarrelling with one another. Live, and serve and obey your Creator!"

The giants came to life at Viracocha's word. They went about in the darkness of that world without sun or moon or stars. But soon they quarreled with one another, and they forgot to serve and obey Viracocha, so Viracocha turned some of them into great stones. Others he destroyed by opening up the earth beneath the giants' feet. The giants fell into the earth which closed over them. Yet others

170

were destroyed by great waves that pulled them out to sea. None of the giants were ever seen again.

Viracocha was dismayed that his creation had failed. He made it rain for sixty days and sixty nights. It rained and rained, and soon the streams and rivers began to overflow their banks. The lakes overflowed their banks. The rain came down, and the water rose, and soon the whole world was covered by the waters of the flood. Everything Viracocha had made was washed away.

When the waters of the flood receded, Viracocha returned to Lake Titicaca. He went to the island that sits in the waters of the lake, the Island of the Sun. Viracocha thought that this time he would begin his creation differently. This time, Viracocha created lights in the heavens before making anything else. He created the sun, the moon, and the stars, and he put them in their places in the heavens.

The sun rose, and it was pleased with its brightness. "I am the brightest thing in the heavens," said the sun. "Everyone will look at me in wonder."

Then the moon rose, and it was even brighter than the sun. This made the sun jealous. The sun reached down and took up a handful of ashes. It threw the ashes at the moon. The moon's face became mottled with the ashes that the sun threw at it, dimming its light.

After creating the lights in the heavens, Viracocha left the Island of the Sun and went to Tiahuanaco. Viracocha took stones that he found on the banks of the lake. He molded the stones into the likeness of people, but he did not make these new people into giants. He gave the different people different features. He gave them different clothes to wear. He gave them languages to speak and songs to sing, and he gave them seeds so that they might grow their own food.

When the people had all been made, Viracocha brought them to life. Then he sent them on a journey below the earth. The people journeyed below the earth, each turning to the way that they must go, according to the dress they wore and the language they spoke. They came up out of the earth when they arrived at the places that Viracocha had given them to live. Some of them came out of the waters of rivers and springs. Some of them came out of the mouths of caves. Some of them came out of the stone of the mountains. Wherever the people emerged, there they made their homes.

Con Tici Viracocha had two sons. One was called Imaymana Viracocha. The other was called Tocapu Viracocha. Before sending the people on their journeys below the earth, Con Tici Viracocha showed them to his sons. Con Tici Viracocha said, "Look at the people carefully. Remember how they look and how they dress. Remember how they speak, and remember the songs they sing. For we will have duties to the peoples of the earth once they have emerged into the places that will be their homes."

Con Tici Viracocha sent Imaymana up into the mountains and down into the jungle. Tocapu Viracocha went to the place where the sea meets the land and went along the coastline. Con Tici Viracocha went along the river valley toward Cuzco. In all those places, each Viracocha proclaimed loudly to all the peoples that they were to obey Con Tici Viracocha Pachayachachic, who commanded that they make their homes in the places they had emerged and that they multiply and people the earth. And it was then that the people came forth from the springs and rivers, from the caves and mountains. They came forth at the command of Con Tici Viracocha, the command that was spoken by his sons and by Con Tici Viracocha himself. As they called to the people to come forth into their new lands, Viracocha and his sons taught the people all the things they needed to know to live. They showed the people how to grow plants for food. They showed the people which plants could be used for medicine. They taught the people the names of all the plants and creatures.

Viracocha then decided to make a journey. He put on his traveling cloak and took up his staff and set off down the road. Northwards Viracocha walked, going toward the city of Cuzco. On his way, he arrived at a town called Cacha. Now, the people who emerged in this place at the call of Viracocha and his sons were called the Cana people. They came into the world armed for war, and they were very fierce and dangerous people. The Cana saw Viracocha coming along the road, but they did not recognize their Creator. They armed themselves and went forth from their village, thinking that they would kill this stranger who dared to come near their lands.

Viracocha saw the armed men coming toward him. He knew that they did not mean him well, and he was angry that they would attack the one who had made them and given them a good place in which to live. Viracocha raised his hands to the heavens and called down a rain of fire. The fire landed on the hillside where the armed men were, setting the grass alight. The Cana people then realized their mistake. They fell down before Viracocha and begged his forgiveness. Viracocha took pity on them. He took his staff and put out all the flames, but he did not cause the grass to regrow. That place remained burnt and dry ever after, and even the stones themselves were altered by the flames of Viracocha: the fire burned away their heaviness so that even the largest of stones could be carried by one man alone.

Leaving the Cana people behind, Viracocha continued walking northwards. Ever northwards he walked until he came to a place called Urcos, where he climbed up the mountain and sat down upon its peak. There he called forth another group of people, that they might live upon the heights of the mountain. He called them forth, and they came, and he explained to him that he was the Creator who had made them. The people worshipped Viracocha. They made a *huaca*, which is a place sacred to the gods, and there they placed an image of Viracocha that was all made out of gold, and they set it upon a bench that was also made out of gold.

When the people of Urcos were well established in their new home, and when the *huaca* had been constructed and properly consecrated, Viracocha resumed his journey northwards. He went along the road to Cuzco, and as he went, he called forth new peoples and instructed

173

them in the ways they were to live. Finally, he arrived at Cuzco, which is the name that Viracocha himself gave to that place. Viracocha called into being a man named Alcaviza, who was made the first lord of Cuzco. Then Viracocha made a command that the Inca people emerge in that place once Viracocha had left to continue his journey.

On and on Viracocha journeyed, going along the road until he came to the place that is now called Puerto Viejo. In Puerto Viejo, the sons of Viracocha came to meet their father. Once they had all gathered, Viracocha and his sons went down to the coast, for that is where they departed from this world. A great crowd of people had gathered to greet their Creator and hear what he had to say to them. Viracocha said, "I must leave you now, but I will tell you of things that are to come. In time, people will arrive in your lands, people who claim to be myself, to be Viracocha the Creator of All Things. You must not listen to them, for they speak falsehood. I alone am Con Tici Viracocha, and I will care for you by sending messengers who will protect you and teach you things I wish you to learn."

After Viracocha spoke to the people, he and his sons walked out onto the ocean. They walked ever westwards until they passed out of sight, and the people marveled to see them walking on the water which they trod as lightly as they had done the solid ground. Thus it is that the people call their Creator Viracocha, which means "foam of the sea."

And that is the tale of how Viracocha created the world and filled it with people.

The Tale of Pachacamac

Whereas Viracocha was a creator-god for the highland Inca, Pachacamac was worshiped by lowland coastal peoples. Unfortunately, most of the mythology pertaining to Pachacamac has been lost, partly because his cult was displaced by sun worship when the Incas took over the area that had worshiped Pachacamac and partly as a result of the Christianization of Peru after the conquest.

Gary Urton notes that the main myth about Pachacamac was preserved by Antonio de la Calancha, a Spanish cleric who wrote a chronicle of the Incas in the middle of the seventeenth century.

Pachacamac is also the name of an important archaeological site that contains the ruins of several temples and other buildings. One of these was the only temple to Pachacamac in the whole of the Inca Empire, and as such, it became a site for pilgrimage. The temple was sacked and looted by the conquistador Hernando Pizarro in 1533.

Long, long ago, in the very beginning of things, there was a son of the Sun, and his name was Con. Con had great power: if he came to a mountain that was too high for him to climb, he would lower it, and if he came to a valley that was too low for him to cross, he would raise it. Con strode about the world creating people to live in it. He created the people, and he also created everything they needed for food. He gave them good land to till, land that was fertile and easily worked, and plenty of rain to water their crops and orchards.

But all was not well with the people. They behaved very badly and did not treat Con with reverence. Con therefore decided he would punish the people. This he did by causing the rain to cease falling. All the fields that the people used to grow their food dried up and became like deserts, and the only water they had came from the rivers and streams that flowed through their lands. The people then had to work many times harder to grow their food because they no longer had enough rain from the sky. They had to dig channels from the rivers to bring water into their fields. It was very hard work, and the crops did not grow as well as they did before Con's punishment.

Con was not the only child of the Sun. A brother he had, child of the Sun and the Moon, named Pachacamac. Pachacamac saw all the people that his brother created, and he thought to himself that if he were the creator, he could do much better. So Pachacamac drove Con out of the world. He then changed all the people Con had created into beasts. Some of them became monkeys. Some became foxes. Some became birds. But when Pachacamac was done, there were no more people to live in the land and to terrace and till the soil.

Pachacamac then created a man and a woman. But he did not provide food for them, and soon the man died. The woman did not know what to do. She was all alone in the world, and she had nothing to eat. She faced the Sun and said, "O Father Sun, I have nothing to eat. I have no family. I do not know what to do. Please help me!"

The Sun looked down upon the woman and saw that she was very beautiful. The Sun desired her, and so he sent his rays down upon her to get her with child. The child grew in the woman's womb and was born after only four days.

Pachacamac saw that the woman had borne a child by the Sun. This made him very angry and jealous. Pachacamac swore revenge, and so he took away the child and tore him into pieces. Pachacamac then scattered the pieces all around the land, and from the pieces, plants useful for food began to spring up. From the teeth sprang maize. From the bones sprang manioc. From the flesh sprang all manner of other fruits and vegetables.

The Sun saw what Pachacamac had done with his child and sorrowed greatly. He decided to make for himself another son, using the parts of the body that Pachacamac had not scattered. The Sun took the penis and the navel of the dismembered child, and from these pieces created another whole boy, whom he named Vichama. Just as the Sun likes to travel across the sky, so Vichama was seized by a desire to travel, and so one day, he set forth, leaving his mother behind.

When Pachacamac found out that the Sun had made another child from the pieces of the first one, he fell into a rage. He went to where the woman was, and he killed her. Then he took her body and gave it to the vultures and condors for their food. Then Pachacamac made a new man and a new woman, and they had many children, and their children had many children, and finally the land was peopled again.

Pachacamac decided that the people needed a way to govern themselves, and so he named some of them to be *curacas*, who had authority over all the others.

After a time, Vichama returned from his journey. He wept to hear that Pachacamac had slain his mother and thrown her body to the vultures and condors to eat. Vichama went out and looked for all the pieces of his mother's body. He carefully put them back together, and when he was done, she was a whole woman again. Then Vichama brought her back to life.

Pachacamac saw that Vichama had come back and that he had brought his mother back to life. He feared Vichama's power and his anger. Pachacamac therefore went down to the seashore where he went out into the waves, going farther and farther until the water swallowed him up and he was lost from sight.

Once Pachacamac was gone, Vichama turned all the people Pachacamac had created into stone. But the ones who had been curacas when they were alive, he turned into *huacas* to be used as shrines for honoring the gods. Thus it was that the curacas kept the high status that Pachacamac had given them.

Yet again was the world unpeopled. Vichama therefore prayed to his father, the Sun, to help him make more people to live on the earth. The Sun gave Vichama three eggs. One egg was made of gold. One was of silver. The third was of copper. One by one, Vichama opened the eggs, and from them sprang different kinds of people. From the golden egg sprang the curacas and the nobles. From the silver egg sprang women. From the copper egg sprang commoners, both men and women, and their children. And in this way, the world was filled with people once again.

Coniraya and the Maiden

In this tale, we see Viracocha going by the name Coniraya in his guise as a trickster, and we also see how very human Inca deities could be, feeling lust and pride, shame and delight. This legend also functions as a just-so story, explaining how certain animals came to have their distinctive traits, for example, why the condor feasts on dead llamas and why the skunk smells so bad.

The Incas, like many other cultures around the world, also told stories of mysterious, miraculous births. In this case, the woman Cavillaca becomes pregnant when she eats an enchanted fruit of the lucuma tree, which is an evergreen that grows in the Andean valleys in Peru and Ecuador.

One day, in the beginning of the world, Coniraya Viracocha had a mind to go on a journey. He had finished creating the land and the plants and the animals, the birds were in the sky, and the people were living in the places he had given them for their homes. His work of creation was done, and so Coniraya felt it was time to journey about the world.

Coniraya took up his staff and gave himself the appearance of a very old, very poor man. His skin was wrinkled, and his hair was white. He leaned upon his staff as though he needed its support. And in this guise, Coniraya set out upon the road. He went to many places, and everywhere he went, the people there treated him ill. "Go away, old man!" they would shout at him. "We have no use for an old beggar such as yourself!"

But Coniraya paid them no mind. He continued on his way, seeing what there was to be seen.

One day, Coniraya came upon a maiden who was sitting beneath a lucuma tree. The maiden was named Cavillaca, and she was a *huaca*, or divine spirit being. Cavillaca was busy at her weaving, and her clever fingers pulled at the threads on her loom, turning the bright wool into something beautiful.

Now, Cavillaca was very beautiful, and all the male *huacas* vied for her favor, but she never paid any mind to their advances, remaining unwed and unknown by any man. Coniraya saw Cavillaca and desired her for himself, but well he knew that she would not have him, so he thought to have a child by her by means of a trick. Coniraya transformed himself into a bird and lit on a branch of the lucuma tree. There he took some of his seed and turned it into a ripe lucuma fruit. He dropped the fruit near the woman and waited to see what she would do. Cavillaca noticed the bright fruit on the ground next to her. She had not eaten for some time and was hungry, so she picked up the fruit and ate it. And in this way Cavillaca became with child without ever having relations with a man.

When her nine months were done, Cavillaca gave birth to a beautiful child. She nursed the child at her breast and wondered often who the father could be. The child grew, happy and strong, and soon was able to crawl about. It was then that Cavillaca decided to find out who the father of her child was. She sent a message to all the other *huacas*, saying, "I wish to know who the father of my child is. If you know him, come and tell me." She told them that she would meet with them on a certain day in a place called Anchi Cocha.

All the *huacas* were overjoyed to hear Cavillaca's summons. They hoped that she would choose one of them for a husband at the meeting. On the day of the meeting, they dressed in their very best finery and took their seats in the place Cavillaca had set aside. Cavillaca showed her child to them and said, "Here is my child. I wish to know who the father is. Do any of you know him? Which of you is the father?"

But all the men sat silently, for none could truthfully claim to be the father of the child.

Now, Coniraya Viracocha also had heard Cavillaca's summons, and he was there at the meeting. He sat at the edge of the group, wearing his beggar's rags and leaning on his staff, his old man's white beard trailing down toward his chest. But even though he knew himself to be the father of the child, he did not speak out, and Cavillaca did not address him, thinking a poor beggar not worthy of her notice.

When none of the fine young men admitted to being the father of the child, Cavillaca said, "If you will not claim the child as your own, the child shall claim his own father. I shall set him down on the ground, and the one to whom he goes must be his father." Then she set the child on the ground and said, "Go and find the one who begot you!"

The child crawled through the crowd of young men, not stopping to greet any of them. He kept going, crawling on all fours as infants do, until he came to Coniraya. There the infant stopped and pulled himself up onto his father's knee.

Cavillaca saw who the infant had greeted and was dismayed. "Alas!" she cried. "Alas that the father of my child is a lowly beggar, a poor man of no account!"

Weeping, Cavillaca snatched up her child and ran from that place, going straight down to the shore where she thought to cast herself and her child into the sea. She ran across the sand and out into the waves and did not stop until she came to the deep water, where she and her child were turned to stone. And to this day, there are two stones in that place that look like people.

When Cavillaca ran away, Coniraya followed her. He ran after her as fast as he could, calling out her name, but she soon was so far ahead of him he did not know which way she had gone. As Coniraya tried to follow Cavillaca, he came upon a condor.

"Brother Condor," said Coniraya, "tell me, did you see a young woman run past here?"

"Yes, I did," said the condor. "She went that way. You should find her soon."

"I am grateful to you," said Coniraya, "and so I shall give you a gift. I will give you a long life. I will let you eat your fill of any dead animals you shall find upon the mountains. And people who kill you will also die."

Coniraya left the condor and returned to his search for Cavillaca. Soon Coniraya came upon a skunk.

"Sister Skunk," he said, "tell me, did you see a young woman run past here?"

"Yes, I did," said the skunk. "She went that way. But I doubt one as old as yourself could catch her; she ran like the wind."

Coniraya felt insulted by what the skunk said to him, so he laid a curse upon her. "Never shall you see daylight! You will go about only at night, and you will smell so bad that no other animals will want to come near you!"

Coniraya left the skunk and returned to his search for Cavillaca. Soon Coniraya came upon a puma.

"Brother Puma," said Coniraya, "tell me, did you see a young woman run past here?"

"Yes, I did," said the puma. "She went that way not long ago. You should find her soon."

"I am grateful to you," said Coniraya, "and so I shall give you a gift. You shall eat many fat llamas, and if people kill you, they will do it so that they can wear your head at festivals. That way you will always get to dance at festivals, too."

Coniraya left the puma and returned to his search for Cavillaca. Soon Coniraya met up with a fox.

"Brother Fox," said Coniraya, "tell me, did you see a young woman run past here?"

"Yes, I did," said the fox, "but that was some time ago. She must be very far from here by now. I don't think you'll ever catch up to her."

What the fox said made Coniraya very angry indeed. "A curse upon you!" said Coniraya. "You will always slink about craftily, and people will say of you that you are a thief and a trickster. If they kill you, they won't even use your body for food, and they won't even use your pelt for clothing or ornament!"

In the same way as he had met the other animals, Coniraya came upon a falcon.

"Sister Falcon," said Coniraya, "have you seen a young maiden running past here?"

"I have indeed," said the falcon, "and not very long ago. I think you must be close behind her."

"A blessing upon you," said Coniraya. "You shall have other birds for your food in great plenty. Sometimes people will kill you, but when they do, they will honor you with the sacrifice of a llama. They will put you on their heads when they dance at festivals. That way you will always get to dance at festivals, too."

Coniraya went upon his way, still chasing after Cavillaca. He ran and he ran until he came across some parakeets. He asked them the same question he had asked the other animals, and they replied, "Oh, she is far away from here. She was running so very swiftly, you'll never catch up with her no matter how hard you try."

"A curse upon you!" said Coniraya. "You will ever fly about screeching and screaming, and people will hate you and chase you away from their fields and orchards."

Everywhere Coniraya went, he asked for news of the maiden Cavillaca. If he was given good news and encouragement, he gave a blessing. But those who gave him bad news, he cursed.

On and on Coniraya ran, chasing after Cavillaca. But he never caught her. Coniraya came to the seashore and found that the maiden and her infant had gone out into the deep ocean where they had been turned to stone.

Seeing that there was no point in trying to find Cavillaca any more, Coniraya turned back inland. He walked until he came to the place where the daughters of Pachacamac lived, along with a giant snake who was their guardian. The mother of the girls was named Urpay Huachac, and when Coniraya arrived at that place, he found the mother was away, for she had gone to visit Cavillaca in her new home in the sea.

Coniraya looked upon Pachacamac's daughters, and he desired them greatly. He went into the house and made love to the eldest daughter, but when he tried to do the same with the younger one, she turned herself into a dove and flew away. And so it was that their mother was called Urpay Huachac, which means "Gives Birth to Doves."

Now, at that time, all the fish that there were in the world lived in a little pond near Urpay Huachac's house. Not a single fish was in the ocean. Coniraya was angry that the younger daughter would not sleep with him, so he took all the fish out of the pond and cast them into the ocean, saying, "Urpay Huachac has gone into the ocean to visit Cavillaca. Why don't you go and join them there!" And that is how the ocean came to be filled with fish.

After throwing all the fish into the ocean, Coniraya went away from that place and continued his journey. But soon Urpay Huachac returned home, and her daughters told her all that Coniraya had done while he was there. Urpay Huachac was furious that Coniraya dared to sleep with her eldest daughter and that he dared to go after the younger one as well, so Urpay Huachac went running after Coniraya as fast as she could go, calling his name all the while.

Soon enough, Coniraya heard Urpay Huachac calling for him, and so he stopped to wait for her. "What do you want of me?" he said.

"I wish to remove the lice from your head," said Urpay Huachac.

"Very well," said Coniraya, and he let her pick the lice from his head.

But Urpay Huachac had a plan. She intended to destroy Coniraya in revenge for what he had done to her daughters. Some say that Urpay Huachac made a great hole open up in the ground so that she could throw Coniraya into it. Some say that she created a great stone that she intended to drop onto his head. But whatever plan she had, Coniraya knew that Urpay Huachac did not mean him well, so he left her, saying that he needed to relieve himself. Once he was out of her sight, he ran off to another village, and thus he escaped Urpay Huachac's wrath.

And so it was that Coniraya went on his journey about the world, seeing what there was to be seen and playing tricks on people and *huacas* alike.

The Tale of Huathacauri

One of the features of Inca mythology is the concept of multi-partite gods. We see this with Viracocha, who seems to have been conceived as a trinity, and also with Pariacaca, a god who apparently is five beings in one. Not only is Pariacaca a complex being, but apparently, he is able to engender a son even before he himself is born: the hero of this tale, Huathacauri, is the son of Pariacaca, but Pariacaca himself is still confined within the five condor eggs of his own genesis.

Although he is the son of a god, Huathacauri is a poor man. He falls in love with a rich man's daughter and manages to marry her, but in doing so, he falls afoul of his wealthy, prideful brother-in-law, whom Huathacauri bests in a series of contests and who is eventually transformed into a deer. This myth therefore also functions as a cautionary tale against both pride and the mistreatment of the less fortunate.

This story and others about the god Pariacaca are recorded in the so-called Huarochirí Manuscript. It is written in Quechua and was compiled in the sixteenth century by Francisco de Avila, a Spanish cleric whose mission was to eradicate traditional Inca beliefs and replace them with Christianity. This manuscript, which was rediscovered in a Madrid library in 1939, was partially destroyed during World War II, although various modern copies of its contents survive. The manuscript is devoted to myths, legends, and religious beliefs from the Huarochirí province, which is an area in west-central Peru in the vicinity of Lima.

Once there was a man named Huathacauri who was so poor that he lived on potatoes he gleaned from others' fields that he then roasted in pits on the hillside. Poor he may have been, but Huathacauri was the son of the mighty god Pariacaca, and so his life was blessed, and he performed many marvels.

Not far away from where the poor man lived there was a very rich man named Tamta Ñamca. Tamta Ñamca lived in a house thatched with the colorful feathers of birds, and the soft, thick thatch gleamed in the sun so that it could be seen from very far away. Tamta Ñamca also owned a vast herd of llamas, but what was astonishing was not their numbers but rather their colors. Just as birds have feathers of red, blue, and green, so too did Tamta Ñamca's llamas have hair of red, blue, and green, so that when they were shorn there was no need to dye the wool before spinning it into fine thread, and the wool from Tamta Ñamca's llamas made the best thread in the whole world.

People from all around that place saw how splendid Tamta Ñamca's house was and how large and colorful his llama herd was, and they said to one another, "Tamta Ñamca is a fine fellow! See how wealthy he is? Surely he must be kin to a divine being, or perhaps he is divine himself! Come, let us go and ask him for advice, for he must know a great many things."

Except Tamta Ñamca wasn't really all that wise, nor was he divine at all, but he was flattered by what the people said about him, and so he pretended to know a great many things that he did not know. So clever and deceitful was Tamta Ñamca that he managed to convince the people of his wisdom, and after hearing them sing his praises continually, he began to think to himself, "Perhaps what the people say about me is true. Perhaps I really am a god!"

This went on for some time until one day Tamta Ñamca became very sick indeed, and despite the efforts of all the best doctors, no one could find a cure for his ailment. Years went by, and still Tamta Ñamca was very ill, so the people began to wonder how wise he really was if he could not find a cure for his own sickness. They also began to wonder whether maybe they had been fooled by him, and so they began to turn against him.

One day, after Tamta Ñamca had been on his sickbed for many years, Huathacauri was sleeping on a mountainside near the rich man's home. In the night, Huathacauri was wakened by voices. Not knowing who was speaking and fearing robbers who might do him harm, Huathacauri held very still and listened. Soon he discerned that the voices were not those of men but rather of two foxes who had met in their prowls that night and were exchanging news of the places they had been.

"Let me tell you what I heard in Upper Villca," said one fox to the other. "You know that rich lord who lives in Anchi Cocha, the one whose house is all roofed with feathers and who claims to be a god?"

"I do indeed," said the second fox. "Have you news of him?"

"Yes," said the first fox. "He has been very ill for many years, and nobody knows what is wrong or how to cure him. But I know the cause, and I know how it might be cured.

"That rich man is ill because one day his wife was toasting maize for another man who had come to visit, and one of the kernels of maize popped out of the pan and fell into her lap. She picked up the kernel and put it on the plate with the others, and the man ate it, which is just the same as if he had slept with her. As a punishment, two serpents have come to roost in the rafters of their home, and a two-headed toad has burrowed its way under their grinding stone, and it is these loathsome things that are causing the rich man's illness."

"That is quite a tale!" said the second fox. "It is too bad for that man and his family; no one will ever happen upon that cure by themselves. His younger daughter will spend the rest of her days tending her father instead of marrying well like her older sister did."

The two foxes talked of many other things before bidding each other good night and going home to their kits, but Huathacauri did not listen to much of it. His mind was full of the plight of the rich man and how he might use this knowledge to his own advantage. Huathacauri also thought about what the foxes had said about the rich man's daughters.

In the morning, Huathacauri went down into the town where Tamta Ñamca lived and began asking after the health of the rich man. One of the people he asked was Tamta Ñamca's younger daughter. "My father is the one who is ill," said the maiden.

"Oh, that is very sad indeed," said Huathacauri.

"Yes," she replied, "for no one has been able to cure him for many years, and he suffers greatly."

"Take me to see your father," said Huathacauri. "Perhaps I can help him."

Together the young people went to Tamta Ñamca's house, where the rich man lay in bed surrounded by doctors who murmured to each other about what a sad case it was and sometimes argued about what cure they should try next.

The daughter, whose name was Chaupi Ñamca, brought Huathacauri to her father's bedside and told him that the young man thought he could cure his illness. When the doctors heard this, they all started laughing. "What is a young beggar like you going to do that none of us wise and learned men haven't already tried? Be off with you!"

But Tanta Ñamca said, "Let him come to me and say what he wants to do. None of you has been able to cure me, so I may as well listen to what this young man wants to try. I don't care that he's poor and dressed in rags as long as he can make me well again."

Huathacauri went to Tanta Ñamca's bedside and said, "Sir, I do think I can cure you, but I will do so only on one condition: you must give me your youngest daughter to be my bride."

"With a good will I shall do this if you can make me well again," said Tanta Ñamca.

Huathacauri explained that Tanta Ñamca's illness was caused by the serpents in the rafters and the two-headed toad beneath the grinding stone, and that they had come to make Tanta Ñamca sick after his wife gave the grain of maize that had fallen into her lap to another man.

"If I get rid of the serpents and the toad, you will get well," said Huathacauri. "And when you have gotten well, you must stop thinking yourself a god, for a god would not let himself get sick. Instead, you must worship my father, Pariacaca, who will come into the world in just a few days."

Tanta Ñamca gladly agreed to all this, so Huathacauri set about hunting the vile animals that were making the rich man ill. First, he went up into the rafters of the house and killed the serpents. Then he went out to where the grinding stone was and lifted it up. When the two-headed toad saw Huathacauri, it ran away into a nearby ravine and made its home in a spring there. And this is why when people go to that spring, they go mad.

Once the vermin had been killed or driven away, Tanta Ñamca became well again. He kept his promise to Huathacauri, and soon his daughter and the poor man became man and wife.

Now, Huathacauri's wife had a sister who was married to a rich and powerful man. This man was ashamed that his sister-in-law had married a wandering beggar, and he vowed to get his revenge. The brother-in-law went to Huathacauri and said, "We should see who of us is the better man. I propose we have a drinking and dancing contest."

Huathacauri accepted his brother-in-law's challenge, and then he went up the mountainside where there were five eggs. In the eggs was Pariacaca, Huathacauri's father. He was still inside the eggs, for the time had not yet come for him to come into the world. Huathacauri went to the eggs and told his father that he had been challenged to a drinking and dancing contest. He asked what advice Pariacaca might have for him.

"Go to that mountain over there and pretend to be a dead guanaco," said Pariacaca from inside the eggs. "I'm expecting a fox and a skunk to visit me tomorrow morning. They usually bring a jar full of maize beer with them. The skunk brings a drum, and the fox also brings his panpipes, but when they see you, they'll set those down and go over to you to start to eat you. When they do that, jump up in the form of a man and scream as loudly as you can. They'll be so frightened that they'll run away and forget their jar and their pipes and their drum. Then you can come here and get those things and take them down to the village to use for the contest."

Huathacauri did as Pariacaca said, and when he had frightened away the skunk and the fox, he picked up their belongings and went down to the village to have the contest with his brother-in-law. The brother-in-law went first in the dance. He danced with all his wives, and he had hundreds of them. Then it was Huathacauri's turn. He danced with only his one wife, but he played the skunk's drum as he danced, and every time he struck the drum, the earth shook. The people declared that Huathacauri had won the dancing contest because while the rich man had many wives to dance with him, the whole earth had danced with Huathacauri.

Then it was time for the drinking contest. The people served cup after cup after cup of maize beer to Huathacauri, but no matter how much he drank, he never became drunk. When it was Huathacauri's turn to serve, he picked up the jar of beer he had taken from the fox and the skunk and went around serving all the people. No matter how much beer he poured out, there was always more in the jar, and when the people drank their cups of beer, they each fell down drunk after only one sip. And so Huathacauri also won the drinking contest.

The brother-in-law was enraged that Huathacauri had beaten him so easily in the drinking and dancing contests, so he proposed another challenge. "Let's dance in the plaza wearing our best puma skins," he said. "Whoever is best adorned and dances best will be the winner."

Now, the brother-in-law was a very rich man, and he had many fine puma skins. He thought that it would be easy to win this contest because there was no way a poor beggar such as Huathacauri would have even one raggedy puma skin, never mind the fine collection that the rich man had.

Huathacauri was undaunted. He went up the mountain where the eggs were and asked his father what to do about this contest.

"Do you see that mountain over there?" said Pariacaca from inside the eggs. "On the side of that mountain is a fountain, and next to the fountain is a fine puma skin. Go there and take the skin. You can wear that for your contest."

Huathacauri did as Pariacaca instructed. Near the fountain he found a fine red puma skin which he put on. Huathacauri returned to the village and announced that he was ready for the challenge. The rich man was astonished that Huathacauri was wearing such a fine puma skin, but he thought to himself that surely the poor beggar would never be able to dance as well as a rich man. And so, the brother-in-law did his dance in his puma skin, and the people thought that he had danced very well indeed and looked very fine in his puma skin. But when Huathacauri danced, a rainbow appeared in the sky above his head, and so the people judged that Huathacauri had won the contest.

The rich man was ashamed and angry that Huathacauri had beaten him yet again, so he proposed a fourth contest. "Let us see who can build a house the quickest," he said.

Huathacauri agreed to the contest, and so the rich man began right away to build the house. The rich man hired many workers to come and build the house for him, but Huathacauri merely saw to the foundations of his and then spent the rest of the day with his wife. At the end of the day, the rich man's house was nearly finished, but Huathacauri's was still only the foundations. But that night, birds, serpents, and many other kinds of animals came to Huathacauri's house and put up the walls for him.

In the morning, Huathacauri's brother-in-law was astonished to see that the poor man's house was nearly finished, just as his own was. So, he proposed that the next challenge would be to see who could build the best roof. Guanacos and vicuñas brought the thatch for Huathacauri's house, and soon the roof was finished. The other man waited for his thatch to be brought on llamas, but it never arrived because a bobcat who was friends with Huathacauri charged the llamas and drove them over a cliff. And so Huathacauri won that contest, too.

Then Huathacauri said to his brother-in-law, "We have had many contests, but you have always been the one to propose them. If I propose a challenge, will you accept?"

"Yes, I will accept your challenge," said the rich man, thinking that he would finally have a chance to defeat Huathacauri.

"Let's put on blue tunics and white breechcloths and dance," said Huathacauri. "Whoever dances best will be the winner."

"Agreed," said the rich man, and so they put on their blue tunics and white breechcloths and went into the plaza to dance.

The rich man danced first, but as he was dancing, Huathacauri ran at him, screaming as fiercely as he possibly could. The rich man was so frightened by Huathacauri that he turned into a deer and bounded away out of the village and up the mountainside. When the rich man's wife saw that her husband had fled in the form of a deer, she went running after him.

"Run all you like!" shouted Huathacauri. "I'm tired of all your contests! I'm tired of you thinking that you're the best just because you are wealthy! You thought you would have revenge on me for being poor? No, it is I who shall have revenge on you!"

So Huathacauri went running after them, and soon he caught up with the wife. He grabbed her and stood her upside down on her head, where she turned into stone. And to this day, in that place is a stone that looks like the lower half of a woman's body, sticking out of the ground as if she were upside down. But the rich man ran away into the mountains in the form of a deer and was never seen or heard from again.

And these are all the deeds that Huathacauri did in the time before Pariacaca emerged from the five eggs.

The Wanderings of Pariacaca

Pariacaca, a primary god of the Huarochirí region, is a water deity that is five beings in one. We see his association with water here when he calls down rain that brings about a mudslide upon people who have disrespected him and also in his work to create canals for irrigation of crops in an area that is experiencing drought. Like many other deities found in myths the world over, Pariacaca also is susceptible to the charms of beautiful women, and here he falls for a female huaca named Chuqui Suso.

When Pariacaca decided to come into the world, he first appeared as a clutch of five condor eggs on the side of a mountain. There he waited until the time was right, and then the eggs hatched into five fine condors. The condors flew out over the mountains, but eventually they turned into men who journeyed throughout the world.

One day, Pariacaca went to a Yunca village. The villagers were celebrating a feast that day. They were rejoicing and eating much food and getting very drunk on maize beer. Pariacaca went to join them, sitting at the very end of the feast in the lowest place, as is fitting for a visiting stranger. He waited and waited, but no one brought him any food or drink. He waited and waited some more, and still the villagers went on with their eating and drinking without offering any to Pariacaca. This went on all day until finally one of the village women noticed poor Pariacaca sitting there and said, "Oh, this is shameful! You have been given nothing to eat or drink! How long have you been waiting?" And so, she filled a large cup to the brim with maize beer and brought it to him.

"Thank you for the drink, Sister," said Pariacaca. "Because you have been kind to me where others have not, I will tell you an important secret. Five days from now, there will be a terrible tragedy here in this village. I am angry with all the people here, but not with you, and I don't want to kill you and your family by mistake. If you want to live, take your family and go far, far away from here. I'm letting you know this because you have been kind to me, but if you breathe a word to anyone else here, you will be killed as well."

Five days later, the villagers still sat at their feast, eating and drinking, but the woman left the village with her husband and her children. Also, their other relations went with them, and so that family was spared the disaster that was to come.

And this was how the disaster came to be: Pariacaca was angered that the villagers had not given him the hospitality due to a stranger and a guest, so he went up to the top of the mountain that stood over the village. There he caused it to rain. Sheets of rain came down in heavy, great drops, and soon the earth at the top of the mountain was so heavy and wet that it slid down the mountainside and into the village. The mudslide came crashing down and swept away all the houses and all the animals and all the villagers. The whole village was washed right into the sea.

Near to the Yunca village that was destroyed by the mudslide was a place called Cupara, and in Cupara, they were suffering from drought. They had had no rain, and the channels for bringing water to their fields were drying up. The maize was dying in the fields, and there was nothing anyone could do about it.

Pariacaca came to Cupara, and there he saw a woman named Chuqui Suso working in her maize field. She was trying to water the maize by hand and weeping because she knew that she could not give the plants enough water no matter how hard she worked, and she was sure that she would die of hunger. Chuqui Suso was very beautiful, and Pariacaca desired her greatly. Pariacaca saw that Chuqui Suso's fields were being watered by a little pond nearby, so he stopped the mouth of the channel there with his cloak and caused the water to stop flowing entirely. Then he went to the woman and asked her why she was sorrowing so.

"I do not have enough water for my maize plants," she said, "and I do not know what I shall do."

"Yes, that is troublesome indeed," said Pariacaca, "but I can give you plenty of water if you sleep with me."

"I will let you sleep with me after you make the water flow," said the woman, "and after I see that my field has enough water."

"Very well," said Pariacaca.

Then Pariacaca removed his cloak from the mouth of the channel. He also increased the flow of water, and soon the field was very well watered indeed. Chuqui Suso rejoiced to see that her maize would now grow well.

"Let's sleep together now," said Pariacaca.

"Not yet," said the woman. "I think it would be better to wait. Maybe tomorrow."

"What if I make a channel that goes from the river to your fields? Then you will never lack for water ever again. Will you sleep with me if I do that for you?"

"Yes, I certainly will sleep with you then," said Chuqui Suso. "Dig the channel from the river, and we can sleep together when it is finished."

"Very well," said Pariacaca.

All sorts of animals came to help dig that canal. There were pumas and foxes, serpents and birds, and they all worked together. But before they started, they decided to choose a leader to direct the work. All the animals wanted to be the leader, but they finally decided that the fox would be best.

Under the direction of the fox, the animals began work on the watercourse. When it was halfway done, the fox accidentally flushed a tinamou bird from its covert. This startled the fox so badly that he jumped in the air and yelped, and then he fell halfway down the mountainside.

"We cannot work under such a leader," said the other animals. "He gets frightened by the smallest things. Let's have the snake be in charge now."

The snake took charge of the work, and soon the new channel was all finished and directing a fine flow of water into Chuqui Suso's maize field.

Pariacaca then went to Chuqui Suso and said, "I have carried out my promise. Your fields now have a good source of water. Your maize plants will grow and yield a fine harvest. Will you now keep your promise to me?"

"Yes, certainly," said Chuqui Suso. "Let's climb up to that high place. There we can sleep together very well."

And so Pariacaca and Chuqui Suso went to the high place she showed him, and there they slept together. When that was done, Chuqui Suso said, "Let's go to a different place."

Pariacaca agreed, and so they started off down the mountainside. They came to a place called Coco Challa, where the mouth of the canal that watered Chuqui Suso's fields was. When they came to the edge of the canal, Chuqui Suso cried out, "I'll go no farther! I will stay here in the mouth of my canal and never go anywhere else!"

With that, Chuqui Suso turned herself to stone, and there she stands to this very day.

The Combat of Pariacaca and Huallallo Carhuincho

The Andes Mountains are the highest mountains in the world outside of Asia. They are also part of the Pacific Ring of Fire and thus are home to several active volcanoes, which are created by the motion of the South American tectonic plate against the Nazca Plate. In the story retold below, we see a traditional conflict between a fire being (probably an anthropomorphized volcano) and a water being who can bring rain, hail, and mudslides.

Once there was a *huaca* named Huallallo Carhuincho. This *huaca* was a fearsome creature made of fire. He ruled over the people, commanding them to have no more than two children and that one of the children must be given to him to eat. The people were greatly afraid of Huallallo, but they had no power to make him go away or to stop eating their children.

Pariacaca knew that Huallallo had been terrorizing the people and eating their children. They set out to find Huallallo and to defeat him, so that the people could live in peace.

Now, Pariacaca was not one single being but five. Pariacaca emerged from five condor eggs, first in the shape of five great condors who then took on human form and wandered about the world. The five Pariacacas met together at Ocsa Pata. They took their bolas and swirled them around, faster and faster. When Pariacaca swung the bolas, freezing cold and a great rain of hail came into that place.

While Pariacaca was swinging his bolas, a man came up the mountainside. The man carried an infant in one arm and a bundle of offerings in the other, and he was weeping very sorrowfully. Pariacaca saw the man and stopped swinging his bolas. "Friend," said Pariacaca, "why is it that you weep so?"

"Sir," said the man, "I am taking my child to Huallallo Carhuincho, for that *huaca* has commanded that we have no more than two children and that we give him one of the two to eat. Otherwise he will destroy us. I am taking this child to Huallallo to be his food, and this is why I weep."

Pariacaca was angered when he heard this. "Do not take your child to Huallallo. Take him back to your village. Give me your bundle of offerings. I will go to Huallallo and defeat him, and then you and your people can live in peace with all your children.

"I will fight with Huallallo in five days. You must come here and watch the combat. I will fight Huallallo with water, and he will fight me with fire. If I am winning, you must call out, 'Our father surely will be victorious!' But if Huallallo seems to be winning, you must declare the fight to be finished."

At first, the man refused to do as Pariacaca said. "I cannot do this thing. Huallallo surely will be angry with me."

"Don't worry about him," said Pariacaca. "I will deal with Huallallo, and you will be safe."

Finally, the day came for Pariacaca to fight with Huallallo. The five beings that were Pariacaca sent down rain upon Huallallo from five directions. They flashed lightning bolts at Huallallo from five directions.

Huallallo roared up in a great column of fire. No matter how much rain Pariacaca sent, the flame of Huallallo could not be extinguished. In this manner, Huallallo and Pariacaca fought all day long, and neither of them was able to get the better of the other, and the water from the rains of Pariacaca rushed down the mountainside and flowed all the way into the sea.

Finally, one of Pariacaca's selves, the one named Llacsa Churapa, knocked down a mountain and blocked the flow of water. Soon a lake had formed behind the dam. Huallallo was caught in the rising waters behind the dam. His fire was very nearly extinguished, and all the time Pariacaca was still hurling lightning at him, never stopping once to give his enemy any respite.

Huallallo saw that he would never be able to defeat Pariacaca, so he ran away down the mountain into the lowlands. The Pariacaca known as Paria Carco followed Huallallo and set himself at the foot of the mountain pass so that Huallallo would never be able to return.

Also, Pariacaca commanded that Huallallo should never again eat children but eat only dogs from then on.

Now, Huallallo Carhuincho had a companion, a woman named Mama Ñamca. Like Huallallo, Mama Ñamca was a being all made of flame. Pariacaca knew that he would also have to defeat Mama Ñamca if his victory were to be complete, so he went to Tumna where he knew Mama Ñamca would be. One of Pariacaca's children, Chuqui Huampo, went with him.

Mama Ñamca saw Pariacaca coming. She knew that he was coming to do battle with her, and so she hurled a weapon at him, but it hit Chuqui Huampo instead. Pariacaca went to Mama Ñamca and fought with her. He defeated her and threw her into the sea.

Once Mama Ñamca was defeated, Pariacaca went back to Chuqui Huampo. Chuqui Huampo was now lame because Mama Ñamca's blow had broken his foot. "I cannot walk properly," said Chuqui Huampo, "so I'll stay here and make sure that Mama Ñamca doesn't come back."

Pariacaca agreed this was a good plan. Chuqui Huampo stayed in that place, and Pariacaca made sure that his child had enough food to sustain him. Pariacaca also said that the people of that place were to bring a tribute of coca leaves every year and to sacrifice a llama that had not yet borne young in Chuqui Huampo's honor.

And thus it was that Pariacaca defeated Huallallo Carhuincho and Mama Ñamca.

PART II: INCA POLITICAL MYTHS

The Tale of Manco Capac

Transformation of an actual historical personage into a larger-than-life mythical character is a common process in many cultures, a process that the Incas also apparently embraced in their stories about Manco Capac, the founder and first ruler of the Inca state. Subsequent rulers, who used the name "Inca" as a royal title, traced their lineage and their claims to the throne back to this mytho-historical figure.

Although Manco Capac may have been an actual historical personage who ruled Cuzco, probably in the early thirteenth century, his story became embroidered into a political myth. There are several versions of this story which were compiled by Spanish redactors from Inca witnesses during the early colonial period. All of these versions of the tale assert some kind of divine origin for Manco Capac and his companions, as well as a variety of superhuman abilities that allow them to conquer the peoples in the various places they make their home on their way to founding the Inca capital city of Cuzco.

Long, long ago, in the place called Pacaric-tombo, which means "Tavern of the Dawn," there was a hill called Tambo-toco, which means "Window of the Tavern." And in the hill called Tambo-toco there was a cave that had three windows. One window was called Capac-toco, which is "Royal Window." The Royal Window was in the center of the three, and it was decorated with beautiful silver and gold. The other two windows were called Sutic-toco and Maras-toco, but the meanings of these names have been lost.

From this cave of three windows came the ancestors of the Incas and of other peoples. They arose within the cave, not having mothers or fathers. From the window called Sutic-toco came the people known as Tampus, and they made their homes in the lands about the hill. From the window called Maras-toco came the people known as Maras, and they dwelt in the lands around Cuzco. From the window called Capac-toco came four men and four women. They came from the Royal Window because they were the ancestors of the Incas, and the founders of that mighty empire. Some have said that these ancestors of the Incas were the children of none other than Inti, the god of the sun, and Mama Quilla, the goddess of the moon.

The people who emerged through the Royal Window were Ayar Manco and his wife, Mama Ocllo; Ayar Auca and his wife, Mama Raua; Ayar Cachi and his wife, Mama Huaco; and Ayar Uchu and his wife, Mama Cura. The men and women were all dressed very richly. Their clothing was made of finely woven wool decorated with gold. The men carried golden halberds, and the women carried all the things needed to prepare and serve meals, and these were also made all of gold.

When the four men and four women emerged from the cave, they looked about them for a place to make their homes. They walked along through the mountains until they came to a place called Huanacauri, which is near Cuzco, where they made their homes and began to grow potatoes. But they were not satisfied that this was the best place, so one day they went up to the top of a mountain to see whether they could find a better land.

When they got to the top of the hill, Ayar Cachi took a stone and put it in his sling. He flung the stone with all his might at a nearby hill. Such was the strength of Ayar Cachi's arm that the stone he threw plowed through the hill, and when the dust cleared, the men and women saw that there was a ravine in its place. Ayar Cachi took three more stones, and with these, he knocked down three more hills and plowed three more ravines.

Seeing this, the others began to worry that with his great strength Ayar Cachi might try to rule them as a lord. They therefore plotted to be rid of him forever. They went to Ayar Cachi and said, "O Our Brother, we have left many things of great value in our cave of origin, things that we will need for our new homes. Will you not go back and fetch them?"

"With a good will I will do this," said Ayar Cachi, and so he went back to the cave.

The others followed Ayar Cachi secretly, and when he had gone into the cave, they took a great stone and covered its mouth. Then they sealed the stone in place by bricking it in with a wall made of many other stones and mud for mortar so that Ayar Cachi would not be able to get out no matter how hard he tried. The three men and four women waited to see whether Ayar Cachi would be able to dislodge the stones and open the mouth of the cave. Soon enough, Ayar Cachi came to the walled-up cave mouth. He shouted and pounded on the stone but could not move it. Satisfied that Ayar Cachi would be confined in the cave forever, the three men and four women went back to their homes at Huanacauri. Since Mama Huaco no longer had a husband, she became a servant to Ayar Manco.

The three men and four women still had not found a suitable place to call their home. They climbed the hill at Huanacauri so that they might look out over all the lands below and see whether any of those places would be better. While they were on the top of the hill looking about, a rainbow came into the sky. The rainbow hovered over the end of the Valley of Cuzco. The Ayars and the Mamas saw the rainbow, and they looked down into the valley.

"This is a good sign," said Ayar Manco. "We should go to the place marked by the rainbow and there make our homes."

The others agreed with this plan, but before they could begin their descent into the valley, a wondrous thing happened. A great pair of wings sprouted from the back of Ayar Uchu. The feathers were long and of many beautiful colors that shone in the light. As the others watched, Ayar Uchu spread his wings and flew up to the Sun. Ayar Manco, Ayar Auca, and the women waited, hoping that Ayar Uchu would come back. They waited for a long time, and just as they had begun to think their brother was lost to them forever, Ayar Uchu returned.

"Have no fear!" said Ayar Uchu. "I have spoken with our Father, the Sun, and he has bid me bring you tidings. He says that you are go into the Valley of Cuzco, where you shall found a new city that will be the beginning of a mighty empire, the empire of the Incas. There you are also to build temples to the Sun, that he might receive the worship and honor that is his due.

"Our Father the Sun says also that Ayar Manco is henceforth to be known as Manco Capac, The Supreme Rich One, for he is to become the founder of the empire and the ancestor of all the great Incas who are to come. Go now into the valley, and begin the work our Father the Sun has bid you to do!"

When Ayar Uchu finished speaking, he was turned into stone. Although Ayar Uchu's family did not mind his transformation, the other people who lived near the hill were frightened to see a stone idol with great wings flying about in the sky. One day, the people threw stones at the idol Ayar Uchu had become. The stones broke off one of his wings so he could no longer fly. He came to earth and the place where he landed became a *huaca*, a sacred place for honoring the gods.

Leaving the idol of Ayar Uchu behind, Manco Capac, his brother Ayar Auca, and the women began their journey into the Valley of Cuzco. Along the way, they took a rod of gold that belonged to Manco Capac and pressed it into the ground. Wherever they went, they found that the rod would not go more than a little way into the soil. By this sign they knew that they had not yet reached the place they were to settle. They journeyed on to a place farther along the valley, testing the soil with the rod all the while. When they were not far from the place where they were to build the city of Cuzco, they thrust the rod into the ground. This time, the ground did not resist at all; instead, it yielded so readily that the rod was quickly swallowed up and buried in the soil. Then the Ayars and Mamas knew they had reached the place that they were to settle, the place in which they were to begin to found their empire.

Manco Capac looked about this new land, and not far off he saw a pile of stones. "Go and look at those stones," he told Ayar Auca.

"With a good will I will do it," said Ayar Auca, who then sprouted a pair of wings just as Ayar Uchu had done and then flew off to the place where the stones were.

Ayar Auca found that the pile of stones was in a place where two streams met in their courses. Flying down, he lit upon one of the stones and there was transformed into stone himself. This was to signify that the place now belonged to the Ayars and the Mamas, and on that spot was built the Temple of the Sun.

Manco Capac traveled onward to Matagua with the three women. By this time, Mama Ocllo had given birth to a fine son, whose name was Sinchi Roca. When their settlement had been built there beneath the peak of Huanacauri, they celebrated for Sinchi Roca the rite called *huarachico*, wherein the ears of the children of the nobility are pierced for the first time, for it is a sign of nobility to wear plugs in the earlobes. They also celebrated the feast of Capac Raymi, the great dance that is made for the turning of the year at the summer solstice, to honor Inti, the god of the sun.

After two years at Matagua, Manco Capac and the women decided that it was time for them to seek a better place to live. To find out which way they should go, Mama Huaco took two golden rods and threw them northwards. Mama Huaco was very strong, and the rods went a very long way. One landed in a place where the land had not been terraced. That rod did not sink into the ground. The other rod landed in a field near Cuzco and firmly planted itself in the soil there. Manco Capac and the women knew that the place near Cuzco would be the best for them to live in for the land there was tilled and fertile.

They went to that land near Cuzco, but when they arrived, they found it was already inhabited by people who grew coca and hot peppers. Those people resisted the coming of Manco Capac until Mama Huaco took her sling and killed one of them. Then Mama Huaco sliced open his body, removed the lungs, and then blew into them, making them swell up. This she showed to the inhabitants of that place, whereupon they all fled, leaving the land for Manco Capac and the women to have for their own.

There it was that Manco Capac and the women settled. They tilled the soil and planted the seeds of maize that they had brought with them when they left the caves. They built a temple to the Sun, which they called the House of the Sun. And they spread their power over the land, going forth from time to time and conquering neighboring peoples. And when Manco Capac was a very old man and his son Sinchi Roca came to manhood, Manco Capac handed the title of Inca to his son so that Sinchi Roca might rule.

And thus it was that the empire of the Incas began, long, long ago.

The Tale of Mayta Capac

In addition to the foundation myth that was intended to grant the Inca political legitimacy, other stories about subsequent Incas also paint them as larger-than-life beings with special powers and divine or semi-divine origins. Here we have the story of Inca Lloque Yupanqui's wish for an heir, which is granted by none other than the

Sun himself. Although the story asserts that Lloque Yupanqui was the father of Mayta Capac, the connection to a divine origin is maintained by the prodigious growth of the young lad, who is already large and strong enough to defeat trained youths and even grown men when he is only two years old.

This story also speaks of Mayta Capac "taking the fringe." Imperial power in the Inca Empire was symbolized by a braided chaplet topped with feathers to which was attached a long fringe made of fine, red wool decorated with gold. "Taking the fringe" therefore is the Inca equivalent to the Western idea of coronation as conveying absolute power.

The grandson of Manco Capac was Lloque Yupanqui, and he ruled wisely and well as the third Inca. But for a long time, Lloque Yupanqui remained unmarried, and so he came into his old age without an heir. One day as he sat sorrowing over his plight, he had a vision of the Sun, who told him that he would surely father a fine son who would be a worthy successor to the throne.

Lloque Yupanqui therefore began to search for a bride among the daughters of the lords of the empire. He found one in the town of Oma, a woman by the name of Mama Caua. Lloque Yupanqui asked whether Mama Caua might become his wife, and her father gladly granted his assent. The Inca Lloque and the family of Mama Caua were very pleased with this match. Mama Caua was a very beautiful woman, and her marriage to the Inca himself was a source of great pride for her and her family.

When the match was announced, there was a great feast held in Oma to celebrate the departure of Mama Caua for Cuzco. And all along the road, there was much feasting and dancing and rejoicing, for the Inca had commanded that his marriage be a time of rejoicing for all his people. Finally, Mama Caua arrived in Cuzco. The Inca himself came to the gate of the city to meet her with all his nobles in his train. They greeted her well and made her very welcome, and the whole city rejoiced with feasting and dancing for many days.

As the Sun had promised, Mama Caua soon found herself with child, and the baby was given the name Mayta Capac. But this was no ordinary child: Mayta was born fully formed after only three months. When he opened his mouth to give his first cry, everyone saw that he already had all his teeth. He grew so quickly that at the end of his first year, he was as tall as an eight-year-old child, and by the time he was two, he was so strong and so skilled at games and feats of arms that he could defeat young men who were much bigger and older than he.

One time, he went to play at rough games with young men from the Alcabisas and Culunchimas, tribes who lived near Cuzco. The youths could not stop Mayta. He wrought havoc amongst them, injuring many and killing a few others. On another day, Mayta and the other youths of the Alcabisas went to slake their thirst at a fountain. A dispute broke out over who had the right to drink first. Mayta broke the leg of the son of the chief of the Alcabisas, and when the other lads fled, he chased them down until they ran into their houses and barred the doors against him.

The chiefs of the Alcabisas and Culunchimas saw how badly Mayta Capac had abused their sons. Surely a child that was so very large and strong at the age of two would be an unstoppable foe once he reached his full growth and manhood. The Alcabisas therefore proposed to rid themselves of both the old Inca and Mayta Capac together. They sent their most skilled men to the House of the Sun in Cuzco with orders to find the Inca and his son and kill them. When the men arrived, Mayta Capac was in the forecourt of the House, playing ball with some of his friends. Mayta saw the approach of his enemies. He took the ball he had been playing with and hurled it at the foremost man. It hit him in the forehead and killed him instantly. Mayta Capac took up the ball as it bounced back to him and threw it at another man, killing him likewise. He then set upon the rest, and although they managed to escape with their lives, not one of them was unwounded.

The Alcabisas and Culunchimas saw how handily Mayta Capac had defeated their finest picked men, and they were very afraid. They therefore summoned together all their warriors into a great army, thinking to attack Cuzco and take it for their own and dispose of the Inca and his wayward son in the bargain, for surely even Mayta Capac would not be able to hold off an entire army. Word of the impending battle reached the ears of Inca Lloque Yupanqui. He called to him his son and said, "What then have you done that the people rise up in rebellion against me? You have called down a bad fate upon me, and I shall die at the hands of rebels."

"Fear not, O Father," said Mayta Capac. "The warriors of the Inca are mighty, and we will defeat this foe."

Inca Lloque Yupanqui protested, for he did not want war to come to his kingdom, but he was overruled by Mayta Capac and by his own nobles, who wanted to obtain glory for themselves by defeating the Alcabisas and Culunchimas.

Soon enough, the armies of the Inca and the Alcabisas and Culunchimas met on the field of battle. Both armies fought hard and well, but in the end, the army of the Inca was victorious. But the Alcabisas and Culunchimas could not be dissuaded from their attempt to unseat the Inca and slay his mighty son. Again, they challenged Mayta Capac and his army to battle, and again, they were defeated. The chief of the Alcabisas was taken in that battle and spent the rest of his life as the captive of Mayta Capac.

After the death of Inca Lloque Yupanqui, Mayta Capac took up the imperial fringe, becoming the fourth Inca. Also, Mayta Capac had in his possession a magical bird that had been brought from the cave of Tambo-toco by Manco Capac. Mayta Capac was able to understand the speech of this bird which could see the future. Many times, Mayta Capac took counsel of the magical bird and used its oracles to determine what courses to take in his rule. Mayta Capac stayed in Cuzco for the duration of his reign, and when he died, the fringe passed to his son, Capac Yupanqui.

Topa Inca Yupanqui and Macahuisa

Topa Inca Yupanqui ruled the empire between 1471 and 1493. He headed the Inca army under his father, Pachacuti, and was involved in a significant expansion of Inca territory. This story mythologizes one of his conquests, legitimizing his rule over the conquered peoples by asserting divine assistance given to Topa Inca Yupanqui's armies.

Topa Inca Yupanqui was a very powerful king. He went up and down the land, conquering all manner of people and bringing them under the rule of the Inca. For a long time after those conquests, there was peace and prosperity, but one day three peoples—the Allancu, the Callancu, and the Chaqui—decided they had had enough of Inca rule, and they rose up against Inca Yupanqui.

Inca Yupanqui mustered his armies. He sent them out to fight against these three peoples. But no matter how many men he sent, and no matter how skilled his warriors were, they were not able to reconquer those peoples. The battles went on and on for a full twelve years, and at the end of that time, Inca Yupanqui began to despair of ever having victory. He thought to himself, "I offer all manner of good things to the *huacas*, to the divine spirits that protect my people. The *huacas* have silver. They have gold. They have the best food and the finest raiment. Surely if I call upon them, they will come to my aid!"

And so, Inca Yupanqui went out, and he summoned all the *huacas*. He commanded them to come to his aid if they had received rich gifts from him. He bade them to meet in the plaza at the center of Cuzco where he would take counsel with them and find out what remedies they might offer against his enemies.

The *huacas* heard the call of Inca Yupanqui. They came from the villages and the mountains all around, riding in litters carried by their retainers. Even the mighty Pachacamac was there. But Pariacaca didn't want to go. He delayed and delayed, but finally he knew he could wait no more. If he did not go himself, some representative of his house must go. So Pariacaca called to himself his son, Macahuisa, and told him to go to the meeting and see what must be done.

Macahuisa obeyed Pariacaca. He went on his litter to the meeting in Cuzco. He sat at the edge of the meeting and listened to what Inca Yupanqui had to say.

"O my Fathers, mighty *huacas*, great *villcas*! O gods, divine beings, and spirits of the mountains! I have served you ever, with rich gifts of gold and silver, of the best food and the finest raiment. Never have I stinted you. Since I have given you all those things, will you not come to my aid?"

But the *huacas* and the other spirit beings said nothing.

"Tell me, why do you not answer? The people who serve me and who serve you are daily being slaughtered by our enemies. Many thousands already have we lost. Answer me, or I shall have you all burned!"

Again, the *huacas* and the other beings kept their peace. Inca Yupanqui grew angry and impatient. He said, "I have served you well and given you of my wealth. Gold and silver and sacrifices of many llamas have been yours. Now that I stand before you and ask for something in return, you sit there silent as though you know me not! Will you not aid me? Will you not aid my people? Speak, or I shall have you all burned!"

Finally, the great Pachacamac spoke. "O Inca Yupanqui, O Sun in the Sky, I would help you if I could, but my power is so great that if I shook your enemies to destroy them, you and your people would be destroyed as well. If I put forth my might in that way, it might even end the whole world. I do wish to help you, but I cannot. That is why I have not spoken."

Then there was another silence. Not one of the other *huacas* spoke. Inca Yupanqui despaired that any of them would offer help at all until finally Macahuisa said, "O Inca, O Sun in the Sky, I will help you. If you stay here and protect your people, I will go forth and conquer your enemies. I shall do this thing right away!"

As Macahuisa spoke, a green-blue vapor issued from his mouth that looked like smoke. Then Macahuisa took up his panpipes and clad himself in his finest raiment. The Inca commanded that a litter be prepared for Macahuisa with the fastest, strongest bearers in all the kingdom so that Macahuisa might come to the battlefield as soon as may be.

Macahuisa went to the place where the enemies of Inca Yupanqui lived. There Macahuisa caused it to rain. The rain came down gently at first, soft and grey. But then the rain grew heavier and stronger. The wind rose. Thunder rumbled across the sky, and forked lightning split the air. The thunder and lightning grew, and the rain grew heavier yet. Soon all the enemies of the Inca were washed away by the torrent of water, but Macahuisa let a few of them escape the flood to take back to Inca Yupanqui as prisoners and proof of his conquest.

When Inca Yupanqui saw that Macahuisa had thus conquered all his enemies, he vowed unending gratitude to Pariacaca for sending his son to help him and gave him fifty attendants to see to his needs and offer him the best sacrifices. Then Inca Yupanqui bowed down in thanks to Macahuisa, saying, "I owe you a great debt, O Macahuisa, for you came to my aid and conquered my enemies. Whatever you ask of me, this shall I do."

Macahuisa replied, "I wish for nothing, save that you worship me in the same way that the Yauyo people do."

Inca Yupanqui replied, "Yes, certainly!" but in his heart he was afraid because perhaps Macahuisa might deal with him the way he had done with the Inca's enemies.

Then the Inca called for food to be brought to Macahuisa, but the *huaca* said, "Oh, I do not eat food such as you eat. Bring to me instead the shells of thorny oysters."

The Inca sent for thorny oyster shells and gave them to Macahuisa. The *huaca* ate them hungrily, all in one bite, crunching and crunching the hard shells.

When Macahuisa was done eating, the Inca said, "We have here many beautiful maidens who would be honored to share your bed. Please choose from among them, as many as you wish!"

Macahuisa replied, "That is most generous of you, but I do not require their services."

Then Macahuisa bade farewell to Inca Yupanqui, and he went back home to tell his father Pariacaca of all that had happened during his sojourn in the land of the Incas.

And from that time forward, the Inca Yupanqui and his successors worshipped Macahuisa, dancing special dances in his honor, and the Inca himself led the dancing in gratitude for what the *huaca* had done for him and his people.

Inca Huayna Capac and Coniraya

This story from the Huarochirí Manuscript is a myth woven around an actual historical personage. The Inca Huayna Capac lived from c. 1464/68 to c. 1525/27 and was the successor to Topa Inca Yupanqui. Conquests achieved during Huayna Capac's reign extended the empire north into Ecuador and Colombia and south into Chile and Argentina. Huayna Capac was the last Inca to rule independently before the arrival of the Spanish.

Not long before the Spanish came to Cuzco, Coniraya decided to go and visit the Inca Huayna Capac. Coniraya went to the Inca and said, "Let us go to Lake Titicaca. I have some things to show you there."

And so Huayna Capac went with Coniraya to Titicaca. When they arrived, Coniraya said, "Summon your magicians and sages. We must send them to the underworld."

"I shall do as you ask," said Huayna Capac.

Soon the magicians and sages started to arrive.

"I am the sage of the condor!" said one.

"I am the sage of the hawk!" said another.

A third one said, "I am the sage of the swallow!"

Coniraya addressed the sages, saying, "You must go to the underworld. There you must ask my father to send one of my sisters to me."

The sages said that they would do as Coniraya asked, and they set out on their road. The first to arrive in the underworld was the sage of the swallow. He told Coniraya's father the message he bore. Coniraya's father gave the sage of the swallow a small chest and told him, "Do not open this. It is for Inca Huayna Capac and no other man."

The man took the chest and left the underworld. Now, it was a long journey back to Titicaca, and the whole way along the road the sage of the swallow burned with curiosity over what the chest contained. Finally, he could bear it no longer. He opened the chest and saw inside it a beautiful maiden with long golden hair and the finest raiment. Because she was inside the chest, she appeared to be very small. But when she saw the sage looking at her, she disappeared!

The sage of the swallow was very frightened. He did not want to go back to Titicaca. He did not want to admit that he had opened the chest that was only for Inca Huayna Capac. But the sage was an honest man, and so he went before the Inca and confessed what he had done.

When Huayna Capac heard the sage's tale, he shouted, "I would have you killed on the spot if you were not the sage of the swallow! Go back to the underworld! And this time bring back the chest without opening it!"

And so, the sage of the swallow returned to the underworld, and again he received the chest. This time, he did not open it on his road. On and on he walked, on the long journey back to Titicaca, and at day's end, he found himself still a long way from any village, and he was very hungry and tired. "Oh, how I wish I had a nice meal and a soft bed!" the sage said to himself.

Suddenly, a table appeared before the sage, laid with a tasty meal. The sage sat down and ate gratefully, and when he was done, the table and the dishes all vanished, and in their place a soft bed appeared. The sage lay down on the bed and slept deeply and well. And so, it went for the five days of his journey back to Titicaca: when he was hungry, the table would appear, filled with good things to eat; when he was tired, the bed would appear, and he would take his rest.

On the fifth day, the sage arrived at Titicaca and went before Inca Huayna Capac and Coniraya. "O Inca, Sun in the Sky," said the sage, "here is the chest that Coniraya's father sent you."

Before Huayna Capac could open the chest, Coniraya said, "Wait! Let us divide the world between us. I'll go to this part. You can go to this part with my sister. You and I cannot be in the same place together."

Then Huayna Capac opened the chest. A brilliant light shone out of it, and out stepped the beautiful woman.

"I will not return to Cuzco," said Huayna Capac. "I will stay here with my beautiful new wife. You!" he said, pointing to one of his kinsmen, "you will return to Cuzco. You will say, 'I am Huayna Capac,' and you will rule in my stead."

Then Huayna Capac and his beautiful wife vanished from that place, and so did Coniraya, and none of them were ever seen again. The man who pretended to be Huayna Capac went back to Cuzco where he ruled as Inca. But when he died, the people quarreled about who was to lead them next. And it was while they were fighting thus that the Spanish arrived.

PART III: FIVE ANDEAN FOLKTALES AND AN INCA PLAY

The Macaw Woman

The legend of the Macaw Woman is the origin tale of the Cañari people, who hail from an area of southern Ecuador. The Cañari were conquered by the Incas and absorbed into the empire in the sixteenth century, not long before the arrival of the Spanish.

Once there was a great flood. The waters rose and rose. They filled the valleys. They climbed up the hills. Soon they reached nearly to the top of the mountains. All the animals and people were drowned, all except for two brothers who managed to climb all the way up to the top of a mountain. There they waited until the flood waters receded, and when they deemed it safe, they went down the mountainside until they found a place that suited them, and there they built a home for themselves.

Every day, the brothers left their home to forage for food. Because the flood had destroyed everything, they could only find various roots and a few herbs to eat. It was but poor fare, and they barely found enough to live on, even though they worked very hard every day.

One day, the brothers returned home after a long day spent foraging to find that someone had lit a fire inside their home, and a meal of good cooked food and maize beer set out on the table. Not waiting to find out who might have given them such bounty, the brothers sat down immediately. They ate every last morsel and drank every last drop, and when they were finished, they collapsed into their beds, content for the first time in many, many months.

The next day, the brothers went out foraging as usual, and when they returned home, they again found their table laid with choice food and drink. This went on for ten days.

Finally, the elder brother said, "Who do you think it is that lays such a table for us every night?"

"I'm sure I don't know," said the younger brother. "I should like to thank them, but they seem not to want us to see them."

"I want to know who it is," said the elder. "Tomorrow, instead of going foraging, I will hide inside the house. I will wait to see who it is that leaves a good meal for us every day. I am tired of living with this mystery."

In the morning, the younger brother went out to search for food, but the elder hid himself in a corner of the house. Soon enough, two women came into the house. But these were not ordinary women: they were actually macaws, and they were the most beautiful beings the elder brother had ever seen.

The macaw women moved about the house, lighting the fire and setting things ready to cook the meal. The elder brother could stand it no longer; he jumped out of his hiding place and tried to catch one of the women. The macaw women were frightened. They evaded his grasp, turned back into macaws, and flew away, leaving no meal for the brothers that evening.

The younger brother came home and found that no food had been prepared. The elder explained what had happened, that he had tried to capture one of the macaw women but failed.

"Tomorrow I shall watch with you," said the younger brother. "Perhaps together we can capture one of the women."

The next day, the brothers hid themselves inside the house, but the macaw women did not return. The brothers continued to keep their vigil, hoping that the women would come back. Finally, at the end of the third day, the macaw women appeared and set to work preparing a meal. This time, the brothers waited until the meal was ready. When all had been placed on the table, they jumped out of their hiding place. The women were angry and frightened and turned back into birds. The younger brother ran to bar the door so that the birds could not escape. The elder brother managed to catch one of the birds, but the other escaped out the window.

The macaw changed back into a woman. She became the wife of both of the brothers and bore them six sons and six daughters. She also had brought with her many seeds which the brothers planted as crops and harvested at their proper times. And so, the human race had a new start, there on the sacred mountain, and all people are the descendants of the macaw woman and her twelve children.

The Condor and the Shepherdess

The Aymara people live in parts of what are now Peru, Bolivia, and Chile, and were absorbed into the Inca Empire in the early sixteenth century during the reign of Huayna Capac. This Aymara folktale shows the importance of the condor to Andean peoples. Some versions of this tale also function as a just-so story for the origin of hummingbirds: instead of many smaller parrots being created out of a greater one at the end of the tale, hummingbirds result instead.

Once there was a shepherdess who would go out onto the mountainside every day to graze her flock. She liked being out of doors, feeling the wind in her hair and the grass and stones under her boots. She also liked being alone, for when she was out with her flock, no one could tell her what to do or speak to her when she did not feel like talking.

Near that same mountain there lived a condor. Every day he would fly out looking for food to eat. He frequently soared over the place where the shepherdess grazed her sheep, and at first, he took no notice of her, for he knew that when a guardian was present, he would not be able to steal a lamb very easily, and he preferred not to have to work too hard for his food. But one day, the shepherdess happened to look up as the condor sailed past. The condor caught a glimpse of her face and instantly fell in love with her. "What shall I do?" he lamented. "She is a beautiful young woman, and I am a great, ugly bird. She will never consent to be my bride."

The condor pined for many days, wondering how to go about getting the young woman to marry him. Then he hit upon it: he would change his form. He would take on the shape of a handsome young man, and then she would surely wish to be his wife. And so, the very next day the condor watched to see whether the shepherdess would take her flock to graze on the mountainside, and when she did, the condor alit on the ground out of sight and turned himself into a young man.

The condor walked over to where the young woman was watching her sheep. He greeted her well and asked, "What is it you are doing out here on the mountainside all alone?"

"I am watching my sheep," she answered. "I keep the foxes and the condors away, and I make sure my sheep get enough good grass to eat."

"Don't you ever get lonely with only the sheep to keep you company?" said the condor.

"Oh, no, never!" said the young woman. "I like being here by myself."

"Well, maybe someday you might change your mind," said the condor. "Perhaps I could help you. I'm good at chasing away foxes and condors. How would you like to have me for a husband?"

"No, thank you," said the young woman. "I don't want to marry anyone. I want to live alone and raise my sheep."

"Very well," said the condor, and then he walked away.

The next day, the condor again took the form of a man and talked with the shepherdess.

"How would you like to come and live with me?" he asked. "I live up at the very top of the mountains. I see the sunrise and the sunset. Sometimes I am even above the clouds. It is very quiet and peaceful where I live. Are you sure you don't want to be my wife? I think you would like my home very much."

"Thank you, but no," said the shepherdess. "I really do not want to get married at all. I prefer to stay here with my sheep, and besides, if I left my mother would be very sad."

"That's all right then" said the condor. "But before I go, do you think you might scratch the itch between my shoulder blades? It bothers me so, and I cannot reach it myself."

"Certainly," said the young woman. She went to the condor and began to scratch the spot between his shoulder blades, but as she did so, he turned back into a condor and flew up into the sky, pulling the woman up with him on his back. The condor flew high up into the mountains, and he did not stop flying until he reached a place where there were many caves. He alighted inside one of them, where his mother lived. The other condors in the nearby caves came out to see who had arrived, and when they saw that the condor had brought a young woman back with him, they danced and flapped their wings for joy.

At first, the young woman was very happy living with the condor because he loved her very much. But soon she began to feel cold and hungry and thirsty. "I cannot stay here like this," she said. "I need fire and food and water, and I see none of that here. If I do not get those things, I will die."

"Do not worry, my love," said the condor. "I will bring everything you need."

The condor flew away from the cave. He circled down toward the valley. He found a place where a fire was burning low on the hearth and no one about to tend it. The condor picked up a coal in his beak and brought it back to the cave so that his wife could build a fire. Then he went to a place in the mountainside near his cave and dug at the rock with his beak. Soon a spring of fresh water leaped out, and his wife was able to drink. That done, the condor went back down into the valley. He collected up pieces of meat from dead animals. He dug up potatoes from an untended field. The condor brought this food back to his bride, but the meat was rank and the potatoes were rotting. The young woman ate these things because there was nothing else and she was so very hungry, but the food was disgusting.

After a time, the young woman's body began to change. She became very thin from the cold and the bad food. Feathers began to sprout from her body, and her hair fell out. She even began to lay eggs. Although her husband was very loving and attentive, she began to feel restless and longed to go home to her mother.

Meanwhile, the young woman's mother was beside herself with worry and sorrow. Her daughter had not come home with the sheep as she usually did, and it was not until the morning after the condor had taken the shepherdess that a neighbor brought the flock back to the young woman's mother. The mother went out onto the mountainside to look for her daughter, but she found nothing, and no one could tell her where her child had gone. Many days passed until the poor woman began to wonder whether her daughter had died.

One morning, the mother sat weeping near an open window. A parrot was flying by and heard the poor woman sorrowing. The parrot flew in through the window and said, "Why do you weep so? What is it that makes you so sad?"

"My daughter has disappeared," said the mother, "and I do not know where she has gone. I do not know whether she is alive or dead, but I fear the worst."

"You need not fear," said the parrot. "Your daughter is alive and well. I know where she is. She has been taken to wife by the great condor. She lives with him in a cave high up in the mountains. If you will let me eat maize from your garden and nest in your trees, I will bring her back to you."

The mother readily agreed, and so the parrot flew away into the mountains. After a short time, he spied the cave where the young woman lived with her condor husband and their chicks. The parrot waited until the condors had all gone out looking for food, then he flew into the cave.

"Have no fear," said the parrot to the shepherdess. "I have come to take you home to your mother." Then the parrot picked up the shepherdess in his claws and flew back to the mother's house.

When the parrot arrived carrying the shepherdess, the mother cried out in sorrow to see how changed her daughter was. The shepherdess was so thin that her bones were peeking out through her skin, and she had feathers all over her body. She smelled very bad, and her hair had almost all fallen out. But the mother embraced her daughter tenderly and brought her into the house, where she bathed the young woman and gave her fresh, warm clothing to wear.

Later that day, the condor returned to his cave and found his wife had gone. "I know who did this," said the condor. "It was the parrot. I shall make him pay for his insolence."

The condor flew down to the mother's garden where the parrot had made a nest in a tree and where he was feasting on grains of maize. Before the parrot even knew what was happening, the condor swooped down upon him and swallowed him whole. But the parrot did not die: he passed right through the condor's body and came out the other end. The condor was furious when he saw this. He captured the parrot again and swallowed him again, but the same thing happened: out came the parrot at the other end, quite alive. Then the condor grabbed the parrot in his claws and tore him to little shreds. He ate the shreds, one by one, but these merely passed through his body and came out the other end as small, lively parrots.

The condor realized he could never get his revenge on the parrot and that he never would be able to get his wife back. In great sorrow, he flew back to his mountain cave. He took ashes from the cold fireplace and painted them all over his feathers so that they turned black. He wept many tears as he did this, and those tears became the flecks of ash that float above fireplaces.

The Maiden and the Three Warriors

The story of the maiden and the three warriors explains how the town of Huanuco and three nearby peaks came to be. Huanuco is about 1,200 km (745 mi) north of Cuzco and lies in a valley through which flows the Huallaga River. Mount Runtuy, which the story says was named after Runtus, a warrior who vies for the hand of the maiden, is located in the Huayhuash range of the Andes, which runs to the west of Huanuco. (I have been unable to identify the locations of the other two peaks.)

Once there was a chief named Pillco-Rumi who had fifty sons and but one daughter. The daughter's name was Cori-Huayta, which means "Golden Flower." She was well named for she was the most beautiful maiden anyone had ever seen, and she was the jewel of her father's heart. So well did Pillco-Rumi love Cori-Huayta that he vowed never to let her marry a mortal man. In this he was transgressing his own law which said that all maidens and young men must marry when they come of age. No one knew of the chief's vow, for he had never spoken of it to anyone, and so when young men from all around became enamored of Cori-Huayta, they told themselves that surely they would be the one chosen to be her husband.

Finally the time came when Cori-Huayta was of an age to marry. Pillco-Rumi went to the High Priest to take counsel on what was to be done.

"O High Priest," said Pillco-Rumi, "I do not wish my daughter to marry. You best know our laws; what might be done to keep her by my side?"

"Well you know the laws, O my chief," said the High Priest. "She may not stay with you. If she take not a mortal husband, then she must join the Daughters of the Sun in the House of the Sun and there spend her days in service to the Sun himself."

But still Pillco-Rumi insisted that there must be a third way, and still he vowed that Cori-Huayta would neither marry a mortal man nor become a Daughter of the Sun. And so Pillco-Rumi prayed to Inti, to the sun-god himself, saying, "O My Father the Sun, no mortal man is worthy of my daughter, and I would not have her spend her days confined to the House of the Sun. I ask that none but you be her husband, if you will have her."

No answer did Pillco-Rumi receive, and so he began preparations for the Spring Festival, at which all maidens and young men who were of age must marry, with a heavy heart.

Word had gone out to all the lands that Cori-Huayta was to be wed at the coming festival. Three warriors, each from a different land, gathered their armies and set out to march to the lands of Pillco-Rumi to see whether they might persuade her father to let her marry them.

The first of these warriors was named Runtus. He was an old man, and his hair had already turned white. "Surely Cori-Huayta will have me for a husband," he said, "for I am a man of age and wisdom, and I will be able to make her happy and care for her well."

The second was named Maray. He was a young man and exceptionally strong. No man had ever defeated him in battle. "I am the best husband for Cori-Huayta," said Maray. "Women are weak and need a strong man to protect them. I am the strongest by far, and therefore she should marry me."

Paucar was the name of the third man, and he was the handsomest man that had ever lived. Every maiden that saw him immediately fell in love with him, but he spurned them all. "Only Cori-Huayta is to be my bride," said Paucar, "for I will only wed the one who can match me in beauty."

On the day the festival was to begin, Cori-Huayta made herself ready, thinking that she was to be given a husband for her father had said nothing to her of his vow that she would never wed a mortal man. Pillco-Rumi, for his part, went to the city walls to pray once more to Inti, hoping that this time the god would hear him. As he walked the walls, Cori-Huayta came to stand with him. She saw that her father was troubled. "What is it, O My Father? What weighs upon your heart? Surely today should be a day of rejoicing," she said.

But Pillco-Rumi made no answer for at that moment he saw three great clouds of dust on the horizon. Soon he realized that these were three armies coming toward his city. As Pillco-Rumi and Cori-Huayta watched, three runners came to the walls, each one sent by his master. The first was from Runtus, the second from Maray, and the third from Paucar. Each of them said that their master was coming to claim the hand of Cori-Huayta, and that if she was not given over, that their army would sack the city and leave nothing alive within it.

"Armies approach!" cried Pillco-Rumi to his people who had gathered in the plaza below to make merry at the festival. "Pray! Pray to Inti that we should be spared!"

The people all immediately knelt and intreated the sun-god to spare them. While they prayed, a rainbow appeared in the sky above them.

Seated on the rainbow was Inti. He heard the prayers, and he saw the armies approaching Pillco-Rumi's city. Inti looked upon Paucar in his army and turned them all into a high mountain covered with snow. The snow melted under the heat of Inti's rays and rushed down the mountainside and into a channel, becoming a mighty river. Then Inti turned his gaze upon Maray and Runtus, likewise turning them and their armies into stone. And so where the three armies had been now stood three new mountains.

Then Inti looked down upon the city of Pillco-Rumi. He uttered a single word, "Huanucuy!" which rumbled through the air like thunder. And the meaning of that word is "Live no more upon the earth." When that word was uttered, Cori-Huayta fell down, dead. Inti stretched out his hand from the heavens and took her to himself to be his bride. And so it was that the daughter of Pillco-Rumi neither wed a mortal man nor became a Daughter of the Sun.

Today the three mountains Inti made bear the names of the warriors who sought to marry Cori-Huayta, and the city bears the name Huanuco after the word uttered by Inti when he took Cori-Huayta to be his bride.

The Llama-Herder and the Daughter of the Sun

The story of the llama-herder is found in a manuscript compiled in 1585 by Spanish missionary Fray Martín de Murúa (1525-1618). De Murúa says that the mountains spoken of at the end of the tale are between Calca and Huayllabamba. Both of these towns are just north of Cuzco, with Calca lying to the east and Huayllabamba to the west.

Once there was a young llama-herder named Acoya-napa who lived in a town called Laris. Every day Acoya-napa would take his flock of llamas out onto the mountainside to graze, and there he would amuse himself by playing his panpipes while he watched over his flock. Not far from where the young man grazed his flock was the House of the Sun, where lived many young women from throughout the Inca Empire, along with their caretakers, and the duty of those who lived there was to ensure the proper worship of Inti, god of the sun. The young women who lived in the House of the Sun were known as the Daughters of the Sun, and it was a law that they were to remain unmarried for their whole duty was to conduct the worship of Inti and give thought to no others.

From time to time, some of the Daughters of the Sun would leave their temple and wander freely about the mountainside. This they were allowed to do as long as they returned by sundown and as long as they did not neglect their obligations within the House of the Sun.

One day, two Daughters of the Sun thought to go for a stroll about the mountainside together. They walked along companionably, enjoying the bright sunshine and the greenery of the fields. As they walked, they heard the lilting sound of panpipes being played nearby. They wondered who it was that played so skillfully, so they went toward the sound. Soon enough, they found Acoya-napa, seated on a large rock, playing his pipes while his llamas grazed. The young women hid themselves from Acoya-napa's view so he never had any inkling that someone was listening to him.

For many days thereafter, the two Daughters of the Sun went to that place to listen to the llama-herder play his music, and they did so in secret. But one day, one of the Daughters, whose name was Chuqui-llantu, had a mind to meet this young man who played so sweetly. She convinced her sister to go with her, and so they went to the rock where Acoya-napa was sitting and greeted him courteously.

Acoya-napa was overcome. He had never seen two such beautiful women in his life, clothed as they were in the raiment of the House of the Sun. The young llama-herder fell on his knees before them, certain that they were divine beings.

The women reassured the young man that they were not divine but human beings just like him. They raised Acoya-napa to his feet, and he kissed their hands, surprised to find that they were warm and solid, flesh and blood, just like him. Acoya-napa and the young women spoke for a little while together, but then he said it was time for him to guide his flock back to his home. The Daughters of the Sun gladly granted him leave to depart, and as he said goodbye to them, his eyes met those of Chuqui-llantu, and her heart was suddenly rent by a great love of this handsome young man who played so well upon his panpipes and who looked after his flock with such good care.

The young people went their separate ways, Acoya-napa to his home with his llamas, and the young women to the House of the Sun. When Chuqui-llantu and her sister arrived at the House of the Sun, they found their sisters preparing the evening meal. Chuqui-llantu excused herself, saying that she was tired and did not feel hungry. She went to her chamber and lay upon her bed, able to think of nothing but the handsome young llama-herder. Chuqui-llantu's sister, meanwhile, ate with the rest of the household, not knowing that Chuqui-llantu was smitten with love for Acoya-napa, for the sister had not seen in him anything very special at all.

Chuqui-llantu lay upon her bed pining for young Acoya-napa, but tired from her long day in the fresh air, she soon fell asleep, and while she was sleeping, she had a dream. In the dream, Chuqui-llantu saw a little songbird that was flitting from tree to tree, singing merrily. The bird saw Chuqui-llantu's sorrow and said, "Why do you weep so?"

"I weep for love," said Chuqui-llantu. "I weep because my heart pines for young Acoya-napa, and I know not what to do, for if I declare my love for him, it will be my fate to be killed. I am a Daughter of the Sun and may never marry."

The bird said, "Have no fear. I know what may be done. Go to the courtyard in the House of the Sun where the four fountains play, and sit you down among them. There you must sing to the fountains what is in your heart. If the fountains sing your song back to you, then you will know that a way will be found for you to go to your young man and be with him forever."

When the bird ceased speaking, Chuqui-llantu awoke. Wrapping herself in her cloak, Chuqui-llantu stole through the House of the Sun and went into the courtyard of the four fountains. The fountains stood for the four provinces of the Inca Empire, and each Daughter of the Sun bathed in the fountain that was named for her home province. Chuqui-llantu seated herself among the fountains and began to sing of her love for Acoya-napa and her longing for him, terrified all the while that she would be found and punished. As she sang, she listened with all ears, hoping beyond hope that what the bird in her dream had said would be true. And sure enough, after she had sung her song once, twice, thrice, the fountains began to sing back to her, singing the song of her love for the llama-herder. Chuqui-llantu was comforted, and she rejoiced that soon she would be able to love Acoya-napa in earnest, if she could but discover whether he felt the same about her.

Acoya-napa, for his part, had been struck by the beauty and grace of Chuqui-llantu, by her courtesy of speech and dignity of bearing, and on his way home with his flock, he could think of nothing else. But his heart was also pierced with sorrow for he knew that the Daughters of the Sun must spend their days in service to the great Inti, never marrying any man, least of all a lowly llama-herder who spent his days playing his panpipes on the mountainside.

When Acoya-napa got home, he went straight to his chamber and lay upon his bed, playing the most sorrowful tunes he could think of. His mother heard this and went in to see what was wrong. There she found her son, tears streaming down his face, playing laments on his panpipes.

"O my son, what is it that ails you?" she said.

"Today I met the most beautiful woman," said Acoya-napa, "and I love her with all my heart."

"Surely that is cause for rejoicing, not sadness," said his mother.

"Alas, no," said Acoya-napa, "for the one I love is a Daughter of the Sun, and she may never marry any man, least of all a lowly llama-herder such as I."

Now, Acoya-napa's mother was a very wise women, learned in all manner of remedies and cures. She said to him, "Take good heart, my son, for I am sure there is a remedy for your sorrow."

Leaving her son in his chamber, the woman went out upon the mountainside to collect herbs that she knew to be a cure for lovesickness and grief. When she returned to the house, she saw Chuqui-llantu and her companion coming toward her.

"Greetings, Mother," said Chuqui-llantu. "My companion and I have walked very far today. Would you have something that we might eat to refresh ourselves?"

"Certainly," said the old woman, and soon she had cooked a dish using the herbs she had culled on the mountainside.

Now, before setting out that day, Chuqui-llantu had learned where it was that Acoya-napa lived and which house was his, so she had not come to the place by chance. As she ate, she gazed about the house wondering where she might find Acoya-napa, but she did not see him for his mother had hidden him under a magic cloak that had once belonged to the beloved of the god Pachacamac himself. And the magic of the cloak was this: anyone or anything hidden underneath it would enter into the cloak and become one with it. Thus had Acoya-napa's mother hidden him, for when Chuqui-llantu looked about the house for her beloved, all she saw were the household things and in one room the beautiful cloak lying upon the bed.

"Oh!" cried Chuqui-llantu. "What a beautiful cloak! I do so wish I had something like it."

"You may have it," said the mother, "with a good will."

Chuqui-llantu took the cloak and arranged it about her shoulders, and with many thanks, she and her companion took their leave of

Acoya-napa's mother and returned to the House of the Sun. Those who dwelled in that sacred House took their evening meal together and then retired to their chambers for the night. Chuqui-llantu took the cloak and folded it tenderly at the foot of her bed and then wept for love until she was fast asleep.

Late that night, Chuqui-llantu was roused by someone softly calling her name. She woke and was startled to see Acoya-napa kneeling at her bedside, weeping many tears.

"O my beloved," said the young woman, "how do you come to be here?"

"When my mother put me under the cloak," said the llama-herder, "I became one with it, and you carried me into the House of the Sun on your own body. But in your presence, I resumed my own form once again, and the cloak became merely a piece of beautiful cloth."

Then the young people embraced one another very tenderly, and they spent the night in Chuqui-llantu's bed, delighting in one another.

In the morning, Acoya-napa covered himself with the cloak and once again became one with it. Pretending that she was going out for a walk as usual, Chuqui-llantu covered herself with the cloak and went out upon the mountainside. When she came to a place she deemed safe, she removed the cloak, and Acoya-napa recovered his own form. But alas, one of the guards from the House of the Sun suspected something was amiss and had followed Chuqui-llantu. He saw Acoya-napa come out of the cloak and take hands with Chuqui-llantu, and he raised the alarm.

Acoya-napa and Chuqui-llantu fled into the mountains, near a town called Calca. Soon they had outrun the guards, but they were very tired from their flight. Acoya-napa and Chuqui-llantu found a place to rest, and soon they were asleep in one another's arms. They had not slept long when a noise awakened them. The young people began to take flight once more, but they did not go many steps before they were both turned into stone.

There the two lovers stand to this day, in a place between Calca and Huayllabamba. And near that place also is a mountain with twin peaks, which is called Pitu-siray, which means "The Couple."

The Legend of Lake Titicaca

Lake Titicaca plays an important role in many Inca creation myths, but here we have the story of how the lake itself came to be, in a flood that was sent as retribution against a proud people who refused to honor the gods. Like many origin legends, the story of Lake Titicaca may contain grains of truth: in 2000, an archaeological expedition found the remains of an ancient temple and other civic structures under the lake, which probably were built by the Tiahuanaco people between 1,000 and 1,500 years ago. The Tiahuanaco people lived on the shores of Lake Titicaca and eventually were absorbed into the Inca Empire. It is possible that this legend is an imaginative just-so story that explains both the presence of the lake and the demise of the people who lived there in pre-Inca times.

Once, long ago, high in the mountains, there was a wide, flat plain. And on this plain was a magnificent city. The buildings were made of the finest timber and stone and were trimmed with gold and silver. The people who lived there were proud and wealthy. They ate the finest food and dressed in the finest clothing. Their lives were good and easy, and they thought that they had the best city in the whole world. In fact, they often boasted of this to one another, and they did so so often that soon they began to think that they were not only the best city but that they were the lords of all creation. Their chief even began to think himself a god.

One day, a group of ragged beggars came to the city. They went through the streets crying out warnings. "The gods have seen your pride and arrogance, and they are displeased! Turn back from your evil ways, or you will be destroyed!"

The people of the city did not listen to the beggars. They laughed and mocked them, saying, "Who are you to tell us what to do? We are wealthy and strong while you are dressed in tattered clothing and have dirty faces. Go back where you came from!"

But the beggars did not stop making their warnings, even when the city people threw rotten vegetables at their heads.

After a few days, the beggars' warnings changed. "You have not listened to our warnings," they said, "so the gods have told us to tell you that you must leave your city. You must go away into the wilderness. You must climb up the mountains and repent of your evil ways, or the gods will destroy you and your city forever!"

The people of the city only laughed harder at this, and they only became more cruel toward the beggars. But the priests in the city temple came together to take counsel over what the beggars had been saying. "Maybe they are right," said one priest. "Maybe we should listen to them."

"Yes," said another. "I think it would be wise to do as they say."

And so, the priests agreed that they would listen to the beggars. They packed the things they would need for the journey, and they went out into the wilderness. They climbed up the mountains and prayed to the gods to be forgiven.

Now, after the priests had left the city, the people neglected the worship of the gods entirely. "If the priests won't stay to help us worship, then maybe there isn't anyone there to hear our prayers anyway. Maybe we are gods ourselves. And if we are gods, we have nothing to fear from these wretched beggars. Let us drive them from our city!"

But when they went to gather up the beggars and cast them outside the walls, they found that the beggars had already gone.

A few more days passed, and the city people said to themselves, "At last we have peace! No more beggars going about shouting at us! We can enjoy ourselves again." And so, they went back to their arrogant, wicked ways.

The next day dawned bright and sunny. But by afternoon, black clouds were gathering on the horizon. The people of the city paid this no mind for the clouds merely looked like rain clouds. Then other clouds began to appear, red clouds the color of blood. "What is this?" said the people. "We have never seen such clouds before. I wonder what it means?"

The black clouds and the red clouds advanced until the sky was covered in them, yet no rain fell. Night came, but there was no darkness because of the glowing redness of the clouds. A great sound of thunder rent the air. The ground shook. It shook and shook and did not stop shaking. Cracks appeared in the walls of the buildings, and soon the houses and shops and temples were falling down.

Rain began to fall from the sky, crimson rain the color of blood. The rivers near the city overflowed their banks. The waters flooded into the city. The people ran into the streets, screaming in terror, but there was nowhere for them to go. They could not escape the flood waters which rushed into the city, drowning the buildings and all the people. The rain fell, and the rivers overflowed until even the tops of the buildings were covered by deep water. And when the storm was over, a great lake stood where the city had once been. Of all the city people, only the priests who had listened to the beggars and gone to the mountains remained alive.

And that is how Lake Titicaca came to be on the great plain in the mountains.

The Tale of Ollantay

Apu Ollantay is a play in the Quechua language set during the ancient Inca Empire. The oldest copy of the play, which dates to about 1770, belonged to Antonio Valdés, who was a priest in Sicuani, Peru. Five other early manuscript copies survive today, with the first published editions dating from the middle of the nineteenth century. For a time, Valdés was believed to have been the author of the play, but now this has largely been discredited.

Scholars also debate the origins of the play. Because both the sources and many of the dramatic conventions of the play date from the eighteenth century, the actual genesis of the work is unclear. Some scholars have suggested that in the absence of sources earlier than the eighteenth century, we must consider Apu Ollantay *to be an entirely colonial product, while others have argued that it is an old Inca tale that received dramatic treatment in colonial times. It is presented here as a prose tale with some omissions from the original play.*

The name "Ollantay" also refers to the ancient stone fortress of Ollantay-tampu north of Cuzco. The early twentieth-century scholar Sir Clements Markham, who thought that the play was based on an ancient Inca legend, assumed that the fortress had been named after the protagonist of the drama.

In the time of the Inca Pachacuti, there was a young warrior named Ollantay. Ollantay was strong and handsome and the most valiant fighter the Inca people had ever seen. Ollantay also was wise, and because of all his good qualities, the Inca Pachacuti trusted him and thought him one of his most valuable advisers and generals.

As a member of Pachacuti's court, Ollantay was often about the royal palace, and so he came to know Pachacuti's daughter, Cusi Coyllur, which means "Joyful Star." It was not long before the two young people fell very much in love with one another for Cusi Coyllur was beautiful and gracious just as Ollantay was brave and strong. Their love should have made them happy, but alas it caused them only pain, for brave and trusted as he was, Ollantay was but a commoner, and none but a man of noble blood might think to wed the daughter of the Inca.

For a long time, Cusi Coyllur and Ollantay contented themselves with brief meetings when they were able to find a few moments to be alone or fleeting glances across the room when they were in company, but finally, they could bear it no longer. They married one another in secret, and for a time, they were very happy, even though they still could not reveal their love to anyone else.

This time did not last, however. One day, Cusi Coyllur came to Ollantay and said, "We should not have to hide like this. We are man and wife, and we love one another. Let us go to my father and plead our case and ask to be formally married."

Ollantay agreed, although his heart warned him that it would be a fool's errand: the laws of the Incas were very strict, and Inca Pachacuti had been relentless in enforcing them. It seemed unlikely that the old man would set aside the traditional ways, even for his own daughter.

And so Cusi Coyllur and Ollantay begged audience of the Inca. They went before him and explained that they loved one another and that they wanted to be wed. But the Inca would have none of it. "Do you not know what it is you do?" he shouted. "No commoner may wed a daughter of the royal house. She is kin to the gods themselves, and you are but a mortal man and a servant. How dare you!"

Then Inca Pachacuti had his daughter taken to the House of the Sun where she was made one of the Daughters of the Sun, who are the women who serve in the temple and who are forbidden from ever marrying any man. Ollantay was told to go to his quarters and remain there, for the Inca was so wroth with him that he could not immediately think of a punishment sufficiently fitting for Ollantay's crime.

Ollantay chafed under his confinement and fretted about his wife. He knew that whatever punishment the Inca devised for him, the one end to it all would be his death. So, one night he escaped from his quarters. He went to his army captains and told them that he would be leaving. "The Inca Pachacuti has turned against me. I have lost everything I ever loved. I commend to you my good soldiers. Care for them well as you have seen me care for them. For myself, I will go far away into the mountains, and live there solitary. There is no longer any reason for me to stay here."

The captains protested at this. "You must not go! But if you cannot be swayed, then we will leave the service of the Inca and go with you, for you alone are our general, and we will serve none other."

"My friends," said Ollantay, "your love and loyalty do you credit. But I cannot ask you to come with me, for if you do, you will be deemed traitors, and the penalty for that is death. I have nothing to lose, for the Inca will take my life no matter what I do, but you have a choice in the matter."

The captains would not be swayed. They swore to accompany Ollantay and cast their lots in with his, whatever might come. And so it was that with a band of doughty men Ollantay made his way out of the capital and into the mountains.

Cusi Coyllur, meanwhile, was treated well by the Daughters of the Sun and their servants. She fell in with their ways and did her best to perform the duties expected of her. However, it soon became clear that she was with child, and when her time came, she was delivered of a daughter, whom she named Yma Sumac, which means "Most Beautiful." But because the Daughters of the Sun were forbidden to marry or have children, Yma Sumac was taken from her mother and raised as a foundling in another part of the temple.

Word came to the Inca that Ollantay had escaped his confinement and disappeared, along with a number of officers and soldiers from the army. Inca Pachacuti called to him Rumi-ñaui, his most trusted general. "Find them at once," roared the Inca, "and bring them to me that I may mete out justice to them! And take Cusi Coyllur and throw her in chains. This perfidy and the threat to my throne is all her doing."

"I will do as the Inca commands," said Rumi-ñaui. He conveyed the Inca's command to the servants of the House of the Sun, and Cusi

Coyllur was imprisoned. Then Rumi-ñaui departed the court to begin his search for Ollantay.

Meanwhile, Ollantay had taken refuge with his men at the fortress of Ollantay-tampu, and there they gathered about them a mighty army. Ollantay had sent his servant back to Cuzco to see what response his flight had engendered with the Inca and to see what news might be had of Cusi Coyllur. Soon enough, the servant returned. "O Ollantay, the Inca is most wroth with you. He has set Rumi-ñaui the task of finding you and returning you to Cuzco, and a thousand men are at his command, searching throughout the empire."

"And of my beloved?" said Ollantay. "What news have you of her?"

"Alas, I could find no trace of her," said the servant. "Both she and the queen seem to have disappeared, and I fear the worst."

Hearing this, Ollantay despaired. Nothing now was holding him back from open rebellion. He rallied his army and the people of the region and spoke to them about the slights they had received at the hands of the Inca and of his own heart's sorrow for the loss of Cusi Coyllur. The people listened well to Ollantay's speech, and when he was finished, they raised up a great shout: "Long live Ollantay! Let Ollantay take the fringe! We will have none other as our Inca!"

When the Inca Pachacuti heard that Ollantay had taken up arms in rebellion, he recalled Rumi-ñaui and the thousand men from their search and commanded them to put his own army in order that they might defend the empire from the rebels. Quickly Rumi-ñaui marshalled his troops, and they headed into the mountains where they encountered Ollantay's army, and battle was joined. Both sides fought fiercely, but in the end, the army of the Inca was defeated, and Rumi-ñaui was forced to flee back to Cuzco, weakened and bleeding from many wounds, while Ollantay and his men returned to their fortress.

Ten years passed, and still Ollantay neither was defeated nor attempted to take Cuzco for his own. Ten years passed, and Yma

Sumac, the baby born to Cusi Coyllur and daughter of Ollantay, grew into a strong young girl in the House of the Sun. Yma Sumac began to wonder why it was that others might come and go freely from the House of the Sun while she herself was forced to remain within its walls.

One night, Yma Sumac was unable to sleep, and so she went to take a walk in the courtyard of the House of the Sun. The entire household was asleep. The winds were calm, and the moon and stars bright in the sky. As Yma Sumac gazed at the night sky, a faint wailing came to her ears. "Surely that is the wind in the trees," thought Yma Sumac, but then she noted that there was no wind. Again, the wail arose, louder this time and followed by words. A woman's voice it was, praying to the Sun.

"O Sun," said the voice, "free me from these chains. I have done no evil. You who see all, take pity on me."

Yma Sumac knew not from where the voice came. She looked in many places but could find neither who it was that was in chains nor where they were held. Puzzled over the mystery and haunted by the wailing voice, she returned to her chamber and an uneasy slumber.

The next day, Yma Sumac sat in one of the gardens of the House of the Sun with a friend, who was a novice preparing to become a Daughter of the Sun. Both girls rose when they saw the Mother of the House approaching. The Mother addressed Yma Sumac, saying, "The time of choosing is upon you. Will you leave the outside world behind you and become a Daughter of the Sun? Or will you leave us?"

"How can I leave behind that which I have never seen?" said Yma Sumac. "Nevertheless, I have made my choice: I will not take the vows. I do not wish to become a Daughter of the Sun. I wish to leave this place as soon as I am able."

The Mother's face darkened for she had hoped to persuade the girl to stay within the House, under her control. "Very well," said the Mother and then turned and left the garden.

Yma Sumac and her friend stood watching the Mother leave. "Spiteful old tabby," muttered the young girl at the Mother's retreating back. Then she turned to Yma Sumac. "You're lucky," she said. "They won't be able to keep you here, and you have no family on the outside to tell you what to do or where to go. But I'll have to stay. My family wouldn't have me back for any money; they'd be too afraid of the Mother and the Priests of the House. I'll be a prisoner, just like that poor woman."

Yma Sumac looked sharply at her friend. "What woman?" she asked, trying to feign only little interest.

"You know, the one they keep in chains. The one who always wails at night. Surely you must have heard her. I have to bring her bread and water every day."

"Will you take me to her?" asked Yma Sumac. "I didn't know they kept prisoners here. I'd like to see the poor thing. Maybe I could bring her comfort."

"Very well," said the friend, "but it will have to be in secret. I'm not supposed to tell anyone else about her."

The friend told Yma Sumac how to get to the prisoner's cell and where she might hide until such time as the friend arrived with food and water for the prisoner. They agreed to meet there that very evening.

At the appointed time, the friend arrived and let Yma Sumac slip into the cell with her. Against one wall lay the form of a woman, dressed in rags and with unkempt hair, her leg in a manacle that was chained to the stone wall. The friend put the bread and water down next to the woman, who looked up wearily.

"I brought someone to see you," said the girl.

"Ah, a new face!" said the woman. "Ten long years have I been here, and only my jailers for company. And scant company at that."

Yma Sumac and the woman regarded one another for a moment. Then the girl spoke. "Why are you here?" she said. "What wrong have you done that they keep you here chained to that wall?"

"No wrong save to have loved the wrong man," said the woman. "I loved him against the wishes of my father and bore my beloved a child, but because I had done so without my father's blessing, the child was taken, and I was placed here, to live the rest of my days in sad misery."

"Oh," said Yma Sumac, "I also have been placed here, for I know neither my mother nor my father, and although I am not chained, yet I am a prisoner, for the Mother and the Priests will not let me leave this House even though I have no wish to become a Daughter of the Sun."

When the woman heard Yma Sumac's tale, she sat up a little straighter and looked long at the girl. "Tell me, if you will, what is your name and your age?"

"I am Yma Sumac, and I am ten years old," the girl replied.

The woman let out a little cry, and then she began to weep with joy. "Come to my arms, child," she said, "for you are my child indeed. You are the babe that was wrenched from me as soon as you drew breath. I am your mother, Cusi Coyllur, daughter of the Inca Pachacuti, and your father is the valiant Ollantay."

Then Cusi Coyllur and Yma Sumac embraced, and they wept many happy tears until finally Yma Sumac's friend reminded them that they could not linger, or Yma Sumac might be found where she had not leave to be and so come to grief at the hands of the Mother and the Priests of the House.

"Never fear, Mother," said Yma Sumac to Cusi Coyllur, "I shall find some way to free you. Give me but a space of a few days to find help, so that once again you may be free."

Then the girls took leave of Cusi Coyllur, and went back to their duties, promising one another not to reveal anything that had transpired in the prison cell.

Not long after Yma Sumac was reunited with her mother, the Inca Pachacuti died, and his son, Tupac Yupanqui, was chosen to succeed him. In a grand ceremony at the House of the Sun, Tupac Yupanqui assumed the imperial fringe and was proclaimed Inca by the Priests and all the nobles of the empire. During the celebration, the High Priest of the Sun prophesied that the rebels would return to allegiance with the Inca.

Among those attending the ceremony was the soldier Rumi-ñaui, who had lived in disgrace ever since his defeat at Ollantay-tambo. Thinking that he might regain some of his lost status with the new Inca by being the one to see the prophecy fulfilled, he begged an audience of Tupac Yupanqui and was admitted into the imperial presence.

"O my Inca, Child of the Sun and ruler of us all, I beg of you a boon," said Rumi-ñaui.

"Speak on," said the Inca.

"I have a plan, a ruse, that surely will deliver Ollantay into your hands and bring his rebels back under your control, as the High Priest said must happen. I ask only leave to do this thing for your greater glory and the safety of the empire."

"You have our leave so to do, but no blood must you shed" said the Inca, and Rumi-ñaui set out immediately to put his plan into effect. First, he readied his army and marched them to a place near Ollantay-tambo where they could lay hidden from the rebels. Then he donned ragged clothes that made him look like a beggar, disheveled his hair, and slashed bloody wounds into his own face. Thus disguised, he went to Ollantay-tambo, where he cried mercy of the rebels.

"Let me in, O let me in," he wailed in front of the gates. "Have mercy, for the gentle Pachacuti has passed, and his son, Tupac Yupanqui, rules us with great harshness."

The guard at the gate did not open directly but first sent for Ollantay. When Ollantay heard the supposed beggar's tale, he bade the gates be opened, for he did not recognize his old foe. Ollantay told his men to give the ragged man fresh clothing and food and medicine for his wounds. Then Ollantay said to his comrades, "Tonight we feast, for our great enemy, the Inca Pachacuti, is dead!"

And so, the rebels feasted, drinking and dancing until well into the night. When they ceased their feasting, besotted with drink, Rumi-ñaui opened the door of the stronghold to his own men, who slipped inside noiselessly and strangled many of the rebels in their sleep, thus keeping the Inca's command that no blood must be shed while reducing the number of rebels. Ollantay and his generals they took captive back to Cuzco.

Blindfolded and in bonds, Ollantay and the generals were brought before the Inca and his counsellors.

"Behold, O Mighty Inca," said Rumi-ñaui. "I bring before you the rebel Ollantay and the other conspirators against your empire and your throne. What judgement should be brought upon them for their treason?"

The Inca looked first to his High Priest, who said, "O Mighty Inca, I beg mercy on these men. Truly they have rebelled against the empire and the throne of the Inca, but they are doughty and resourceful. If you could win their allegiance, they would be useful allies."

Then the Inca looked to Rumi-ñaui, who said, "O Mighty Inca, I say that no mercy ought to be used. Rebels and traitors, they are, and remain a threat to your realm. Put them to death at once!"

"So shall it be," said the Inca. "We shall take them to a high place and have them thrown down to their deaths. Let us depart at once."

Ollantay and the generals were taken to a high place near Cuzco. They could feel and hear the wind swirling about them, and they knew that soon they would meet their fate. They were herded to the edge of the precipice and prepared themselves to be cast over, but instead of finding themselves falling, the blindfolds were taken from their eyes and they found themselves facing the Inca Tupac Yupanqui. They fell on their knees before him, and he said, "See now what mercy we use toward our enemies. We declare you not only to be free men but raised in station. Ollantay shall be a general of our armies and our chief deputy in Cuzco, and these others are to receive preferments as well, although lesser than those of Ollantay."

Hearing the merciful words of the Inca, the men bowed before him in gratitude and promised to him their everlasting loyalty. Rumi-ñaui, for his part, was shamed by the generosity of the Inca. He left Cuzco that very day and was never seen nor heard from again.

When they returned to Cuzco, Ollantay begged an audience of the Inca. "O Mighty Inca," he said, "you have been generous beyond measure to me. Let me show my loyalty and steadfastness by leading your armies into battle. We shall conquer many peoples and thus increase your realm and your store of treasure."

"That is a generous offer, O my deputy," said the Inca, "but such deeds shall I only call for when they are needed, and today is not that day. Take you a wife, and live quietly and serve me here in Cuzco."

"Alas," said Ollantay, "never shall I marry, for once I had a wife, and we had but a few days together before she was taken from me. Ever have I lived in sorrow since, and I will have no other wife for the rest of my days."

As Ollantay finished speaking, the door of the audience chamber swung open, and a young girl rushed in and prostrated herself before the Inca. A servant ran in close behind and bowed low, saying, "A thousand pardons, O Mighty Inca, but this young one from the House of the Sun evaded me, and before I could stop her, she came in here. I ask your mercy on us both for this disturbance."

"Never fear," said the Inca, "We will not have it said that we do not listen even to the youngest of our subjects. What is it you need of us, little one?"

"O Mighty Inca," said the girl, "my name is Yma Sumac, and all my days I have lived as a foundling in the House of the Sun. Lately I have learned who my parents are. My mother is cruelly held in a prison cell where she languishes and must die soon if she does not receive your mercy. I swear to you and to your Father the Sun that my mother has done no wrong. I beg you to come see for yourself how she has been treated, that you might be moved to pity and release her."

"We will not have it said that we hold prisoners who are guiltless," said the Inca. "Show us where your mother is kept, and we will make judgement proper to the situation. Our deputy also will accompany us in this."

Now, Yma Sumac had never seen her father, and even though he was present in the audience chamber, the Inca had never pronounced his name. Nor had Ollantay ever seen his child; and thus it was that neither recognized the other, and so as strangers they went together with the Inca on his mission of mercy.

When they arrived at the House of the Sun, the Inca commanded the Mother of the House to appear before him and to show him where the prisoner was kept. Together they went to the prison cell. The Mother of the House opened it, and all beheld the wasted form of Cusi Coyllur.

"Release her from her bonds, and have her stand before us," said the Inca.

This was done, and soon Cusi Coyllur was standing, trembling in her rags, with her head bowed before Tupac Yupanqui and his companions, her long, unkempt hair covering her face. The Inca instantly took pity on her and was wroth with the Mother of the House. "You have used this woman very ill," he said. "Even though she were your prisoner, still you had a duty to keep her well. This you did not do, and so we release you from your office. Another shall have the station of Mother of the House."

The Mother could do no other than bow to the Inca and depart. Once she was gone, the Inca said to Cusi Coyllur, "Tell me, if you can, who you are and why you have been imprisoned here?"

"O Mighty Inca," said Cusi Coyllur, "I beg of you your mercy. My name is Cusi Coyllur, daughter of the Inca Pachacuti. I was imprisoned here by my father's order for I loved the valiant Ollantay against his wishes and bore of him a child, the very one who has brought you to this place. As soon as the child drew breath, she was taken from me and I was chained here, to spend my days in misery, although my crime was nothing other than love."

The Inca and Ollantay stood thunderstruck at what the woman had said. So wretched was her state that the Inca had not recognized his sister, nor had Ollantay known her as his very own beloved wife.

"Is this true?" said the Inca.

"It is," said Cusi Coyllur. "I swear by the imperial fringe you wear and by the Sun Himself that I tell no lie."

"Look at us, and let us see your face," said the Inca.

Cusi Coyllur lifted her head and brushed her hair aside. Although she was thin and wan, Ollantay and the Inca both knew her, and both cried out with joy and pity.

"Bring fresh robes for this woman," commanded the Inca, "and bear her in state back to our own dwelling. Give her a chamber and all refreshment, for she is our noble sister and the wife of our trusted deputy."

Ollantay went to Cusi Coyllur and embraced her tenderly. "I had not thought to see you again," he said, "and it pains me that you have been so ill used. But perhaps now the Inca will pardon you for having married a commoner, and we will be able to live together in peace."

"A commoner you may have been when you were wed," said the Inca, "but a nobleman shall you be as of this moment. We raise you in station and wish you long life and much joy with the wife of your heart, whom we also love, for she is our sister, and with your dear daughter, for she is our niece."

Yma Sumac had been standing aside, watching all of this in silence, for she was overcome with joy and gratitude for the mercy of the Inca and also with the knowledge that the man who had accompanied her and their lord to the prison cell was none other than her own father.

Ollantay turned to Yma Sumac. "Come here, child. Let me look on you, for I am your father and am grateful for your courage and steadfast love of your mother."

Then Ollantay embraced his daughter, and the family, now reunited after ten long and bitter years, shed many tears of joy.

True to his word, the Inca gave a pleasant dwelling to his sister and her family within the palace. He saw that they never wanted for the least thing, and there Ollantay, Cusi Coyllur, and Yma Sumac lived for the rest of their days, in peace and harmony.

Section 4: Central American Mythology

Captivating Myths of Gods, Goddesses, and Legendary Creatures of Ancient Mexico and Central America

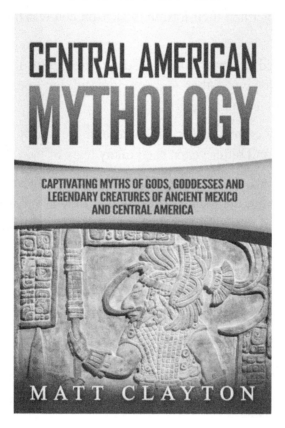

Introduction

Mexico and the Central American states are home to many indigenous peoples, each of whom speaks their own language and lives according to their own customs. These diverse peoples have rich storytelling cultures, passing down myths about gods and the work of creation, and about the humans who for good or ill interact with these otherworldly beings. The loving god Olocupinele creates the world of the Cuna of Panama, while the goddess Nakawe' destroys and then remakes the world of the Huichol of Mexico. In the story "Mother Scorpion Country," from the Miskito of Nicaragua, we learn that even the goddess of the land of the dead cannot break the bond of love between a husband and wife.

Tricksters also figure in many tales told by indigenous peoples. Although tricksters sometimes cause harm, in the two trickster stories presented here, the tricksters use their wiles to help others. The opossum steals fire and brings it to the people in a Mazatec story from Mexico, while Uncle Rabbit saves his friend Bull from being eaten by Tiger in a story from Nicaragua.

Landscape and geography play vital roles in these stories, since ideas about how the world came to be are shaped by the place in which people live. Thus, the ocean figures prominently in creation stories from the Cuna of Panama and the Cabécar of Costa Rica, while life in a desert environment impacts the story "Yomomuli and the Talking Tree" from the Yaqui people, who live in northwestern Mexico and the southwestern United States.

For any culture, an important function of stories is to explain the origin of certain customs, to reinforce right behavior, and to discourage bad actions. We see this in several of the stories retold here. In the Miskito tale, "The Invisible Hunters," three brothers learn a hard lesson about keeping promises and the pitfalls of greed, while in "The King of the Peccaries" from the Bribri of Costa Rica, we receive instructions in ethical hunting practices. The origin of the Chatino tradition of parents bringing their newborn babies into a sweat bath to receive the blessings of the old grandmother is explained in the myth, "The Childhood of the Sun and Moon," and in "How the Sea Was Made," we get a brief glimpse into the burial customs of the Cabécar people of Costa Rica.

The stories presented in this volume are but a small sample of the abundant variety of myths and legends from Mexico and Central America. Nevertheless, they give us important glimpses into the ways people from this part of the world see themselves, as humans trying to understand their place within a larger universe containing beings both seen and unseen, and as people doing their best to live ethical lives that respect their fellow humans and the other creatures that live alongside them.

Note about tribal names: Where available, tribal names are given after the title of each story, along with the name of the country the people live in. Because names used by outsiders sometimes are different from the ones the people use to name themselves, I am giving first the name the people use and then the name that is more familiar to readers from outside those cultures. These are stated in the format "people's own name/attributed name, country." So, for example, the Huichol of Mexico call themselves *Wixáritari*, so their attribution would be "Wixáritari/Huichol, Mexico."

Olocupinele Creates the World (Dule/Cuna, Panama)

The Cuna people live in parts of the Isthmus of Panama, with some communities stretching south into what is now Colombia. Their primary deity is a being known as Olocupinele, who creates the world and everything in it. A striking feature of this myth is the insistence on love as the reason behind Olocupinele's act of creation.

Olocupinele it was who created the world. He created the Earth, the waters, the sky. He made a land that runs between two oceans. He gave the land hills and valleys, and on the land, he planted many trees and grasses and plants that are good for food. On the land, Olocupinele made animals to live. In the waters, he placed fish. In the skies, he placed birds. Olocupinele created clouds to make rain. He made refreshing pools of water and waterfalls and streams and rivers bearing water across the land and into the sea. And everything Olocupinele was made from his love. All creation comes from Olocupinele's dream, a dream of love.

Olocupinele also wanted to make people, beings like him. He wanted the people to have a good place to live. Olocupinele placed all manner of beautiful things in the world he had made: gemstones and precious metals, spices to flavor food, dyes to make bright cloth. All these he made and more, so that when the people came, they might have many good things, for Olocupinele loved the world he made, and he loved all his children.

Not until all was ready did Olocupinele create the people. Not until the mountains and valleys were green with trees and plants. Not until the birds and beasts and fish were thriving in their homes. Not until all the beautiful and useful things had been put in their places did Olocupinele create the people, and these people he called the Cuna.

The Cuna were made in the image of Olocupinele. He made men and women, beautiful and tall and strong. He gave to each of them a special gift. One was skilled in the hunt. One was the best maker of cloth. One was the best singer. One was the best dancer. Each of them had a special gift that they could share.

When the beautiful Cuna men and women were all created and given their gifts, Olocupinele put them on the Earth. The Cuna opened their eyes and found themselves in a bright garden. There were many beautiful trees, and the birds were all singing their songs. There were many good smells, of earth and rain and flowers. But the Cuna had never seen or heard or smelled any of this before, and they were frightened. The sun was too bright. The world was too green. The birds were too loud. The people hid themselves in the shadows.

Olocupinele looked upon his poor Cuna, who did not know how to live in the beautiful world he had made them, a world all made out of love. Then he decided to make one more Cuna man, a man he called Piler *(Pee-lair)*. To Piler, Olocupinele gave all manner of knowledge. Olocupinele sent Piler to the other Cuna, where they were hiding from the sun and the brightness of the world.

Piler went to the Cuna. He stood in the sunlight and laughed in delight. "Look!" he said. "Look at all the good things Olocupinele has made for us! Do not be afraid. This world is our home. There are so many good things here that Olocupinele has given us, and I will teach you how we should live. We must care for the Earth, always. We must care for each other, always. The Earth is ours to live in and to look after. Our Father Olocupinele says that this is what we are to do."

And so it was that the Cuna began to live in the place Olocupinele had made for them, the land between the two oceans, on the Earth made from a dream of love.

Watakame' and the Great Flood
(Wixáritari/Huichol, Mexico)

The Huichol people of west-central Mexico are known for their vibrant yarn paintings that depict myths and other stories and concepts that are important and sacred to them. Like many cultures throughout the world, the Huichol have a flood myth in which everything is destroyed and then remade anew.

Once there was a poor farmer named Watakame'. One day, he went out into his fields to work. He needed to clear a field of trees and bushes so that he could plant new crops. Watakame' took his sharp machete and chopped away at the trees, felling them. He chopped away at the bushes, felling them. It was very hard work, and at the end of the day, he was very tired. Watakame' went home, quickly ate a meal, and flopped down into his bed to sleep.

The next morning, Watakame' went out to chop down some more trees on the field he was clearing. When he arrived at the field, he couldn't believe his eyes: every tree and bush that he had chopped down the day before was back in its place, as if nothing had ever happened. He cut them down again and went home. For five days, this happened. Watakame' would clear part of the field, and in the morning, everything would be back the way it was.

"This cannot go on," said Watakame'. "If I cannot clear that field, I will not be able to plant, and if I cannot plant, I will have no crop to harvest, and I will starve. I must find out who is doing this to me."

In the morning, Watakame' went to the field as usual, but instead of going home at the end of the day, he hid himself to lie in wait for whoever or whatever was undoing all his hard work. Soon enough, an old woman appeared in the middle of the field. The old woman carried a long staff. Wherever she pointed with the staff, all the trees and bushes replanted themselves and came back to life.

Watakame' sprang out from the place he was hiding. "Aha!" he shouted. "You are the one who keeps undoing my work. Why do you do this? Do you not know that I will starve if I cannot plant my crops?"

"Oh, there are much worse things coming than starvation," said the old woman. "I am Nakawe', the goddess of the rain. I have come to tell you that the world will end soon. A great flood is coming that will cover the whole Earth, and it will not matter whether this field is cleared or not. The Sun has decided that the people on the Earth are too wicked, and he wants to kill them all and start over. But I have decided that I will save you, and save the animals, and that I will do the destruction myself."

"Tell me what I must do, Mother," said Watakame'. "I do not wish to drown."

"Do you know the place where the great fig tree grows?"

"Yes," said Watakame'. "I know it well."

"Cut down the fig tree, and use it to make a big box," said Nakawe'. "You must put yourself into the box. Take with you seeds of corn of all colors and beans of all colors. Take squash seeds, and your good black dog. Put a fire in your box, and keep it fed with squash stems. This must all be completed in five days."

Watakame' did what the goddess told him. He chopped down the fig tree and made a big box with it. He gathered the seeds and stems and a brazier to keep the fire in. On the fifth day, he put everything into the box, then climbed in with his dog. Nakawe' appeared and put the lid on the box. She caulked all the seams closed. Then Nakawe' called to her macaw. The goddess sat on top of the box with the macaw on her shoulder.

When all was ready, the wind began to blow. The wind howled through the trees. It roared through the valleys. It whipped around the mountaintops. Wherever the wind howled, the people were turned into animals. They became frightened and started fighting and killing each other. Soon, all the bad people were dead, and it was then that the sea began to rise. Up, up, up it climbed onto the land, filling the valleys, overtopping the hills, and finally covering even the highest mountain. Watakame' sat snugly inside his box with his dog, keeping the fire lit as the goddess had told him.

The box floated all around on the flood waters. It went east. It went west. It went north. It went south. The box went as far as it could go in each direction, measuring the breadth of the Earth. It took four years for the box to travel the whole Earth. In the fifth year, it rose straight up with the ever-rising waters, and it came down when the water started to recede. Finally, the box came to rest on the top of a mountain. Watakame' removed the lid of the box. He saw that the earth was all covered with water, except for the tip of the mountain where he was. But this didn't last long. The macaws and parrots were flying to and fro, digging new valleys and new channels for the water to run in so that the sea would return to its proper place and so that the Earth could dry out.

When all was ready, Nakawe' told Watakame' he could get out of his fig-wood box. "Use the seeds you brought with you to plant crops," she said. "Whenever you come home from your work, you will find tortillas prepared for you. I must go now, for I also have work to do, and in five days, all will be in readiness."

Watakame' did as Nakawe' told him to do. He tilled the soil and planted the seeds he brought with him. He found a cave for himself and his little dog to live in. Every evening when he came home from the fields, he found tortillas made for him. This was strange. He knew that Nakawe' was busy elsewhere, so who could have prepared this good food?

In five days, all was ready, as Nakawe' had promised. The Earth was full of new plants and animals. The trees were full of new birds. A whole new world had been made. Everything was fine and new and wonderful, except one thing: there were no people except Watakame', and he felt lonely.

On the sixth day, Nakawe' visited Watakame'. "Thank you for remaking the world so wonderfully," said Watakame'. "This is a good place to live. The soil is easy to till. My plants are growing quickly and well. The birds sing in the trees. And I have plenty to eat, but I do not understand where the food comes from. Is there someone else here with me? I should like to know, for I miss my family and my friends and would like some company."

Now, what had been happening was this: when Watakame' went to work in the fields, Nakawe' came to the cave. Nakawe' taught the dog how to transform herself into a woman. Then Nakawe' taught her how to cook and do other work that needed doing. And in the evening, when all was done and Watakame' was on his way home, the woman transformed herself back into a dog.

When Watakame' told Nakawe' that he wanted to know where the tortillas came from and that he was lonely, Nakawe' replied, "Tomorrow morning, instead of going to the fields to work, hide yourself somewhere about the cave. Watch what happens. You will know what to do."

Watakame' did what Nakawe' told him. He pretended to go out to the fields, but instead, he hid himself within the cave. As he looked, he saw the little dog rise out of her bed at the side of the cave. She slipped off her dog-skin and became a woman. The woman tended the fire and began preparing food.

Watakame' jumped out of his hiding place. He seized the dog-skin and threw it on the fire. The woman cried out in pain as though she was being burned. Her cries sounded like those of a dog. Watakame' then took the *masa*, the dough for making tortillas, that the woman had prepared. He threw it into the water she had set on the fire to boil, then he used this as medicine for the woman. He laved her whole body with it, and soon, she stopped crying and was healed. It was then that she turned into a real woman. She became Watakame''s wife. They were very happy together and had many children. And all the people in the world are the descendants of Watakame' and his wife.

Yomomuli and the Talking Tree (Yoeme/Yaqui, Mexico)

This Yaqui legend combines the myth about the creation of the world with Yaqui feelings about the Spanish Conquest, an event in history that led to much suffering and displacement of the Yaqui under colonial rule and later under the independent government of Mexico. The Yaqui people live in the northwestern Mexican state of Sonora and in the southwestern United States. They preserve many versions of this myth, but all of them center on the little Surem people and the humming tree or stick that tells the future.

There was a time when there were no people as there are today. The world was the way Yomomuli had made it. She made animals to live on the land and birds in the sky and fish in the waters, but instead of the tall people, she made the Surem. The Surem were little people, maybe only two or three feet high. They lived quite happily in their village.

In the center of the village was a large tree. One day, the tree began to hum. It hummed and vibrated and sometimes waved its branches gently. The Surem gathered around the tree, wondering why it was making these sounds. Surely there must be a reason, they thought, but they could not understand what the tree was saying to them.

The leader of the Surem spoke to the tree. "O Tree," he said, "we want to understand you. What are you saying?"

But the tree did not change its speech. It simply stood under the sky, humming.

The Surem tried many times to understand the tree and to speak to it, but nothing changed, until one day Yomomuli came to their village and said, "I understand what the tree is saying, and I will tell you if you will listen.

"This is what the tree is saying," Yomomuli said. "It is telling all the animals how they are to live. It says that some animals must eat plants. Some must eat other animals and birds. It is telling the waters what they must do, that the streams and rivers must flow downhill into lakes and into the sea."

"Oh!" said the Surem. "Those are wise sayings. Does the tree tell what will become of us?"

"Yes," said Yomomuli, "but you must believe that what I tell you is true, even though you will not like to hear it."

"Tell us anyway," said the Surem. "We will believe you."

"The tree says that the world will change. Strange people will come from far away. They will have many weapons. They will take away your lands and make you live according to their laws. They will make you worship their god. They will have many things all made of metal and many houses all made of stone."

"This is terrible!" cried the Surem. "Surely there are no such people in this world. Surely they will not come here. This cannot be what the tree says."

"Think what you like," said Yomomuli, although she was angry that the Surem did not believe her. But Yomomuli believed what the tree had said. She did not want to stay in the land of the Surem. She did not want to be there when the strange people from far away came to conquer everything and make the Surem worship their god.

Yomomuli went to the river. She rolled it up and took it away with her. Yomomuli walked ever northwards, away from the Surem, with her river tucked under her arm.

As for the Surem, many of them ran away from their village. Some went to live in the rivers and the sea, and the ones that did this turned into dolphins and whales. Some went to live under the hills or in the desert, and the ones that did this turned into ants. The Surem that stayed in their village grew very tall, and these became the Yaqui people.

It is said that if a Yaqui gets lost on the waters, the whales and dolphins will help them get home. And if a Yaqui gets lost in the hills or the desert, the Surem will help them there, too.

How the Sea Was Made *(Cabécar, Costa Rica)*

Costa Rica is a small Central American country with coastlines on both the Pacific Ocean and Caribbean Sea. This geographical reality is reflected in the Cabécar myth of the creation of the sea; the world starts out as a rock in the void, around which the sea eventually is created by the god Sibú, a deity the Cabécar share with the neighboring Bribri and Boruca tribes, and it is the presence of the new sea that allows Sibú to continue his work of creating a world with creatures in it.

This story also mentions Cabécar burial customs. Anthropologist Doris Stone reports that when someone has died among the Cabécar, their bodies are wrapped in the large leaves of the bijagua *(also known as the Cuban cigar plant), and this burial package is then covered with thorny material to prevent the body being disturbed by animals. Only when nothing but the clean bones are left is the body recovered and buried near the village.*

Before the world was made, there was only a great rock that stood in the middle of the void. Sibú the Creator thought to himself that there should be an Earth with people living on it and that maybe he could use the rock to make the Earth. Sibú knew that this would be a long and difficult task. He wanted someone to help him with it. He called to a woman named Sea and asked her to take a message to Thunder.

"Go to Thunder," said Sibú, "and tell him to come to me. I want to create an Earth with people on it, and I need his help and advice."

Sea went to Thunder and told him that Sibú wanted help creating the Earth and putting people on it, but Thunder refused to go. Sea went back to Sibú and told him that Thunder would not help.

"Maybe if I give Thunder my staff, he will help me," said Sibú. He gave the staff to Sea and told her to take it to Thunder. "Tell him that this is my good staff. He can use it to help him in his journey here to see me."

Sea took the staff to Thunder, but still he would not go to help Sibú. "Use the staff yourself on your journey back," said Thunder, "but take care not to misplace it. Never put it down, even for a moment."

Sea thought that Thunder's instructions were very odd, but she tried to obey them. But at one point in her journey, she did put the staff down, and when she went to pick it up again, she found that it had vanished. She looked for it everywhere. When she went to a patch of tall grass to see whether the staff was there, a venomous serpent darted out of the grass and bit her. A brief moment later, Sea was dead.

Sibú wondered what was taking Sea so long to return to him, so he went out searching for her. Soon, he came across her body. He prepared it for burial, wrapping it in *bijagua* leaves as is proper, but the body began to swell very strangely. Sibú put a frog on top of Sea's burial shroud to hold it in place, but when an insect flew by, the frog jumped up to snap at it. Sea's body continued to swell, growing larger and larger until it began to take a new shape. Her body became the trunk of a great tree. Her hair became leaves. All manner of bright birds began to nest among the leaves.

The tree grew and grew and grew. Finally, it became so tall that it pushed its way through the sky, which was where Sibú lived. "Oh!" said Sibú, "I do not want this tree inside my house! I must do something about this."

Sibú called to some birds. "Go to the top of the tree, and grab the branches at the top. Pull them around until they make a circle."

The birds went and did as Sibú commanded. They took the branches at the top of the tree and made a circle with them. When the circle was complete, the tree fell down and turned into water. The nests that were in the tree became turtles. The leaves of the tree became crabs. And everywhere around the rock that was in the void there was now water. Waves washed up onto the edge of the rock and crashed against it.

"There!" said Sibú when he saw the water the tree had become. "I have my house back. And now I can make an Earth and put people on it because now I have a sea with crabs and turtles in it."

And so Sibú made the Earth and put people on it, but to this day, the people know that the sound of the waves crashing on the shore is really the sound of the wind rushing through the leaves that were made out of Sea's hair.

Mother Scorpion's Country
(Miskito, Nicaragua)

The Miskito people live along the Caribbean coast of Nicaragua and were first contacted by the Spanish in the early eighteenth century. Later, many of the original Miskito people intermarried with black slaves who escaped from various Caribbean plantations. One result of this mixture of many cultures is that several languages are spoken by the Miskito: their indigenous tongue, Spanish, and a Miskito-English creole that resulted from contacts with British traders.

This legend about Mother Scorpion's country gives us insight into Miskito beliefs about the afterlife and about the loving bond between husband and wife.

Once there was a man named Nakili. He had a wife named Kati. They loved each other very much, and for a time, they lived happily together. But one day, Kati became very ill. Nakili cared for her as tenderly as he could and got her the best medicines he could find, but to no avail. After a few days, Kati died.

Every day, Nakili went to visit Kati's grave. He sat there, weeping many bitter tears and mourning her. He neglected his body and his work. One day, he arrived at the grave and saw the spirit of his dead wife hovering there.

"I am going to Mother Scorpion's country now," said the spirit.

"Oh, please, please, take me with you!" cried Nakili. "Don't leave me here all alone!"

"You cannot come with me," said Kati's spirit. "Mother Scorpion's country is the place for the shades of the dead. You are still a living man. You must stay here on the Earth."

Still Nakili begged and begged to be allowed to go with her, and finally, Kati gave in. "Follow me," she said and set off down the trail that led to Mother Scorpion's country. After they had walked a little way, they came to a place where there were many moths flying about in the air. The air was so thick with the little flying creatures that it was impossible to see what lay beyond them.

"Oh!" cried Kati. "I do not like this place. I am afraid of the moths. I do not want to have to walk through them."

"Have no fear," said Nakili. "I will make a path for us. Stay close to me."

And so, Nakili waded into the crowd of moths with Kati close beside him. Nakili waved his arms about, shooing the moths away, and soon, husband and wife had passed safely to the other side where there were no more moths.

They went a little farther until they came to the place where two great trees grew next to each other in the middle of the path. The trees were so close together that only Kati could pass between them. Nakili had to go around.

Next, they came to a gorge. At the bottom of the gorge was a lake of boiling water, and the only way across was a bridge that was so narrow and light that it looked like it was made from a single hair. Because Kati was a spirit, she was able to walk across the bridge, but Nakili knew he was too heavy to go that way. He looked from where he stood to the other side of the gorge and thought that perhaps he might be able to jump the gap. Nakili got a good running start then gave a great leap when he got to the edge of the gorge. He landed safely on the other side, where his wife's shade stood waiting for him.

Leaving the gorge behind them, husband and wife continued on their way. They walked for a very long time without encountering any other difficulties. Finally, they came to a wide river, the river that flows along the border of Mother Scorpion's country. Nakili and Kati paused on the banks of the river and looked across it. There, in Mother Scorpion's country, they could see the souls of the dead. Everyone on the other side of the river appeared to be happy.

Nakili and Kati looked about for a way to cross the river. Some way along the bank, they saw a canoe. In the canoe were four toads.

"Please," said Nakili to the toads, "can you take us to the other side of the river in your canoe?"

"With a good will," croaked the toads, "but our canoe cannot carry the body of a living person. That body is too heavy, and the canoe will capsize." So, Kati got into the canoe, and the toads began to paddle her across the river while Nakili swam alongside.

As they crossed, Kati looked into the water. "Oh!" she cried out, "the water is full of sharks! I am so frightened! Surely my husband will be devoured!"

Nakili looked about him in the water, but all he saw were small fish. "Never fear," he said. "Those are not sharks, just fish. I will not be harmed."

The toads looked over the side of their canoe and saw Nakili swimming there among the little fish. "Ah," said the chief toad, "you must be a good man. Because if you had been a wicked person, those fish would have turned into sharks and gobbled you right up!"

Soon, Nakili and the canoe arrived on the far bank of the river. Nakili helped his wife's spirit out of the canoe, and they both thanked the toads for their help. When both husband and wife were standing on the shore and the toads had gone back, a very tall, very stout woman came striding over to where Nakili and Kati stood. The woman had many breasts, from which the souls of the dead sometimes suckled. This was Mother Scorpion, and it was her country in which all the spirits of the good people lived after death.

"Welcome, my child," said Mother Scorpion to Kati. "Welcome to my country. Here you will have no pain or sorrow. You will always have plenty to eat, and you will not have to work. I am glad to receive you and for you to join my other children here."

Then Mother Scorpion turned to Nakili. She frowned angrily at him and said, "You, however, are not welcome. You are still alive. You should not be here. Go back to the land of the living where you belong!"

"Please, Mother Scorpion, let me stay!" begged Nakili. "I love Kati more than life itself, and I do not wish to be parted from her."

At first, Mother Scorpion would not listen to Nakili's pleas, but finally, she relented and let him stay.

For a time, Nakili and Kati lived very happily among the other souls, but one day, Nakili realized that he missed his children and wanted to see them again.

"I must go," Nakili said to Kati. "Mother Scorpion was right; I do not belong here. But one day I will come back, and we will never be parted again."

Nakili went to Mother Scorpion and told her that he wanted to go home to his children. Mother Scorpion cut down a big stalk of bamboo and put Nakili inside it, telling him that he must never return to her country until he had died himself. Then Mother Scorpion put the bamboo into the river, and it floated away.

After a time, Nakili realized that he was no longer on the river. He was being tossed about by waves. The river had emptied into the ocean, and now, the waves were carrying him back to the shore. Finally, the bamboo washed up onto the beach, and Nakili climbed out. He looked about and saw that he was standing in front of his own house, with his children running out to greet him.

The Childhood of the Sun and the Moon *(qne-a tnya-e/Chatino, Mexico)*

The Chatino people live in the state of Oaxaca in southern Mexico. This legend explains how the sun and moon got into the sky, and it also establishes the old woman who care for Sun and Moon during their childhood as the protector of newborn babies through the old woman's transformation into ashes in a sweat bath. According to author Lulu Delacre, Chatino parents still bring their newborn babies into a sweat bath that they might receive the protection of the old woman who cared for Sun and Moon when they were children.

There once was a time when the Sun and the Moon did not travel the sky but lived on the Earth as human beings. They were brothers, twins, and they walked about together as human brothers do.

One night, a Night Terror came upon the twins and tried to catch and eat them. Night Terror hated Sun and Moon because he was jealous of them. Sun and Moon ran from Night Terror. They ran until they came to a river. Sun and Moon plunged into the water and hid themselves there, hoping that Night Terror would not find them. But they had hidden near the mouth of the river, and when the tide of the ocean went out, the water of the river began to dry up. Night Terror was nearly upon the twins when an old woman passed by.

"Help us!" cried the children. "Night Terror is chasing us! He wants to kill and eat us!"

The old woman took pity on the children. She picked them up and put them in her mouth, one in each cheek. Her face became terribly swollen.

Once the children were safely hidden away, the old woman started walking back to her home. On her way, she met Night Terror.

"Have you seen two children anywhere near here?" said Night Terror.

"No, I haven't," said the woman.

Then Night Terror said, "Why is your head so big and round?"

"I have a terrible toothache," said the woman. "It has made my whole head swell up."

Night Terror believed the woman and went on its way, still hunting the children, not knowing that the old woman had fooled him by putting the twins in her cheeks.

When the old woman got home, she let the twins out of her cheeks. Since the children seemed to have no family, the old woman began to care for them herself. The children were very mischievous. The old woman could never finish her spinning properly because the boys would take the spindle and make a great tangle out of the thread. But the old woman was patient with them, and after a time, the children began to think that the old woman was their mother.

Sun and Moon lived happily with the old woman. They grew into fine, sturdy boys. They began to make their own bows and arrows, and when they had practiced using these, they went out into the forest to hunt for food. They often caught pigeons that they would bring home for the old woman to cook.

From time to time, the old woman would leave their home and go off into the forest. When the twins asked her where she was going, she always told them that she was going to visit her husband. Then one day, the twins asked her, "You are our mother, but who is our father?"

"My husband is your father," she replied.

"Why do we never see him?"

"Oh, he lives deep in the forest. He feels much happier and safer there," said the old woman. "But you must never see him, for I am afraid you might kill him."

The children became even more curious about their father after this, and so, they decided that the next time the old woman went to visit him they would follow her and see for themselves who their father was. Soon enough, the old woman announced that she was going to visit her husband. She told the children to stay at home and behave themselves.

"Yes, Mama," said the twins, but they had no intentions of staying behind. They secretly followed the old woman into the forest because they were determined to find out who their father was.

Deeper and deeper into the forest went the old woman, with Sun and Moon following after her. The children left behind them a trail of ashes so that they could find their way back out of the forest on their own. After a long time, they came to a little clearing where the old woman stopped and gave a strange cry. From their hiding place in the bushes, the children saw a great deer come into the clearing. The old woman greeted the deer and gave it some leaves and grass she had brought with her.

As soon as the children saw the old woman feed the deer, they followed the trail of ashes back to the house. They arrived there before the old woman and pretended that they had never left.

Some days later, the old woman asked the children to mow some fresh grass for her to take to her husband. The children fashioned a scythe out of wood and went into a meadow where there was a quantity of long, green grass. Sun took the scythe and swung it with great speed and force. It sliced through the grass very easily, but it frightened a young rabbit that had hidden itself in the grass. The rabbit leapt up out of the grass and hit Moon in the face so hard that an imprint of its body remained there, and this is why we can see the shape of a rabbit in the moon even today.

The next day, the twins decided they would go to the clearing and see whether they might meet their father for themselves. They followed the trail of ashes, and when they got to the clearing, they called out in the same way they had heard the old woman do. Soon enough, a great deer came into the clearing.

"This can't possibly be our father," said Sun to Moon. "It is such an ugly creature."

"Yes," said Moon. "Look at its great spindly legs. It looks quite out of proportion."

The twins decided to kill the deer. They shot it through the heart with their arrows, and when it was dead, they skinned it and took out its organs. They set aside the liver to take home to the old woman but used some of the other organs to make a dish called *skualyku*. They cooked it right there in the clearing and ate it all up. Then they took the empty deer hide, filled it full of wasps, and sewed it shut. They left the wasp-filled hide there on the floor of the clearing, and it looked like the deer was lying there, asleep.

When the children were done eating and sewing up the deer hide, they took the liver back to the old woman. She thanked them for their gift and prepared to eat it. Just as she was about to bite into the liver, it cried out, and a nearby frog started to sing, "You are eating your husband, you are eating your husband." It sang that song three times.

Then the old woman looked at the children. "Is this true? Did you kill my husband?"

"Of course not!" said the children. "Frogs never know what they are talking about. You shouldn't listen to them."

But the old woman's suspicions were not allayed. She went to the clearing where she saw the deer hide on the forest floor. She thought that her husband was being lazy, and this made her angry. The old woman took her staff and began beating the deer hide. She hit it so hard that the seams split wide open, and hundreds of angry wasps swarmed out. They attacked the old woman, stinging her all over her body.

Screaming in pain, the old woman ran back home. She ran past the field that the children had mown the other day. The baby rabbit called out to her as she went by. "Jump in the water! Jump in the water!" said the rabbit.

"No, that will not help," said the old woman. "I need my children to make a sweat bath for me."

When the woman arrived home, the children saw that she was covered in wasp stings. They lit a huge fire and put many medicinal plants in it so that it would make a healing smoke to soothe her wounds. The old woman sat before the fire. At first, she started feeling better, but then she felt too hot. "Children, please take me out of the sweat bath," she said.

"No, Mama, we cannot do that," said the children. "You must stay there. This is how you will become the protector of all new children."

The old woman stayed in the sweat bath. She became so hot that she burned up into ashes. Once they saw that the old woman was nothing but ashes, the children took up the old woman's staff and a skein of her thread then left their home and started climbing into the hills.

While they were climbing, Sun turned to Moon and said, "I am feeling very sad. Our mother had to live and die in a world without light. I wonder what we could do to honor her now that she is dead."

Moon said, "I know what we could do. We could climb to the very highest mountain we can find. We could shine our light on her from there."

Sun agreed that this was a good plan, so they started walking up the highest mountain they could find. On their way up, they came across a great serpent that had glowing eyes. The children looked at it for a moment then decided to kill the serpent. Sun hit the serpent with the staff. Moon strangled it with some of the thread. And when the serpent was dead, the children took out its eyes. Moon kept the right eye, which was the brightest one. Sun kept the duller, left eye.

Up, up, up the mountain the children climbed. Presently, they came upon a hollow tree that had a beehive in it. Moon took some of the honey and ate it. It was very good and very sweet, but it made him very thirsty indeed. Sun took the old woman's staff and drove it into the ground. Where the staff entered the soil, a spring of water spurted out.

"Give me some of that water to drink," said Moon. "I am terribly thirsty after eating all that honey."

"I will not give you any water unless you trade your serpent's eye for the one that I have," said Sun.

Moon was angry that Sun would do something like this because he wanted to keep the brighter eye. But in the end, he traded with Sun because he could no longer stand how thirsty he had become. And this is why the Sun is brighter than the Moon.

Up, up, up the children climbed, until they reached the very top of the mountain peak. Sun took the skein of thread and threw one end into the sky. The thread made a path for the children to follow into the heavens. Sun went first because he had the brighter serpent's eye and could see the way more easily. Moon followed Sun with his lesser serpent's eye. When they arrived up in the heavens, they started their travels across the sky.

And this is how Sun and Moon came to be in the heavens and how light came to be on the Earth.

The Invisible Hunters (*Miskito, Nicaragua*)

In the legend of the invisible hunters, three Miskito men learn a hard lesson about greed. This cautionary tale also bears the imprint of indigenous Miskito contact with Europeans since the goods offered by the traders seem to be European products and the hunters must make a choice between their traditional manner of hunting with spears or using modern firearms, which were introduced by European colonizers.

Once there were three brothers who lived in the village of Ulwas on the Coco River. They were very good hunters. They never failed to come back from their hunt with something to share with the rest of the village. One day, they decided to go hunting for *wari*, a kind of wild pig that has the most delicious meat of any animal in the forest. The brothers took up their spears and went out into the forest. They walked for a long time, not seeing any wari at all.

Suddenly, they heard a strange voice. "Dar, dar, dar," said the voice.

"Did you say that?" asked the eldest brother.

"No, we did not speak at all," said the other two.

The brothers waited for a moment to see whether they might spy on who or what the voice belonged to, but all they heard were the usual forest sounds.

As soon as they started to go back to their hunt, they heard the voice again. "Dar, dar, dar," it said.

"Did you say that?" asked the youngest brother.

"No, we did not speak at all," said the other two.

They looked around them and saw a vine swinging from a tree nearby. "Dar, dar, dar," said the vine.

The three brothers went over to the tree where the vine was swinging. The first brother took hold of the vine, and suddenly, he disappeared! Then the second brother also took hold of the vine, and he disappeared as well. The youngest brother was very frightened indeed. "Give me back my brothers!" he shouted at the vine.

"I haven't taken them anywhere," said the vine. "They're right here in front of you. All they need to do is let go of me, and you will be able to see them again."

The two invisible brothers let go of the vine, and suddenly, they reappeared. The three brothers looked at the vine in wonder. "Who are you?" they said.

"I am the Dar, and whoever touches me becomes invisible to others. Neither humans nor animals will be able to see you at all."

The brothers thought about what the Dar had said.

"If we each take a piece of this vine," said the eldest, "we will be the greatest hunters in the world. We will be able to stalk any animal we want."

"Yes," said the second brother. "Let us each take a piece of the vine. Let us do that now."

The brothers all lunged for the vine, but it swung far out of their reach and disappeared. Then the brothers heard the voice of the Dar again. "I will let you take me," it said, "but first you must promise me two things."

"Very well," said the brothers. "You have our word."

"First, you must never sell the wari meat. You must give it away to those who need it. Second, you must never use guns in your hunt. You must use only spears."

"We promise," said the brothers. "We will do exactly as you say."

Then the Dar reappeared and swung down in front of the brothers. The Dar allowed each of them to cut off a small piece with their knives. The rest of the Dar then vanished, and the brothers continued on their hunt.

That day, they took many, many wari. Before they left for home, they returned their pieces of the Dar to the tree where they had found the vine. They left the pieces of vine on a branch of the tree. Then they brought the wari back to their village and gave the meat away to everyone who needed food.

The people in Ulwas were astonished to see so many wari killed in a single hunt. Soon, they had skinned and cleaned the animals, and then they cooked them and ate them in a great feast. Everyone was very happy and very content when the meal was done.

After the meal, the village elders summoned the brothers. "We would like to know how you had such great fortune in the hunt. Never has anyone brought back so many wari on the same day."

"We went into the forest the way we often do," said the eldest brother, "and then we heard a voice. It was the Dar, a magical vine that makes things invisible. After we promised to hunt only with spears and to give the meat away, the Dar let us each take a little piece of itself, and so, we became invisible to the wari. That is how we caught so many."

"Ah!" said the elders. "That is truly good fortune. The legend of the Dar is very, very old. You were very lucky to have found it. But be sure you keep your promises to it!"

It was not long before the fame of the brothers from Ulwas had spread up and down the Coco River. One day, a boat full of strangers arrived in Ulwas. The boat carried a cargo of well-woven cloth and barrels of wine.

"Greetings to you!" said the strangers. "We have come from far away to meet the famous hunters from Ulwas. We have come to trade you our fine cloth and our good wine for some wari meat."

"We cannot sell the meat to you," said the second brother. "Our people need it for food."

"Of course they do!" said the strangers. "We only want to buy the portion they do not need."

The brothers stood aside to talk about what the strangers had said.

"Maybe we could sell just a little bit," said the eldest brother.

"No, we should not do that," said the second brother. "We made a promise to the Dar. Surely it will know if we have not kept our word."

"Yes, we did promise," said the youngest brother, "but surely these traders also have power since they can make such fine cloth and so many barrels of wine. Maybe they are more powerful than the Dar."

The other brothers thought about what the youngest one had said and agreed with him. They went to the traders and exchanged wari meat for cloth and wine. The traders left the village, apparently content with the exchange.

It was not long before the traders came back with more cloth and more wine to trade for wari meat. This they did many times, making bigger and bigger exchanges, until finally the brothers realized that they were trading too much. Soon there would not be enough meat to feed the people.

One day, the traders arrived with more cargo to trade. The three brothers met them at the riverbank. "We can no longer trade with you," said the eldest brother. "We do not have enough meat to feed the people."

"That is because you only hunt with spears," said the traders. "If you used guns, you would be able to kill more wari more quickly, and then you'd have enough both to feed your village and to trade with us."

The brothers decided that what the traders had said was wise. They bought guns and used those to hunt in the forest. With the guns, they were able to kill enough wari both to satisfy the traders and to feed the people. And the brothers no longer gave any thought to their promise to the Dar.

Again and again, the traders came back. Always they brought rich things to trade for the wari meat. The brothers greedily took whatever the traders brought, and soon, they found that there was not enough meat to satisfy both the traders and the hunger of the village.

The village elders watched what the brothers were doing and became concerned. They called the brothers before them to account for their deeds. "You are trading too much," said the elders. "Our people are going hungry while you become rich with the traders' wares."

"Well," said the brothers, "if the people want to get more meat from us, maybe they should pay for it like the traders do."

But the people of Ulwas were poor people. They did not have finely woven cloth. They did not have barrels of wine. They had no money to trade for the meat.

One day, the brothers returned from the hunt to find the people of the village waiting for them at the end of the path.

"Give us the meat," said the people.

"Pay us for it then," said the brothers.

"We cannot pay," said the people. "We are poor villagers."

So, the brothers gave the villagers the bad parts of the meat which they knew the traders would not take. The people became very angry at this, but the brothers only laughed at them and went about their business.

For many months, the brothers continued to hunt with guns and sold what they had caught to the traders. The people of the village became ever more hungry because the brothers would not share their catch with them.

One day, the brothers returned from their hunt laden with wari. But as they came to the entrance to the village, the assembled people did not run up to them and beg for meat. Instead, they all screamed and ran away because they saw only a line of dead wari floating along through the air by themselves. The elders heard the commotion and went out to see what was wrong. "Ah!" they said. "The Dar has made the hunters invisible."

The brothers halted in their tracks when the people started running away from them. Then they looked at each other. Nothing could they see but the dead wari floating in the air.

"What has happened?" asked the eldest brother.

"We left our pieces of the Dar on the tree like we always do," said the second.

"We are still invisible, just the same!" said the youngest. "Oh, this is very, very bad."

They dropped the dead wari there on the path and raced back to the Dar's tree where they fell on their knees. "What has happened to us?" they cried. "Why are we still invisible?"

But the Dar did not answer them, no matter how they begged for mercy. The only thing it said was "Dar, dar, dar, dar," over and over.

"We have done this to ourselves," said the brothers. "We did not keep our promise to the Dar. We were greedy and treated our people very badly. We must go back to our village and beg forgiveness of the elders and the people."

The brothers went back to the village. They went down on their knees before the elders and begged for forgiveness. But the elders would not forgive them for what they had done. Instead, they banished the invisible hunters from the village forever.

The invisible hunters went back into the forest. They wandered up and down the river, looking for the Dar and begging it to make them visible again. Some say that the brothers wander there still, for hunters on the trail sometimes swear that they have heard three tearful voices crying out, "Dar, dar, dar."

The King of the Peccaries *(Bribri, Costa Rica)*

An important part of indigenous subsistence is hunting the animals and birds that live near human settlements. This legend from the Bribri people of Costa Rica concerns itself with ethical hunting of animals for food. In this cautionary tale, the unskilled hunter who falls afoul of the King of the Peccaries does pay a price but only a temporary one: the King's goal is instruction and reform of the hunter's ways, not revenge.

One day, two Bribri hunters went out with their bows and arrows to see what they might catch to eat. They walked quietly through the forest, bows at the ready, in case they saw an animal or bird. For a long time, they crept along the forest path, not seeing anything, until one of them spied a peccary. He let fly with his arrow, but he did not shoot well. The animal was hit, but it was only wounded. The peccary bounded off into the forest, and the hunter ran after it. The hunter's companion soon lost sight of both his friend and their prey. Eventually, he gave up looking and went back home, thinking that his friend would come home when he had caught and killed the peccary.

But the first hunter did not come home. He chased after the peccary, going deeper and deeper into the forest, but no matter how quickly he ran, the peccary went even faster, and soon, the animal was lost to sight. The hunter decided to give up the chase. While he was resting and catching his breath before returning home, a man appeared before him. The man was very tall and very stately. He had fine black hair and was dressed very well.

"Follow me," said the tall man, who then strode off toward another part of the forest.

The hunter thought it wise to go with this man since he seemed to be very powerful. He followed the tall man through the forest until they came to a large house.

"This is my home," said the tall man. "Please come in."

The hunter went into the house and saw that it was very finely built and beautifully decorated and furnished with many well-made hammocks. But the most surprising thing is that the house was also full of animals of all kinds, and every one of them seemed happy and very well cared for.

"Do you see all these animals here in my house?" said the tall man. "These are my subjects, for I am the King of the Peccaries. When hunters wound animals but do not kill them, the animals come to me to be healed, or else I find them in the forest and bring them here. But if they cannot be healed, I use them for food for myself and my guests.

"Listen to me," said the King, "and listen well: when you go into the forest to hunt, you must do that duty very, very well. It is not right to shoot at an animal and leave it wounded without killing it. You must try to kill the beast with the very first shot. That is the proper way to do things."

"That is what I shall do, always, from now on," said the hunter. "I did not know how much harm I was doing before. I shall change my ways."

"That is very good," said the King. "Now, come here and have a seat, and eat and drink. You have had a long and weary day, and you need refreshment before you can go home."

The hunter sat in the place the King prepared for him and ate of the peccary he had wounded earlier, which the King had found and then killed and cooked. The King also served good maize beer to his guest.

When the meal was done, the hunter said, "I thank you, O King of the Peccaries, for my meal and for my lesson. I will try to do as you ask and be a better hunter."

"This I know you will do," said the King. "But there is yet a price to be paid for your error." He handed a piece of cane to the hunter. "You must take this back to your home and plant it in front of your house. You will not be able to speak until the cane has fully grown. And when the cane is grown, you must tell all your people what happened to you, and give them my instructions about hunting."

The hunter thanked the King once more, then took the piece of cane and returned home. He did as the King of the Peccaries had instructed him, planting the cane in front of his house. The hunter could not speak until the cane was fully grown, and when it was, he told all the village what had happened to him.

How Opossum Stole Fire *(Mazatec, Mexico)*

The trope of an animal using its tail to bring fire to people is common to many cultures. In James George Frazer's book of fire-origin myths from around the world, animals as varied as snakes, dogs, and hummingbirds use their tails to bring fire to the people. In this trickster myth from the Mazatec people of Oaxaca, Mexico, the fire-bringer is the opossum, and he pays for his trick by losing all the fur on his tail.

A long time ago, fire did not exist on the Earth. Fire only was found in the sun and the stars. One day, some fire fell from the heavens onto the Earth. An old woman saw it fall. She went to where the fire fell and collected some up. She brought it home with her, placed it in her hearth, and tended it with care. The people saw that the old woman had fire. They asked whether she might share it with them, but she always refused. She wanted to keep the fire for herself alone.

And so it was that all the people were cold and had no way to cook their food. Again and again, they asked the old woman to share her fire, but every time they asked, she told them to go away. This made the people very sad indeed.

One day, an opossum ambled by a village of people. He saw that the people were all very cold and were eating uncooked food. He also saw that they were very sorrowful.

"Greetings, cousins," said the opossum. "What is it that makes you so very sad?"

"We do not have fire to keep us warm or to cook our food. The old woman has some, but she won't share it with us. That is why we are sad," said the people.

"If I went and stole some fire for you, would you promise not to hunt and eat me?" said the opossum.

The people looked at the little opossum and burst into laughter, but the opossum was not bothered by it. "I know you think I am quite amusing," he said, "but I will do as I said I would. I will steal fire for you."

When night fell, the opossum visited all the houses of the people. He told each household that he was going to steal fire for them so they needed to be ready and waiting for his return.

The opossum went to the old woman's house where he found her sitting before her hearth. On the hearth was a large fire, merrily blazing away. "Greetings, mother," said the opossum. "How fortunate you are to have a fire! It is so cold outside I am sure it will be the death of me. Can I sit by your fire with you and warm myself?"

The old woman looked down at the small, shivering opossum and felt sorry for him. "Yes, indeed," she said. "You may sit by my fire and warm yourself with me."

The opossum sat down a little distance from the fire. Bit by bit, he inched closer and closer to the hearth. Because he only moved a little at a time, the old woman didn't notice what he was doing. Now, it is important to remember that at this time the opossum had a fine, furry tail, much like a fox or a squirrel. Soon, the opossum got close enough to touch the fire. He took his fine, furry tail and put it into the flames. Instantly, the opossum went running out of the old woman's house, his tail ablaze.

The old woman was furious. She tried to chase the opossum, but he was too quick for her. The opossum ran back to the village with his burning tail. He gave some of the fire to each of the households until finally the fire was spent. All the fine fur on the opossum's tail was singed quite away, and that is why today opossums have naked tails.

Uncle Rabbit and Uncle Tiger (*Nicaragua*)

Animal tales are common to cultures the world over, and Central America has its share of these fun stories. One character that commonly appears in their animal tales is wily Uncle Rabbit, the primary trickster in stories widely told in both Costa Rica and Nicaragua, stories that are not confined to one particular indigenous group. This story about Uncle Rabbit's victory over Uncle Tiger comes from Nicaragua, and it is a cautionary tale about helping harmful and ungrateful people.

Tiger was walking down the path on a very windy day. How the wind howled through the trees! Even Tiger could not roar so loudly. But Tiger didn't pay the wind any mind until suddenly a large branch was blown off a tree. The branch landed right on top of Tiger. The branch was so heavy that Tiger couldn't move.

"Oh, dear, oh, dear," said Tiger. "I shall never get free. I shall be stuck here forever, and I shall die of hunger and thirst."

As Tiger lay under the branch lamenting his predicament, Bull came trotting down the same path. He was hurrying to get home because he did not like the wind one bit.

Tiger heard Bull and called out, "Uncle Bull! Uncle Bull! Oh, come quickly and help me! I am trapped here under this branch, and I cannot get out."

Bull went over to Tiger and said, "Oh, my. You are stuck indeed. But maybe I shouldn't help you, for surely as soon as you are free, you will leap on me and eat me."

"I promise with all my heart that I will not eat you," said Tiger. "Please lift the branch so that I can go free."

"You promise?" said Bull.

"I promise. I swear most solemnly," said Tiger.

"Very well," said Bull. "I'll help you. But don't you forget your promise!"

Bull put his horns under the branch. With his strong neck, he tossed the heavy branch aside. But as soon as Tiger was free, he leapt upon Bull and started biting him.

"Tiger!" said Bull. "You promised! You said you would not eat me!"

"Well, I'm hungry," said Tiger. "And you look so very tasty. But I'll stop for now. Instead, we'll go along the path and ask for advice. We'll see whether anyone agrees that I should eat you or whether they think I should let you go free. We will abide by the judgement of whoever makes the best argument."

"Very well," said Bull, and so they set off down the path.

Soon enough, they came across a very old Ox.

"Uncle Ox," said Tiger, "we need your advice. If someone does a good deed, how do they get repaid?"

Ox scoffed. "Not with kindness, that's certain," he said. "Look at me. I worked and worked and worked for a farmer. I pulled his plow year after year. I worked so hard, but when I became feeble, he sent me away instead of caring for me in my old age. I did so many good deeds for him, but he only repaid me with a bad one."

Tiger and Bull bade Ox farewell and continued down the path. "Ha!" said Tiger. "We already found one person who agrees with me. I wonder what the next one will say?"

Soon enough, Tiger and Bull came upon a very old Horse.

"Uncle Horse," said Tiger, "we need your advice. If someone does a good deed, how do they get repaid?"

"Well, all you need to know to answer your question is to look at me," said Horse. "I worked so very, very hard for the man who owned me. I carried him everywhere on my back. I pulled his cart. I pulled his plow. I carried his children. Every night he would go out drinking, and I would carry him home safely when he was too drunk to stand. But now that I am old and feeble, he has turned me out of my stable instead of caring for me. I did so many good deeds for him, but he only repaid me with a bad one."

Tiger and Bull bade Horse farewell and continued down the path. "Ha!" said Tiger. "That's two people who agree with me!"

Bull began to feel very afraid. If the next person also agreed with Tiger, surely Tiger would eat him all up.

Tiger and Bull continued down the path. Suddenly, Rabbit jumped out in front of them.

"Uncle Rabbit," said Tiger, "we need your advice. If someone does a good deed, how do they get repaid?"

"Hmmm," said Rabbit. "That's an important question. And a difficult one. What kind of good deed did you have in mind?"

Bull said, "Today I was walking down the path, and I came across Uncle Tiger. He was trapped underneath a very heavy branch. He asked me to help him out, so I did. And now he wants to eat me. So, we're asking for advice about whether he should do that or not."

"Oh, that is a difficult question," said Rabbit, "but I'm not sure I understand what happened. Can you explain it again?"

This time Tiger told Rabbit how Bull had freed him.

"Yes, but I still don't understand how Bull managed to set you free. I think I need to see what happened. Can you take me to the place where the branch is?"

Tiger, Bull, and Rabbit went back to the place where Tiger had been trapped under the branch.

"Oh, that is a very large branch," said Rabbit, "but I still don't understand how you could have been trapped by it. Lie down in the path. Then Bull can put the branch back on top of you, and then he can show me how he pushed it away. Then I'll understand, and I'll be able to answer your question."

Tiger lay down in the middle of the path. Bull picked up the branch with his horns and put it back on top of Tiger.

"Now we run!" Rabbit said to Bull, and the two of them ran away, leaving Tiger trapped once again and roaring with anger at having been tricked.

When Rabbit and Bull were safely away, Rabbit said to Bull, "Don't go back there. And think twice before helping someone who is likely to harm you."

Bibliography

Bierhorst, John, ed. *The Deetkatoo: Native American Stories About Little People*. New York: William Morrow and Company, Inc., 1998.

———. *The Mythology of Mexico and Central America*. New York: William Morrow and Company, Inc., 1990.

Conzemius, Eduard. "Ethnographical Survey of the Miskito Indians of Nicaragua and Honduras." *Smithsonian Institution Bureau of American Ethnology, Bulletin 106*. Washington, DC: United States Government Printing Office, 1932.

Delacre, Lulu. *Golden Tales: Myths, Legends, and Folktales from Latin America*. New York: Scholastic, Inc., 1996.

Endrezze, Anita. *Throwing Fire at the Sun, Water at the Moon*. Tucson: University of Arizona Press, 2000.

Evers, Larry, ed. *The South Corner of Time: Hopi, Navajo, Papago, Yaqui Tribal Literature*. n. c.: University of Arizona Press, 1980.

Fabrega, H. Pittier de. "Folk-Lore of the Bribri and Brunka Indians in Costa Rica." *Journal of American Folk-lore* 16 (1903): 1-9.

Foss, Flora. *World Myths and Legends II: Mexico.* Belmont: Fearon/Janus/Quercus, 1993.

Frazer, Sir James George. *Myths of the Origin of Fire: An Essay.* London: Macmillan and Co., Ltd., 1930.

Friesen, Alyssa. "The Legend of the Miskito Indians: A Literary Translation Project." *SWOSU Journal of Undergraduate Research* 2 (2018): 24-34.

Giddings, Ruth Warner. *Yaqui Myths and Legends.* Anthropological Papers of the University of Arizona 2. Tucson: [University of Arizona Press], 1959.

Love, Hallie N. *Watakame's Journey: The Story of the Great Flood and the New World.* Santa Fe: Clear Light Publishers, 1999.

Loya, Olga. *Momentos Magicos/Magic Moments: Tales from Latin America Told in English and Spanish.* Little Rock: August House Publishers Inc., 1997.

Lumholtz, Carl. "Symbolism of the Huichol Indians." *Memoirs of the American Museum of Natural History* 3 (1907): 1-228.

Nava, Yolanda. *It's All in the Frijoles: 100 Famous Latinos Share Real-Life Stories, Time-Tested Dichos, Favorite Folktales, and Inspiring Words of Wisdom.* New York: Simon & Schuster, 2000.

Pittier, H. Fabrega de. "The Folk-Lore of the Bribri and Brunka Indians in Costa Rica." *The Journal of American Folk-Lore* 16 (1903): 1-9.

Porras, Tomas Herrera. *Cuna Cosmology: Legends from Panama*. Trans. Anita McAndrews. Washington, DC: Three Continents Press, 1978.

Rohmer, Harriet, Octavio Chow, Morris Viduare, Rosalma Zubizarreta, and Alma Flor Ada. *The Invisible Hunters/Los Cazadores Invisibles: A Legend from the Miskito Indians of Nicaragua*. n.c.: n.p., 1987.

Sáenz, Adela de Ferreto, *La Creacion de la tierra y otras historias del buen Sibú y de los Bribris*. San Jose, Costa Rica: Editorial Universidad Estatal a Distancia, 1982.

Schmitt, Martha. *World Myths and Legends II: Central America*. Belmont: Fearon/Janus/Quercus, 1993.

Stone, Doris. *The Talamancan Tribes of Costa Rica*. Cambridge, MA: The Peabody Museum, 1962. Repr. 1973.

Suárez-Rivas, Maite. *Latino Read-Aloud Stories*. New York: Black Dog & Leventhal Publishers, 2000.

Zingg, Robert M. *Huichol Mythology*. Tucson: University of Arizona Press, 2004.

Bellos, Alex. "Ancient Wonder: Pre-Inca Ruins Found in Lake Titicaca." *The Guardian*, 23 August 2000. <https://www.theguardian.com/world/2000/aug/24/bolivia>, accessed 11 January 2019.

Betanzos, Juan de. *Narrative of the Incas*. Trans. and ed. Roland Hamilton and Dana Buchanan. Austin: University of Texas Press, 1996.

Bierhorst, John, ed. *Latin American Folktales: Stories from Hispanic and Indian Traditions*. New York: Pantheon Books, 2002.

————. *The Mythology of South America*. New York: William Morrow and Company, Inc., 1988.

————, ed. and trans. *Black Rainbow: Legends of the Incas and Myths of Ancient Peru*. New York: Farrar, Straus & Giroux, 1976.

Brinton, Daniel G. *American Hero-Myths: A Study in the Native Religions of the Western Continent*. Philadelphia: H. C. Watts & Co., 1882.

Carpenter, Frances. *South American Wonder Tales*. Chicago: Follett Publishing Company, 1969.

Cobo, Bernabe. *Inca Religion and Customs*. Trans. and ed. Roland Hamilton. Austin: University of Texas Press, 1990.

————. *History of the Inca Empire*. Trans. and ed. Roland Hamilton. Austin: University of Texas Press, 1979.

Colum, Padraic. *Orpheus: Myths of the World*. New York: Macmillan, 1930.

Cossins, Daniel. "We Thought the Incas Couldn't Write. These Knots Change Everything." *The New Scientist*, 26 September 2018. <https://www.newscientist.com/article/mg23931972-600-we-thought-the-incas-couldnt-write-these-knots-change-everything/>, accessed 26 November 2018.

Dixon-Kennedy, Mike. *Native American Myth & Legend: An A-Z of People and Places*. London: Blandford, 1996.

Elliot, L. E. "Ollantay: An Ancient Inca Drama." *The Pan-American Magazine* 33/1 (1921): 281-290.

Gifford, Douglas. *Warriors, Gods and Spirits from Central and South American Mythology*. New York: Peter Bedrick Books, 1983.

Hills, Elijah Clarence. *The Quechua Drama* Ollanta. *Romanic Review* 5/2 (1914): 127-176.

Kuss, Daniele. *Myths and Legends of Incas*. New York: Marshall Cavendish, 1991.

La Barre, Weston. "The Aymara: History and Worldview." *The Journal of American Folklore* 79/311 (1966): 130-144.

Markham, Clements R., ed. *The Incas of Peru*. New York: Dutton, 1910.

————, ed. *History of the Incas, by Pedro Sarmiento de Gamboa, and the Execution of the Inca Tupac Amaru, by Captain Baltasar de Ocampo.* Farnham: Ashgate Publishing Ltd., 2010.

————, ed. *Narratives of the Rites and Laws of the Yncas.* Farnham: Ashgate Publishing Ltd., 2010.

————, ed. *The Second Part of the Chronicle of Peru by Pedro de Cieza de Leon.* Farnham: Ashgate Publishing Ltd., 2010.

————, ed. *The Travels of Pedro de Cieza de Leon, A.D. 1532-50, Contained in the First Part of His Chronicle of Peru.* Volume I. Farnham: Ashgate Publishing Ltd., 2010.

Osborne, Harold. *South American Mythology*. Feltham: The Hamlyn Publishing Group, Ltd., 1968.

Pan-American Union. *Folk Songs and Stories of the Americas*. Washington, DC: Organization of American States, 1971.

Roberts, Timothy R. *Myths of the World: Gods of the Maya, Aztecs, and Incas*. New York: Friedman/Fairfax Publishers, 1996.

Salomon, Frank, and George L. Urioste, trans. *The Huarochirí Manuscript: A Testament of Ancient and*

Colonial Andean Religion. Austin: University of Texas Press, 1991.

Schmitt, Martha. *World Myths and Legends II: South America.* Belmont: Fearon/James/Quercus, 1993.

Steele, Paul R., with Catherine J. Allen. *Handbook of Inca Mythology.* Santa Barbara: ABC-CLIO, Inc., 2004.

Suarez-Rivas, Maite, ed. *Latino Read-Aloud Stories.* New York: Black Dog & Leventhal Publishers, 2000.

Urton, Gary. *Inca Myths.* Austin: University of Texas Press, 1999.

Vega, Garcilasso de. *First Part of the Royal Commentaries of the Yncas.* Trans. Clement R. Markham. 2 vols. London: Hakluyt Society, 1869-71.

Witherspoon, Anna. *Let's See South America.* Dallas: The Southern Publishing Company, 1939.

Alexander, Harley Burr. *Mythology of All Races.* Vol. 11, *Latin-American.* Boston: Marshall Jones Co., 1920.

Allan, Tony, and Tom Lowenstein. *Gods of Sun & Sacrifice: Aztec & Maya Myth.* London: Duncan Baird Publishers, 1997.

Bancroft, Hubert Howe. *The Native Races of the Pacific States of North America.* Vol. 3, *Myths and Languages.* San Francisco: A. L. Bancroft Co., 1875.

Bierhorst, John, trans. *History and Mythology of the Aztecs: The Codex Chimalpopoca.* Tucson: University of Arizona Press, 1992.

Brinton, Daniel G. *American Hero-Myths: A Study in the Native Religions of the Western Continent.* Philadelphia: H. C. Watts & Co., 1882.

Burland, Cottie Arthur, et al. *Mythology of the Americas.* London: Hamlyn Publishing Group, 1970.

Carrasco, David. *The Aztecs: A Very Short Introduction*. Oxford: Oxford University Press, 2012.

Clendennin, Inga. *Aztecs: An Interpretation*. Cambridge: Cambridge University Press, 1991.

Coe, Sophie D. *The True History of Chocolate.* London: Thames and Hudson, Ltd., 1996.

Dalal, Anita. *Myths of Pre-Columbian America*. Austin: Steck-Vaughn Company, 2001.

Durán, Diego. *Historia de las Indias de Nueva España y Islas de Tierra Ferme*. Ed. José F. Ramirez. Vol. 1. México: J. M. Andrade y F. Escalante, 1867.

Faiella, Graham. *Mesoamerican Mythology.* New York: The Rosen Publishing Group, Inc., 2006.

Ferguson, Diana. *Tales of the Plumed Serpent: Aztec, Inca and Mayan Myths*. London: Collins & Brown, Ltd., 2000.

Hunt, Norman Bancroft. *Gods and Myths of the Aztecs*. London: Brockhampton Press, 1996.

Jonghe, Édouard de, ed. "Histoyre du Mechique: Manuscrit français inédit du XVIe siècle." *Journal de la société des américanistes* 2 (1905): 1-41.

Léon-Portilla, Miguel, ed. *Native Mesoamerican Spirituality: Ancient Myths, Discourses, Stories, Doctrines, Hymns, Poems from the Aztec, Yucatec, Quiche-Maya, and Other Sacred Traditions*. Mahwah: Paulist Press, 1980.

——— . Trans. Jack Emory Davis. *Aztec Thought and Culture: A Study of the Ancient Nahuatl Mind.* Norman: University of Oklahoma Press, 1963.

Markman, Roberta H. and Peter T. Markman. *The Flayed God: The Mesoamerican Mythological Tradition*. New York: Harper Collins Publishers, 1992.

McDermott, Gerald. *Musicians of the Sun*. New York: Simon & Schuster, 1997.

Mendieta, Gerónimo de. *Historia eclesiástica indiana*. Joaquin Garcia Icazbalceta, ed. n.c.: F. Diaz de Leon y S. White, 1870.

Miller, Mary, and Karl Taube. *An Illustrated Dictionary of the Gods and Symbols of Ancient Mexico and the Maya*. London: Thames & Hudson, Ltd, 1993.

Nardo, Don. *Aztec Mythology*. Farmington Hills: Lucent Books, 2015.

Phillips, Henry. "Notes Upon the *Codex Ramirez*, With a Translation of the Same." *Proceedings of the American Philosophical Society* 21 (1883): 616-651.

Radin, Paul. "The Sources and Authenticity of the History of the Ancient Mexicans." *University of California Publications in American Archaeology and Ethnology* 17/1 (1920): 1-150.

Roberts, Timothy R. *Myths of the World: Gods of the Maya, Aztecs, and Incas*. New York: MetroBooks, 1996.

Roy, Cal. *The Serpent and the Sun: Myths of the Mexican World*. New York: Farrar, Straus & Giroux, 1972.

Sahagún, Fray Bernardino de. *The Florentine Codex: General History of the Things of New Spain*. Book 3: *The Origins of the Gods*. Trans. Arthur J. O. Anderson et al. *Monographs of the School of American Research* 14/4. Santa Fe: School of American Research and the University of Utah, 1952.

Schuman, Michael A. *Mayan and Aztec Mythology*. Berkeley Heights: Enslow Publishers, Inc., 2001.

Smith, Michael E. *The Aztecs*. 3rd ed. Chicester: Wiley-Blackwell, 2011.

Torquemada, Juan de. *Primera parte de los veinte i vn libros rituales i monarchia indiana: con el origen y guerras, de los indios ocidentales, de sus poblaçones: descubrimento, conquista, conuersion, y otras cosas marauillosas de la mesma tierra.* Vol. 2. Madrid: Nicolas Rodriquez Franco, 1723.

Taube, Karl. *The Legendary Past: Aztec and Maya Myths*. London: British Museum Press, 1993.

Alexander, Harley Burr. *Mythology of All Races*. Vol. 11, *Latin-American*. Boston: Marshall Jones Co., 1920.

Allan, Tony, and Tom Lowenstein. *Gods of Sun & Sacrifice: Aztec & Maya Myth*. London: Duncan Baird Publishers, 1997.

Bierhorst, John. *The Mythology of Mexico and Central America*. Revised edition. Oxford: Oxford University Press, 2002.

———, ed. *The Monkey's Haircut and Other Stories Told by the Maya*. New York: William Morrow and Company, 1986.

Brinton, Daniel G. *American Hero-Myths: A Study in the Native Religions of the Western Continent*. Philadelphia: H. C. Watts & Co., 1882.

Christenson, Allen J., trans. *Popol Vuh: Sacred Book of the Maya People*. 2007. Electronic version of original 2003 publication (Alresford: O Books). Mesoweb: www.mesoweb.com/publications/Christenson/PopolVuh.pdf.

Craine, Eugene R., and Reginald C. Reindorp, trans. and eds. *The Codex Pérez and The Book of Chilam Balam of Maní*. Norman: University of Oklahoma Press, 1979.

Edmonson, Munro S., trans. *The Ancient Future of the Itza: The Book of Chilam Balam of Tizimin*. Austin: University of Texas Press, 1982.

Elswit, Sharon Barcan. *The Latin American Story Finder: A Guide to 470 Tales from Mexico, Central America and South America, Listing Subjects and Sources*. Jefferson: McFarland & Company, Inc., 2015.

Ferguson, Diana. *Tales of the Plumed Serpent: Aztec, Inca and Maya Myths*. London: Collins & Brown, Ltd., 2000.

Goetz, Delia, and Sylvanus Griswold Morley. *Popol Vuh: The Book of the Ancient Maya*. Mineola: Dover Publications, 2003.

Green, Lila, ed. *Tales From Hispanic Lands*. Morristown: Silver Burdett Company, 1979.

Knowlton, Timothy, and Anthony Aveni. *Maya Creation Myths: Words and Worlds of the Chilam Balam*. Boulder: The University Press of Colorado, 2010.

Markman, Roberta H. and Peter T. Markman. *The Flayed God: The Mesoamerican Mythological Tradition*. New York: Harper Collins Publishers, 1992.

Menchú, Rigoberta, with Dante Liano. *The Honey Jar.* David Unger, trans. Berkeley: Groundwood Books, 2006.

Milbrath, Susan. *Star Gods of the Maya: Astronomy in Art, Folklore, and Calendars*. Austin: University of Texas Press, 1999.

Miller, Mary, and Karl Taube. *An Illustrated Dictionary of the Gods and Symbols of Ancient Mexico and the Maya*. London: Thames & Hudson, Ltd, 1993.

Nelson, Ralph, trans. *Popol Vuh: The Great Mythological Book of the Ancient Maya*. Boston: Houghton Mifflin Company, 1976.

Rice, Prudence M. *Maya Calendar Origins: Monuments, Myth History, and the Materialization of Time*. Austin: University of Texas Press, 2007.

Roberts, Timothy R. *Myths of the World: Gods of the Maya, Aztecs, and Incas.* New York: MetroBooks, 1996.

Roys, Ralph L. *The Book of Chilam Balam of Chumayel.* New ed. Norman: University of Oklahoma Press, 1967.

Sawyer-Lauçann, Christopher, trans. *The Destruction of the Jaguar: Poems from the Books of Chilam Balam.* San Francisco: City Lights Books, 1987.

Schmitt, Martha. *World Myths and Legends II: Central America.* Belmont: Simon & Schuster Education Group, 1993.

Schuman, Michael A. *Maya and Aztec Mythology.* Berkeley Heights: Enslow Publishers, Inc., 2001.

Sexton, James D., trans. and ed. *Mayan Folktales: Folklore from Lake Atitlan, Guatemala.* New York: Doubleday, 1992.

Taube, Karl. *The Legendary Past: Aztec and Maya Myths.* London: British Museum Press, 1993.

Glossary

Translations of Nahuatl names given when available.

Name	Literal Meaning	Function
Aztec	"People from Aztlan"	Peoples who lived in Central Mexico and established an empire there
Aztlan	"Place of the White Heron"	Mythical place of origin of the Aztecs
Cacatepec/Cacatepeca		Mythical enemies of the Toltecs
Centzon Huitznahua	"Four Hundred Southerners"	Sons of Coatlicue who represent the stars
Chalchiuhtlicue	"Jade Skirt Woman"	Goddess of waterways; wife of Tlaloc
Chapultepec	"Hill of the	Ancient Toltec city on

	Locusts"	the shores of Lake Texcoco
Chichimecs		General term for non-Aztec peoples; often has connotations of barbarism
Cihuacoatl	"Woman Serpent"	Goddess of midwifery
Cipactli		Giant fish whose body was turned into the earth by Quetzalcoatl and Huitzilopochtli
Cipactonal		First man (or woman)
Coatepec	"Serpent Mountain"	Home of Coatlicue
Coatepec/Coatepeca	"Hill of Snakes"/ "People of the Hill of Snakes"	Mythical enemies of the Toltecs
Coatlicue	"Serpent-Skirt"	Mother of the moon, stars, and Huitzilopochtli
Cochtocan	"City of Sleepers"	Place in Quetzalcoatl's journey from Tula
Copil		Son of Malinalxochitl and enemy of Huitzilopochtli and the Mexica
Coyolxauhqui	"Precious Bells"	Daughter of Coatlicue whose head becomes the moon

Cozcaapan	"Place of Jeweled Waters"	Place in Quetzalcoatl's journey from Tula
Culhuacan		Ancient Toltec city
Ehecatl	"Wind"	Aspect of Quetzalcoatl as god of wind
Huehuequauhtitlan	"Place of the Old Tree"	Place in Quetzalcoatl's journey from Tula
Huemac		Mythical last king of the Toltecs
Huitzilopochtli	"Hummingbird of the Left" or "Hummingbird of the South"	God of war
Itztlacoliuhqui	"Curved Obsidian"	God of cold and obsidian; transformed aspect of Tlahuizcalpantecuhtli
Ixtapalapan		Place along the shore of Lake Texcoco where the Mexica settle as part of their journey
Ixnextli	"Ashen Eyes"	Transformation of Xochiquetzal when she is exiled from Tamoanchan
Iztac tepetl	"White Mountain"	Mountain in the Valley of Mexico
Lake Texcoco		Ancient lake in Central Mexico; now the site

		of Mexico City
Macehuales		Aztec farmers; commoners
Malinalco		Mythical city founded by Malinalxochitl
Malinalxochitl	"Wild Grass Flower"	Daughter of Coatlicue and enemy of Huitzilopochtli and the Aztecs
Mayahuel		Goddess of the maguey cactus
Mexica		One of the tribes of Aztlan who migrated to Central Mexico
Michoacán		Region of Mexico; stopping-place of the Mexica on their journey south
Mictecacihuatl	"Lady of Mictlan"	Consort of Mictlantecuhtli
Mictlan		Land of the dead
Mictlantecuhtli	"Lord of Mictlan"	God of the dead
Mixcoatl	"Cloud Serpent"	God of hunting and the Milky Way; inventor of blood offerings and ritual warfare
Nahuatl		Language spoken by the Aztecs
Nanahuatzin	"Full of Sores"	God of disease;

		sacrifices self and is transformed into the Fifth Sun
Ollin Tonatiuh/Tonatiuh	"Movement of the Sun"	God of the sun; transformed aspect of Nanahuatzin
Ometeotl	"Dual God" or "God of Duality"	Main creator-god
Oxomoco		First man (or woman)
Pantitlan		Mythical place where the daughter of the Mexica king is sacrificed in the legends about Huemac
Patzcuaro		Stopping-place of the Mexica on their journey south
Piltzintecuhtli		Son of Oxomoco and Cipactonal
Popocatepetl	"Smoking Mountain"	Volcano in the Valley of Mexico
Quauhtitlan	"Place of the Tree"	Place in Quetzalcoatl's journey from Tula
Quetzalcoatl	"Plumed Serpent"	God of knowledge, crafts, and the Morning Star
Quetzalpetlatl		Sister of Quetzalcoatl
Tamoanchan	"Land of the Misty Sky"	Mythical paradise where the gods live and human beings are

		remade under the Fifth Sun
Tecuciztecatl	"The One from the Place of the Conch"	God of the moon
Temalpalco	"Place Marked by Hands"	Place in Quetzalcoatl's journey from Tula
Tenochtitlan	"Place of the Nopal Cactus"	Ancient city on the waters of Lake Texcoco; capital city and ritual center of the Aztec Empire
Teotihuacan	"Place of the Road of the Gods"	Ancient Aztec city and ritual center
Tepanoayan	"Place of the Stone Bridge"	Place in Quetzalcoatl's journey from Tula
Texcalpan		Place mentioned in the stories of Titlacauan and Huemac
Tezcatlipoca	"Smoking Mirror"	God of night, enmity, and strife
Titlacauan	"We Are His Slaves"	Aspect of Tezcatlipoca; appears as a sorcerer in stories about Huemac and the fall of the Toltecs
Tizapan		Place given to the Mexica by the king of Culhuacan

Tlahuizcalpantecuhtli	"Lord of Dawn"	God of the Morning Star
Tlaloc	"He Who Makes Things Sprout"	God of rain; husband of Xochiquetzal
Tlaloque		Servants of Tlaloc; associated with rain, thunder, lightning, and hail
Tlaltecuhtli	"Earth Lord"	Monster from whose body Quetzalcoatl and Tezcatlipoca remake the heavens and the earth
Tlapallan	"Red Land"	Legendary place that was the goal of Quetzalcoatl's journey from Tula
Tlachtli		Mesoamerican sacred ball game
Toltecs	"People of Tula"	Ancient civilization in Central Mexico that was replaced by the Aztecs
Tonacacihuatl	"Lady of Our Sustenance"	Female aspect of Ometeotl; consort of Tonacacihuatl
Tonacatecuhtli	"Lord of Our Sustenance"	Male aspect of Ometeotl; consort of Tonacacihuatl
Tonacatepetl	"Mountain of Food"	Mythical mountain in which Quetzalcoatl

		finds maize and other foodstuffs
Tozcuecuex		Mythical king of the Mexica in legends about Huemac
Tula	"Place of the Rushes"	Capital city of the Toltec Empire
Tzatzitepetl	"Mountain That Speaks"	Mythical mountain outside of the Toltec capital
Tzitzimitl (pl. tzitzimime)		Goddess(es) of the stars
Xipe Totec	"Flayed God"	God of agriculture, growing plants, and seasons
Xochimilco	"People of the Flower Field"	Nahuatl-speaking tribe who migrated into Central Mexico
Xochiquetzal	"Flower Quetzal Feather"	Goddess of fertility, beauty, and young mothers; wife of Tlaloc
Xochitlan	"Place of the Flower"	Toltec garden city

Check out more mythology books by Matt Clayton

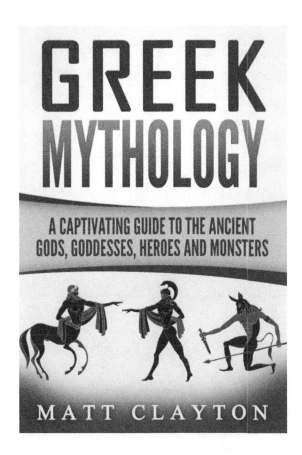

GREEK
MYTHOLOGY

A CAPTIVATING GUIDE TO THE ANCIENT GODS, GODDESSES, HEROES AND MONSTERS

MATT CLAYTON